W9-ACM-942

Where To From Here

A Path to Canadian Prosperity

Bill Morneau
with
John Lawrence Reynolds

Published by ECW Press
665 Gerrard Street East
Toronto, Ontario, Canada M4M 1Y2
416-694-3348 / info@ecwpress.com

Editor for the Press: Jennifer Smith
Substantive Editor: Karen Milner
Cover design: Made by Emblem

LIBRARY AND ARCHIVES CANADA CATALOGUING IN PUBLICATION

Title: Where to from here : a path to Canadian prosperity / Bill Morneau with John Lawrence Reynolds.

Names: Morneau, Bill, author. | Reynolds, John (John Lawrence), author.

Description: Includes index.

Identifiers: Canadiana (print) 20220428999 | Canadiana (ebook) 20220429057

ISBN 978-1-77041-714-4 (hardcover)
ISBN 978-1-77305-985-3 (PDF)
ISBN 978-1-77305-986-0 (Kindle)
ISBN 978-1-77305-984-6 (ePub)

Subjects: LCSH: Morneau, Bill. | LCSH: Finance ministers—Canada—Biography. | LCSH: Finance, Public—Canada. | LCSH: Canada—Economic conditions—21st century. | LCGFT: Autobiographies.

Classification: LCC HJ793 .M67 2023 | DDC 336.092—dc23

This book is funded in part by the Government of Canada. *Ce livre est financé en partie par le gouvernement du Canada.* We also acknowledge the support of the Government of Ontario through the Ontario Book Publishing Tax Credit, and through Ontario Creates.

Canada

PRINTED AND BOUND IN CANADA

PRINTING: FRIESENS 5 4 3 2

To my wife Nancy and our children Henry, Clare, Edward and Grace. Thanks for enduring my political adventure and for sharing my views on the value of public service.

"What great and enduring achievement has the world ever accomplished that was not based on idealism?"

— Sir Wilfrid Laurier

Contents

Introduction

Federal elections in Canada are historic events, and the election of 2015 proved to be both historic and unique for a variety of reasons.

Eleven weeks passed between the day Prime Minister Stephen Harper dropped the writ and election day on October 19, resulting in the longest election campaign in the country's history. Besides setting a record of dubious merit, this meant Canadians were subjected to more days of political tirades than they had been in any prior campaign. The election also marked the entry of a neophyte Liberal party leader in Justin Trudeau, whose political bona fides at the time were more closely linked to his family name than practical experience.

The results were equally historic. After being knocked back to third place in the 2011 election, Liberals scored an upsurge of 148 new seats. Along with delivering a firm majority in Parliament, it marked the biggest numerical increase for a single party since Confederation and the first time a party rebounded from third place in the Commons to a majority government. And with an equal number of men and women among the original 30 ministers, Canada could boast the first gender-balanced cabinet in its history.

Amidst all these notable factors, the election confirmed that Canada is basically a centrist country, choosing a different path than the one followed by the Harper Conservatives. Canadians demonstrated, not for the first time, an aversion to extremist views and politics while generally tolerating their existence and to some extent their role in government. How many other democracies in the world find a place for a political party whose platform is firmly fixed on secession? This tradition of seeking the comfortable and stable centre explains how a sea change in political power can occur in Canada, free of violence and heated rejection of the results. It's a quality we should not only take quiet pride in possessing, but we should also recognize in it a particular Canadian advantage.

The 2015 election confirmed all of this. It also confirmed that Canada can attract fresh faces and new talents to the highest political arena in the land, people who bring ideas, enthusiasm and determination with them.

People like me.

Everyone who enters public life arrives with goals. Some make the choice to satisfy their need to "be" someone. Others arrive determined to "do" something. Political parties, to my mind, should strive to attract the latter group. The former will find their way naturally.

Whatever the motivation, we all arrive convinced that we can make a difference, either individually or within the structure of a political party. Seated somewhere on the floor of the Commons and witnessing the give-and-take across the aisle during Question Period is never enough. Nor is attendance at committee meetings, where a good deal of theatre happens alongside important scrutiny of government. As clichéd as it sounds, we need people driven by visions of doing things today that will improve the lives of other Canadians and pave the way for the country's success tomorrow.

I shared those ideas and visions. Mine were rooted in W.F. Morneau & Associates, the business my father launched in 1966. The company's original plan had been to provide employers and employees with the means to fund benefits through their working years and into retirement. I focused my efforts on building the company from its Southwestern Ontario roots and national presence into an international, publicly traded firm. Expanding our services to include the administration of health and pension programs as well as assistance for employees going through personal challenges made me aware of social problems that I was lucky enough never to have encountered first-hand, and so had never dealt with — problems like financial jeopardy, prejudice, addiction, psychological stress and more.

Writing cheques was one way to respond to needs like these, but that struck me as too easy, too effortless. I chose instead to volunteer my time and energy to organizations such as St. Michael's Hospital in Toronto, Covenant House, the Loran Scholars Foundation and many others committed to providing health care, youth guidance and educational opportunities. My work on their behalf was satisfying, but I was always aware that government represented the ultimate instrument to address major social challenges.

So, with encouragement from people whose opinions I respected, as well as some astonished responses from close friends and family who thought I was crazy, I stepped away from leadership in the corporate and charitable sectors and into the federal political arena. I was somewhat different from most other electoral candidates in Canada because key leaders in Trudeau's team actively backed me, seeing my business background and familiarity with important social concerns as assets. Mind you, I was a willing recruit, having put up my hand after acting as an advisor to the Ontario government; but being sought out by those at the top made me an exception. Political parties in this country cling to the concept of leaving the selection of nominees up to local constituency members exclusively. I realized that a good deal of residual resistance exists against party leaders favouring individuals for nomination in ridings, a practice dismissed as "parachuting." The reaction is understandable, but my view was (and is) that without at least some degree of pre-selection, the makeup of a government — and thus the personnel available for specific functions in cabinet — becomes haphazard. That was the state of affairs prior to the 2015 election.

I managed to win election in an admittedly traditional Liberal riding. When a revived Liberal Party won a clear parliamentary majority, I was appointed minister of finance, taking my seat in a cabinet populated overwhelmingly with first-time MPs and led by a first-time prime minister. I hesitate to use the word euphoric, but the level of eagerness and excitement among all of us was that intense. We represented a resurgence in federal Liberal power, prepared to break new legislative ground, set new standards and realize much of Canada's promise that (we argued) had been neglected and squandered under Stephen Harper's leadership.

There was much to be done, determined by a plan prepared and agreed upon over the months leading up to the election. We would, the prime minister had declared, create "an economy that benefits us all." Ours would be a different federal government, its achievements marked by more than the innovation of a gender-balanced cabinet, as noteworthy as it may be. We had been handed a mandate for change, and our plans outlined the areas in which we would honour that mandate by keeping promises made during the election. They included initiatives to deal with the rising challenge of populism through a recalibration of social benefits, to address the existential challenge of climate change, to reduce gender inequalities, to reconcile with Indigenous Peoples — and many other priorities that had not been core in the Harper era.

Our platform and policies were only one facet of the promised change that had generated so much enthusiastic support for the return of the Liberal Party to the national stage. The other was the presence of a new Liberal leader whose personal qualities appealed to wide factions of Canadians regardless of age, income, language or geography. Echoing the dramatic rise of U.S. president Barack Obama seven years earlier, Justin Trudeau's engaging style was genuine and sincere. He relished the chance to greet large crowds of people, basking in the glow of their affection and admiration. They knew him, after all. Like the nice boy down the block, he had emerged from the shadows of his often-aloof father as a dynamic young man who shared a hug as easily as he shared a smile. Among Canadians who harboured even a small inclination toward Liberals, he was revered because he made them feel good, and that is a laudable quality in politicians of any stripe.

But, of course, success in government demands more than that alone.

We started on our path with the sure view that all of our stated priorities deserved attention, and to a great extent we did follow through on our many promises. One authoritative study confirmed that out of 353 pre-election promises made by the party, at least 90 percent were fulfilled over the four-year first term.[1]

I took as much pride in our achievements as everyone else in the party, but I felt there was more to be done, a narrower set of worthy goals that looked beyond today into the needs of the future. Chief among them was the need to focus on growing the economy by recognizing our challenges and opportunities. We wanted to develop and implement policies that would unleash renewed capacity for Canadians to find not only meaningful work, but work that supported the steadily improving standards of living experienced by previous generations.

The promise and possibility of Canada were not, to my mind, being realized. Many of our efforts were aimed at enabling more people to have a piece of the economic pie. All well and good. But the recalibration of benefits, in my view, was only the start. We needed a larger pie, one that not only could help more people share in it but expand each slice available. That's not only a goal within our grasp; it's a goal that will prove essential for Canada in

1 Centre for Public Policy Analysis, *Assessing Justin Trudeau's Liberal Government: 353 Promises and a Mandate for Change*, Lisa Birch and François Pétry, eds. (Quebec: Presses de L'Université Laval, 2019).

the coming years, and one that I hope this book and my ongoing efforts make a small contribution to achieving.

Still, all of us took justifiable pride in what had been accomplished early on, and that pride carried us through the first year or so of the mandate, riding a crest of generally widespread approval. But beneath the surface, something was happening. The hope and excitement that propelled us to early success gave way to the reality of governing and managing. The plan we started with needed constant refreshing from a leadership group that had no experience in federal government. The gaps in our plan to generate prosperity for Canada were challenging to handle for a government predisposed to think about how to share the existing pie rather than how to grow it. Errors occurred, targets were missed, individuals were slighted and the declared Sunny Days began growing clouded and stormy. What was the cause? Hubris in response to the country's massive rejection of the Harper government and its policies? A learning curve too sharply angled to be negotiated by first-time players? An overly optimistic view of what could and should be done by government? Or merely the reality of governing, made more challenging in an era of increasing partisanship and endless media scrutiny?

Perhaps all were to blame to one degree or another. The overriding cause, in my opinion, was the manner in which these and other challenges were managed or, more correctly, not managed on a daily basis at the highest level.

That kind of backroom activity is rarely discussed in the media unless a scandal is involved, nor should we expect it to be. Results, after all, are more important than process. But an essential aspect of governance involves being concerned about how things are managed. It's our job. Spending five years at the centre of the federal government taught me much about what works and what doesn't work in Ottawa. More important, I learned *why* so many things don't work there, and I will share that knowledge here on a practical level, along with suggestions on how to ensure responsive and responsible governments in future years.

Define the process of governing in any manner you choose, but at the core of it all are the ability and the impetus to manage. We do not need figureheads in our politics. The governor general serves that purpose as a representative of the monarchy, an individual who can command our loyalty and respect without retaining executive power. But a national entity with 38 million stakeholders, plus global representation and an operating budget of several hundred billion dollars, needs leaders who also act as managers; who share the vision, the expertise and the impetus to assemble a team, provide it with direction, make decisions and see them executed.

Every political structure needs management. That's a given. So is the fact that the challenge of governing a democracy has changed in lockstep with every other aspect of modern life, from cyber-based communications to concerns about minority rights. Things have grown swifter and more complex as a result, and the process of governing may appear almost too complex for anyone to perform effectively.

I don't buy that. Complexity doesn't make something impossible. It makes it essential for government, however, to understand changing demands, set new priorities to deal with them and find new means of getting things done. Anything less than this should be construed as abdication of duties.

Some may link the term *management* more closely to business than to government. Governments tend to operate via decrees, legislation, statutes, codes and other means. In the realm of human resources, governments make use of codes of conduct, ethics commissioners, regulations and party whips. Even the verb to discuss their operation changes: businesses, we say, are managed; governments are run.

The language can lead you to conclude that change is possible in business, but perhaps less so in government. Nothing could be further from the truth. The need for goals, for focus, for management, for discipline, and the search for improved outcomes even in the face of increased scrutiny and partisanship, is in my estimation absolutely as important in the public sector as in the private sector.

Every internal decision made by any organization, private or public, is a gauge of management ability. The assessment and application of talents available from the people within the organization represent an accurate measure of competent management. Some observers suggest that corporations enjoy the benefit of choosing personnel from a universe of qualified applicants. Government leaders, the argument goes, do not enjoy that privilege. It's voters, not company executives, who choose the candidates for cabinet positions, leaving government decision-makers handcuffed in comparison with businesspeople.

Is this a valid argument? Not necessarily. In the wider picture, as I'll explain later, the voters' choices can prove as much a benefit as a handicap. And it is entirely possible — I would argue essential — for the leader of a political party to spend significant time and energy recruiting the best candidates for political office and for senior internal political roles.

Effective governing and managing demand a focus on people — recruiting them, developing relationships among them, collaborating with them on objectives and holding them to account for results. None of this is news for anyone who has spent a career in management, but it was strangely absent from the thinking at the political level of the Trudeau government.

This lack of collaborative and effective management at the cabinet level over the five years between September 2015 and August 2020 was a significant problem and represents a challenge for a future government to overcome. Parties in power must do more than create a starting plan; they also must ensure that the structure is in place to continually update and refresh objectives. Only by getting that right can they ensure that key elements of their policies and platform are implemented in an ever more difficult political environment.

Much of what was accomplished over those years was crafted to expand our social benefits and create a foundation for more inclusive growth, a vital step to ensure an economically stable Canada. The foundation was built over the first term with a good deal of attention paid to delivering social equity and security across the board.

—

I wrote this book to provide a record of the many successes and multiple stumbles that occurred over the years immediately following the 2015 election. It stands as an assessment of the style of extreme partisan government that prevails in the 21st century, by someone who endured that particular gauntlet, along with my considered proposals on what is needed to deliver prosperity in our highly charged environment. The goals we set in 2015 to ensure a more inclusive economy that respected our climate change commitments remain valid, and reaching them while growing our collective wealth has become, in my mind, more critical than ever.

It also stands as testimony to the immense contrast between the nature of decision-making in public service and private industry.

I entered the political arena with my eyes wide open and my feet on the ground. Much of my experience to that point had been about getting things done, not just in business but in non-profit organizations where I had volunteered my time to serve on boards dedicated to helping those in need — the ill, the homeless, young people in search of an education, seniors in search of comfort and immigrants building a new life in a strange land.

You don't become involved in such groups just to see your name on a letterhead. You become involved to accomplish things. I was well-versed in the importance of defining goals and assigning responsibility. Performance must be measured and confirmed before being celebrated, and the most binding force among team members is total trust in each other.

So I brought this perspective with me to politics, including a determination to make a positive impact, an emphasis on building relationships and perhaps a smattering of idealism. What I didn't bring was naivety — I was prepared to play the game as vigorously as was needed to justify my presence in Ottawa, and I did.

That, too, is what this book is about.

—

We Canadians too often minimize our assets and achievements, preferring modesty over nationalism. And that's fine. History overflows with tales of disasters inspired by hubris and jingoism. There is a time and a place, however, for Canadians to recognize and appreciate our distinguishing qualities, which much of the world admires. Among them are our ability, proven over time, to resolve our differences peacefully, to find the middle path and to work together to create a more robust economy and a more just nation. We may not always have been number one, but there are few who would deny that we have built a place that is envied the world over. We just need to make sure that in the face of new challenges, and an energy transition that will be much more difficult than we yet appreciate, we apply our considerable resources and resourcefulness to the task of ensuring our children and grandchildren see the best opportunities here in Canada.

This mindset can be difficult to nurture among those Canadians who tend to focus on the country's faults and challenges. Nevertheless, we persist in our efforts to correct our problems and shortcomings and continue serving as a model for much of the world, leaving our children an economic future that will be brighter and more widely available. The key to fulfilling this goal is dependent for the most part on our economic growth.

In the pages of this book, I propose ways in which we can achieve that lofty goal, and why it's one worth striving for.

The vision is at hand. We need to make it a reality. And we can.

One

Conversation in an Empty Room

Rideau Cottage hardly seemed a suitable location for making major decisions in government. Nor did it look like an appropriate residence for the leader of a prosperous G7 nation.

It was my first visit there, and I was struck by the building's lack of architectural charm or grace, despite it serving as temporary living quarters for the prime minister of Canada. With no plans afoot to renovate or replace the PM's official residence, 24 Sussex Drive, "temporary" sounded more like a euphemism for semi-permanent.

I couldn't help reflecting that one of my earliest efforts as finance minister had been to find a way of either restoring or replacing 24 Sussex, creating a residence in keeping with the status that a leader of a G7 nation deserves. The address, after all, represented more than a dwelling for the prime minister and his or her family. Visiting world leaders and dignitaries were routinely entertained and housed there when in Ottawa. The country deserved a showplace for its leader. Rideau Cottage wasn't it.

Tales about the decrepit state of the prime minister's official residence had been traded for years, either embarrassing or amusing anyone familiar with the place, yet no one seemed motivated to do something about it. I actually proposed setting up a group of former prime ministers to review the condition and upkeep costs of both 24 Sussex and Rideau Hall, the governor general's residence, with an eye toward correcting the situation. I received little or no response to my idea, which I attributed to an unfortunate fear of backlash from various quarters against spending public funds on what were essentially two private residences.

On Monday, August 17, 2020, I arrived at Rideau Cottage at the appointed time to tender my resignation as minister of finance to Prime Minister Justin Trudeau. He would not be surprised. My intention to step down had been passed on to him and his staff the previous week. We would spend the next half hour or so turning the page on things.

The prime minister answered the door and welcomed me inside. Despite the weather — bright and cool on one of those late summer days that appear to be preparing us for autumn — my mood was bleak, a feeling reflected by the dark, almost unlived-in rooms of the building.

We settled in the sitting room. No coffee was served and no time was spent on sidebar issues. There were no sidebar issues. There was only one reason for our meeting: I was walking away from a job I had loved, one that fulfilled my wish to make a positive impact on the lives of Canadians at every level and across every province and territory. Why else would anyone choose to enter federal politics?

Our conversation was cordial and formalities were maintained. As on every other occasion I addressed him as "Prime Minister," never as "Justin." It was a mark of my respect for the office, and for the role he played in governing the country. Yet as affable as our conversation was throughout the meeting, I could not help reflecting on an unusual aspect. It was one of the few — the very few — times we had met to discuss matters in private, without the presence of advisors or other sources of counsel. That kind of thing simply didn't happen in Justin Trudeau's world. Virtually any topic you wanted to discuss with the prime minister — official or informal, strategy or gossip — had to be shared in the presence of members of his staff.

This was an acknowledged fact among everyone who had reason to converse with him. While he appeared as a charming individual who could mingle among crowds of strangers, sharing hugs, smiles and selfies, he seemed to avoid solitary encounters. On the one hand, it was understandable and, to some extent, judicious for a political leader. Having another listener or two in the room would be useful to confirm what had or had not been said about a subject or policy. On the other hand, there are times when the presence of others, not only in the room but in the conversation, inhibits frank exchanges of ideas and opinions. Occasions arise in business and in politics where an individual welcomes private access to a leader, an event almost unheard of within the Trudeau government. More to the point, solid relationships are built not among crowds but in the private exchange of personal expressions and in the give-and-take of shared views and experiences. None of these appeared to occur with any frequency. Opportunities for frank exchanges are the basis for building relationships, whether personal, professional or political. Everything of value we achieve in life is based on relationships, and relationships are built on a one-to-one basis. Speak to a crowd of a hundred or a thousand people and you may get your point across and generate applause, but that's not a relationship that builds the kind of two-way trust and partnership that's essential in managing a business or governing a country.

The lack of that kind of rapport between the prime minister and members of his cabinet didn't appear to be a critical factor until problems emerged. That's when the absence of personal connections sowed the seeds for a breakdown among many members of the team. In retrospect it's easy to see how the quandaries involving

Jody Wilson-Raybould, Jane Philpott and me grew in scope and impact; it was difficult for each side to fully grasp the other's case and their reasons for clinging to their position.

This was especially galling to me. I have made relationships the key to the successes I achieved in family, business and public life. The absence of opportunity to build deep, meaningful connections in the political arena was both discomforting and dangerous.

It was also a serious flaw in the roles that the prime minister and I were entrusted to play.

As others had cautioned prior to my assuming the finance portfolio, the relationship between the two positions is rife with tension. How can it not be? Prime ministers deal with a variety of factions seeking solutions, almost all of them with a cost attached. For the cabinet itself — 30-plus ministers focused on satisfying the demands of their sector of responsibility — as well as in regards to social groups, economic issues, geographic inequities and other pressures and causes, the prime minister represents the source of solutions. And the finance minister? He or she is often viewed as an electable Scrooge, guarding the coffers and at least initially denying the expenditure.

That's a situation that cannot be avoided, nor should it be. Dynamic tension is not only inevitable; it's essential as a means of exerting effective management in government. The key to making things work is to build a solid relationship between the two individuals, one wide and deep enough for each side to understand the other's position and cooperate on finding an acceptable point of agreement.

The final decision rests with the prime minister, as it must. But it's easy to see that the only way to encourage the necessary give-and-take and accept the practical solution is via a close relationship between the two individuals occupying these positions, and this simply did not exist between Prime Minister Trudeau and me.

I had accepted this particular quirk during my five years in cabinet. But it had troubled me deeply. My consolation, if that's the term, was the recognition that he in fact had created few, if any, relationships of the kind I felt essential with other members of cabinet.

—

On this day, with his family away holidaying at Harrington Lake, and our two voices echoing within the sparsely furnished rooms of Rideau Cottage, I welcomed the chance to connect directly with the prime minister. My reasons for resigning were linked to the actions of those who might otherwise be present — not his family, but members of the Prime Minister's Office, PMO staffers.

I began by explaining to the prime minister that the leaks from his office about me and my ministry had become intolerable. They had grown in both number and degree of malice, fed to the media with the apparent intent — there was no other way to put it — of limiting the potential for my team and me to advocate for and implement the policies and programs that, from our research and analysis, we believed would most appropriately address the acute economic challenges we were facing in the midst of the COVID-19 pandemic. A story by Reuters claimed the PMO considered me stingy about the cost of pandemic recovery plans, and that I was reluctant to invest in green initiatives — this at a time when we were proposing programs dealing with the climate crisis that were more significant than at any other time in Canada's history.

The *Globe and Mail* quoted another source criticizing my overly conservative approach to COVID-19 relief measures. Yet both the prime minister and I knew my role was to come up with appropriate policy options and recommend the path that made the most economic sense — to be judicious in determining the best solution to fit the problem. My fiscally cautious nature was not a new development. It had been a successful part of our relationship in the early days — my team and I would do the analysis, and his team would push and prod to reach a politically acceptable conclusion.

But the most recent leak had gone even further. A week earlier the *Globe and Mail* reported that my job could be in jeopardy. A series of clashes between the prime minister and me, the newspaper claimed, were behind his plans for a cabinet shuffle that would lead to my departure from cabinet and giving up my seat in Parliament.[2]

This was not the first such story predicting my removal — that sort of speculation is just part of being a federal minister — but it was easily the most direct and credible, and I was no longer prepared to shrug it off as just another of the slings and arrows aimed at politicians from time to time. The truth was that there were differences, but they could have been reconciled — or should have been — by a functioning partnership operating within the pressurized environment of battling the COVID-19 crisis. Both of us needed to focus on the challenge of dealing with the impact of the pandemic on Canada, and we had. Our problem was not any clashes between us but the absence of both a shared agenda and a working relationship. Without a robust relationship to fall back on, we couldn't get beyond the stress of the situation.

Once I lost control of the process, there was no future for what had been generally a successful partnership. To be sure, he had been the senior partner, but we had worked together in a shared endeavour. The leaks and planted stories had poisoned the atmosphere to the point where there were few, if any, alternatives available beyond submitting my resignation.

Let's make it clear: Justin Trudeau has many talents as a politician, all of them apparent to anyone who observes him in a public

---

2 Robert Fife, "Finance Minister Bill Morneau's Job Could Be in Jeopardy after Clashes with Prime Minister, Sources Say," *The Globe and Mail*, August 10, 2020.

forum. But he also possesses a number of weaknesses. These had become evident during discussions of programs dealing with the pandemic, and one of the most striking was his lack of focus on policy details. Leaving the development of policy responses to his PMO staff meant that debates were conducted and conclusions reached without his presence. The real clashes happened over things that we had never discussed.

I tend to remain cool in almost any circumstance. It takes a lot of provocation for me to let my emotions override my generally placid response to unfair commentary, but this one qualified. Knowing the prime minister was on vacation wasn't enough to quell my anger, and so I called him, demanding to know why such a story had been leaked and who leaked it.

He replied that he was not aware of the leaks, and he had no idea where they had come from.

Really? For weeks, I and the rest of Canada had been absorbing a barrage of revelations about a supposedly growing rift between the two of us, information that could only have originated within the PMO. The prime minister's claim that he had not been aware of them and had no idea of their source could only be interpreted in one of two ways: Either he was mismanaging the PMO, permitting it to function free of his knowledge and direction while it spread false rumours about one of his top appointees. Or he was purposefully not telling me the whole truth. If he wanted me gone, there was a direct and civil way to do so. He had always been respectful toward me, so I was pretty sure this was not a malevolent attempt to exit his most senior minister, but a question of his control over the PMO.

Justin Trudeau boasts a raft of qualities critical to a career politician's success. He inherited sharp intelligence and charisma from his father, and an ability to attract and maintain attention no doubt from his reality of being the focus of interest from an early age. Add substantial physical attractiveness along with a childhood spent in the presence of heavyweight decision-makers, and you have built yourself an ideal career politician. No one, including me, can question the power of these aspects of Justin Trudeau. Nor can anyone deny that they are largely responsible for his electoral success.

Enhancing these characteristics are his talent as a performer and his knack for building public rapport and affection via warm smiles and hasty hugs with strangers. As far as I could tell, they are not conscious efforts on his part. The empathy, the tears shed at hearing stories of hardship and suffering are real. The media frequently compared this aspect of his early appeal to the kind of adoration rock stars receive. Politicians can provoke worse reactions among voters. Here was a leader whose personality would leave Stephen Harper's stilted nature in his shadow. Coupled in the 2015 election campaign with innovative and progressive solutions to the raft of social and economic challenges facing the country, he would prove unbeatable.

He fulfilled my, and almost everyone else's, expectations in that contest. Soon after the election, however, I came to realize that while his performance skills were superb, his management and interpersonal communication abilities were sorely lacking. In particular, his inability or lack of interest in forging relationships with those critical to his and his government's success — me and, as far as I could tell, the rest of his cabinet — was a management issue that caused repeated difficulties, leaving problems in its wake.

In some ways we were an odd couple based on our backgrounds — my experience forged by business and economics, his linked to teaching — and our personalities. Justin Trudeau is often referred to as *hip*, to use a well-worn term, and appears comfortable with the label. I'm not hip, nor would I ever pretend to be. If I did, my kids would gleefully call me out on it. Justin Trudeau exploits it, perhaps a means of concealing an introverted nature behind an extroverted facade.

I consider myself capable of building relationships rather quickly on a one-to-one basis. Among large groups in a public setting, however, I tend to remain private, and there is no more public setting in life than federal politics. Justin Trudeau is at the opposite end of that particular teeter-totter, choosing to appear open and revealing among crowds, but being largely guarded and distant in face-to-face situations. Still, I felt that we meshed when and where it was important to get the job done. His political instincts are first-rate, but they can drive his decision-making too fast and too far. Often, when discussing a program or initiative, I had the sense that his major concern was linked to what he understood intuitively: how he would sound speaking about the subject onstage, and the immediate reaction from progressive voters.

It's not that he didn't discuss policy with others, but that he often did not come to the table with a fully formed opinion. He came to listen to the people in the PMO, and frequently adopted their perspective with little input or pushback, letting their points of view prevail with limited exceptions.

Key to many decisions shaped in the PMO was reaching a judgment about who would front programs in the media. "If we're going to launch this program," the thinking would go, "we need this kind of person to get the coverage we want in the press."

This created a cast of cabinet members chosen not necessarily for what they brought to the business of governing but to the needs of promotion, and I realized that those of us in cabinet had been chosen because we fit in a box. Depending upon the PR goals at the time, the appropriate box was trundled into the spotlight and the lid removed. My box held someone who gave the business community a representative, an individual who spoke their language, who knew what a reasonable rate of return on an investment should be and who grasped the upsides and downsides of regulations. I hadn't been recruited as a smooth and polished politician because I wasn't, nor did I ever claim to be. I was there to fill one of several boxes which, stacked together, created a structure with something to appeal to everyone across the country.

In spite of our differences in background, style and philosophy, the rapport between me and the prime minister had been generally smooth. As I mentioned earlier, we were respectful of each other — I in recognition of his position, and he for the business abilities and experience I brought to the role of finance minister. There appeared to be little such respect, however, at the heart of his claim that he had been unaware of leaks announcing my imminent exit from government.

None of these subjects came up during our brief meeting at Rideau Cottage that day. Both of us knew it was the end of our political partnership, and our meeting would serve to confirm the fact.

My initial comment to him was to ask if it would be a hard or a soft landing. A hard landing would see me walking away without the immediate opportunity to play another role in public service. A soft landing would involve his support for me in my quest to become secretary-general of the Organisation for Economic Co-operation and Development (OECD).

Winning that position, we agreed, would be a long shot. Donald Johnston had served admirably in that capacity from 1996 to 2006. Having another Canadian fill the role in such a relatively short time was unlikely, but we had a good and open discussion about how positive it would be to have a Canadian in that seat. Both of us expected the OECD would begin focusing on issues that the prime minister and I actively supported, including the pricing of carbon, carbon border adjustment taxes and other climate-related concerns. As a government, we had been engaged in all of these issues and more, including the taxation of digital giants like Apple, Google, Facebook and Amazon. Our experience and public position on these topics would add credibility to the OECD's position, even if the geopolitics weren't putting the odds in our favour. It would also add to our considerable legacy, reinforcing Canadian leadership on issues of global import.[3]

From my perspective, I knew the role would allow me to have an impact on issues that I cared about deeply, without some of the frustrating realities of life as a politician and public figure. I presumed I'd be able to go out for a nice dinner with my wife or friends without having to debate tax policy with strangers. Canadians are generally polite, and I had signed up for the role of finance minister, but I couldn't honestly say that there weren't some tiring moments. Trying to do the right thing is great — it's just that not everyone agrees with your conclusions, and in a democracy they have every right to express their views.

We reminisced about the achievements we had made together. The ones that gave me the greatest pride and satisfaction were the introduction of the Canada Child Benefit program, reforms to the Canada Pension Plan and the implementation of a national policy on carbon pricing. None of these would have happened without collaboration between us.

The unfortunate articles that had spread throughout the media plus the underlying struggles for control of the policy agenda during the weeks leading up to my resignation couldn't be ignored, and they weren't. The prime minister repeated that he had been unaware of the leaks and the friction they caused between the PMO and me and my office. Again, I had difficulty accepting this as completely genuine. Whether he indeed knew the source of the leaks or not, he had to be clearly aware of the tension they caused.

Eventually there was little more to say. About half an hour after I arrived, we shook hands and parted.

---

3 A few months later I chose to drop out of the race for the position when it was clear that the organization favoured an Australian over a Canadian, which was not a huge surprise. In my announcement I noted: "I am proud to have used this campaign to talk about issues that matter to Canadians and to the world — the recovery from the COVID-19 pandemic, the fight against climate change, inclusive growth and seizing the opportunities of the digital world."

—

What occurred that morning reflected a view I had acquired almost from my first day in Ottawa. It appeared, in many instances, that the prime minister floated above the issues he confronted, choosing not to get his hands dirty in dealing with the mechanics and implications of the issues before him. Many senior executives play a similar role, trusting specialists to deal with inner details. This does not, however, free them from understanding and grappling with the often-messy details of getting things done. Nor should it. Good management, in any capacity, is not about conveniently turning a blind eye to remain above the fray. It's about keeping both eyes open to foresee risks and consequences, and taking steps to avoid or at least minimize them.

I hadn't witnessed the prime minister taking any of these steps. As someone who had made the move from business to politics and remained keenly aware of the differences and similarities between the two, I was repeatedly frustrated and disappointed. And, in the bigger scheme of things, I was worried that the increasing partisanship in our country, with its focus on politics over policy, means that future leaders will be unlikely to possess the experience and skills required for effective governance of our country. The long-term stewardship of our economy will be threatened unless we address this larger issue head-on. We will need to rethink our institutions to keep up with the changing nature of politics and politicians.

Many people assume that operations at the highest levels of business are ruthless in nature, teeming with boardroom betrayals and backstabbing strategies. They believe that success in business demands doing whatever it takes to reach the goal, and if careers and reputations are battered in the process, that's just collateral damage.

It's a concept that seems to work well in bestselling novels and Hollywood dramas, but it's generally uncommon in business.

Things are competitive, yes, but intentionally trashing individuals and their reputations, in the rare instances where this occurs, seldom proves successful. More to the point, far more is achieved in business through understanding and cooperation than through cutthroat actions and purely selfish motives.

Politics is a different game, played under vastly different rules. Electability is the thing, with images and impressions taking centre stage. Almost everything else is superfluous. It couldn't be more different from business, where results are the currency: goals, strategies and tactics are developed; competitors are defined and assessed; responsibility is allocated and apportioned; all with a clear set of objectives. Working with a team and supporting mutual efforts to create positive results is a sensible and effective approach to reaching defined goals.

In theory, the same emphasis on results takes place in the cabinet room. But in reality, the main focus is to influence two audiences: the media and the voters. And it means that the tactics can be entirely different, including the willingness to attack adversaries, or even colleagues, if it better defines the issue and creates distinctions with electoral advantage. This has always been the way of politics, but the advent of social media, permitting and even encouraging anonymity, has led to harsher commentary and vile personal attacks.

That changes everything. Spill the beans on decisions made in a corporate boardroom and most of the news will be absorbed and assessed by business commentators and shareholder groups. Doing the same thing in the political arena prompts headlines to be written and commentators to pose intense questions. The broader the influence, the more dramatic the response, and no political game in Canada exerts wider influence than the federal government. So the game becomes dramatically different, especially when it comes to securing broad support for programs and measuring the performance of individuals assigned to carry them out. In that arena, leaks can be used to cast the top level of decision-makers (the prime minister and PMO) in a positive light, within which they are able to shift public opinion in their direction at the expense of others. This tactic can be used to apply pressure to specific sectors within the government or to satisfy a multitude of other motives. It is rarely apparent to those outside government, but it is keenly evident to all who work within that environment.

Things become even more sharp-edged in the absence of open discussions regarding political goals and strategies. In my experience, no CEO of any business achieved success without seeking other points of view, especially from departments and their heads responsible for piloting the program. But I saw this disregard of other opinions frequently occurring in government, with political operatives deciding on a direction to take and manipulating the outcome through well-placed leaks, stories planted in the press and on social media. Carefully crafted and strategically employed, they drove conclusions before an elected cabinet minister could finish reading the briefing documents, let alone reach a reasoned conclusion on the subject and consider the best way forward.

Decisions were too often made first, with discussions on how to execute them coming later. Once things got underway, effective reviews on the progress of the program were rarely if ever conducted, at least at the political level.

These and other management missteps, in my opinion, were almost impossible for Justin Trudeau's government to overcome in its second term and beyond, leading to less than satisfying results — that is, two consecutive minority governments — and adding to the polarization of political views among Canadians. Yet this was the same regime that had vaulted the federal Liberal Party from third place to a clear majority in 2015 — a victory achieved thanks in no small part to the irresistible blend of Justin Trudeau's personal appeal, the failing allure of Stephen Harper and a Liberal agenda that captured the imagination of Canadians worried about rising inequality, the impact of climate change and their country's place in the world.

Let's be clear about this: I was both proud and eager to take part in the Liberal team that secured a majority in the federal election of 2015 and that set out to achieve a range of clearly established and historically significant objectives well beyond its first term.

So, what happened?

Good management involves the ability to execute the elements in plans and programs to meet specific goals. If the ability to take these steps is missing, or not enough time is made available to devise and apply them, disaster is often imminent.

When the political talent responsible for much of the Party's 2015 election success was put into management roles at the PMO, without the advantage of a team of experienced colleagues, the writing was on the wall: the plan that led to political success was not refreshed, the execution of initiatives was constantly behind and the ability to attract and retain new talent was not prioritized.

More importantly, there was no healthy tension between policies that focused on growth versus policies that focused on fairer distribution of wealth. The team that won was directed by one set of objectives, avoiding contrasting perspectives that might have led to a more balanced set of policies. When key people left, inevitably burned out or just burned by politics, there was no capacity to ensure that a breadth of perspectives was considered in managing some of the most important files in the country — the ones that would lead to increased growth and opportunities for Canada.

Prime Minister Trudeau had scored a brilliant electoral success in part by assembling a well-qualified team to shape and execute the campaign. Unfortunately, during the first year or so after securing his majority he apparently failed to ask himself if the team that had contributed to his success was also the best to help govern the country. These are, after all, two distinctively different functions. A team that works well to achieve a sharply defined, specific short-term objective rarely succeeds at helping to formulate and execute long-term goals across a wide range of issues.

Good managers make those kinds of decisions as part of their duties. They evaluate who demonstrates the best skills for the job at hand, assigning duties to match capabilities. The job doesn't end there; they make sure the team is up to the task, and they make decisions to upgrade or augment the team when needed.

That's not a duty to take lightly, in politics or business. It's the nuts-and-bolts aspect of getting things done in a leadership role. Personnel assessment and, where necessary, reassignment are a form of preventive maintenance for good managers. Unexpected and unwelcomed events require handling in a direct and effective manner, with minimum improvising. The process should not rely on orchestrated media leaks or anticipated deniability to get the job done.

You don't need a Harvard MBA to grasp this concept. The essential component in understanding and applying it is an ability to develop collaborative relationships, engaging people with proven abilities into your orbit not as supporters but as allies working toward achieving defined goals. Without a focus on building a broader team and generating meaningful discussions around the right goals for the country, we moved down a path that started with great promise and ran headfirst into an inevitable challenge: How do you refresh your agenda to consider the most important next set of priorities?

Two

Lessons in Real Life

My father taught me two primary lessons and a secondary one, not by preaching but by example.

The first is: *There is no substitute for hard work and the drive to succeed.* Nothing new there, but my father exemplified that old axiom in dramatic fashion. He started his career at William M. Mercer, an international benefits consulting company that dominated the field in North America for many years. It occurred to him that, while Mercer was undoubtedly successful, they were missing a number of opportunities to expand their business. The most promising move was to provide similar services to more companies by targeting trade associations. These had been neglected by Mercer, which focused its attention on giant international corporations. Trade associations tended to include smaller companies with smaller groups of employees, requiring different levels of service, yet still in need of professional assistance to deliver employee benefits.

Servicing 20 organizations with 100 employees each would definitely be more time-consuming than providing the same service to one company with two thousand employees. But in my father's vision, if he could bring those smaller companies together in acquiring employee benefits through their trade associations, they would save money thanks to the economies of scale, and his company would generate significant income from the same expansion in services. It was an astute observation, and the basis for a remarkable career.

So in 1966 he launched W.F. Morneau & Associates to do just that. It was an example of ultimate entrepreneurial action: A 26-year-old guy with no financial resources, several dependants (including my mother and four young children) and a determination to succeed rolled the dice in search of success. What he lacked in money he made up for with enormous reserves of energy.

Despite the bumps in the road encountered along the way, he managed to build the business steadily thanks to applying the second lesson I learned: *Never underestimate the value of strong relationships in your business and personal lives.*

He practised this second point in many ways. One was to include business colleagues in our family events, inviting them to our home and later to our cottage. Meeting these people and studying their personalities and character proved something of an apprenticeship to me. I understood how my father's energy and ambition both encouraged and grew out of those relationships. When you understand people well enough to see them not as clients or suppliers but as individuals with shared concerns and goals, you gain a resolve to help them achieve their aspirations while enabling you to share in the rewards. Of all the lessons I applied in both business and politics, none exceeds the importance of mutually beneficial relationships to me.

The other lesson I acquired from my father? I discovered that all of us are susceptible to human frailties, including those who, like my father, achieve spectacular success. No matter how committed we may be to reaching our goals, there are physical limits to accomplishing everything we strive to do. And building a team of people with complementary skills is essential to create real success.

By my teenage years, I understood that my father had reached enormous success in spite of the odds against him. In my eyes, he was unstoppable. Which is when, in effect, he hit a wall. Call it exhaustion, call it burnout, but he had to take several months away from work to regain his strength and recharge himself. When he returned, he was no less determined to succeed, but he was much more realistic about the limits of his energy, both mental and physical.

He also seemed to recognize — and this was another lesson for me — that a significant gap exists between the talents needed to be a successful entrepreneur and those necessary to function as an effective manager. He started recruiting capable managers to both expand the business and leverage his impact. Entrepreneurs embrace risk; they understand there is no reward without it. Good managers, however, are able to maneuver around risk. Recognizing and measuring risk becomes a means of advancing a company's business while preserving its assets. That difference, and those complementary talents, laid the groundwork for what would be our extremely successful partnership in furthering the development of the firm he created.

I have always seen myself more as a manager than as an entrepreneur. This didn't prevent me from probing my own entrepreneurial abilities. As a teenager I bought a small swimming pool business, which introduced me to the challenge of scrambling to meet customer demands while managing the people I relied upon to get things done. It was fun, but hardly a true introduction to dealing with the serious side of running a business, which I saw as my career path. I had no early inclination to venture into politics. That seed was planted when I left home to attend school in Europe.

When I was 20 years old, I seized on the opportunity to spend a year studying at the University of Grenoble. I wanted to learn French, and have some fun in the process. I managed to succeed at both, but perhaps the most telling effect on me was the chance to gain a new perspective on Canada — from a distance. I loved and admired much about France while living and studying there, but my appreciation for my home country grew in many surprising ways.

Canadians are not known for bragging about their nation. We tend to downplay its positive aspects, often looking elsewhere for models of achievement. I'm fine with that; there are too many examples in history where nations have paid a price for excessive hubris. From the perspective of Europe, however — even while living in near-idyllic France (I skied 57 days that winter!) — all the facets of Canada's features shone in sharper focus for me.

I saw Canada serving as something of a model for the world, a nation that managed to succeed despite, in the words of Lord Durham's report, often appearing to be two warring nations within the same state. We manage to muddle through our differences, reflecting our tolerance for contrasting points of view, which also sustains the country's multiracial and multicultural values. Difficulties arise from time to time, periodically generating tensions, but our ability to resolve them peacefully represents a unique source of strength. As much as, and perhaps more than, any nation in the world, the ability of Canadians to accept, absorb and support our differences provides us with the means of understanding and appreciating other societies, other cultures and other values.

The word that most easily comes to mind when I think about these qualities is openness. We tend to be lenient in assessing the differences between us, and generally respectful of those differences. Not always, and not perfectly, but well enough for the rest of the world to judge us by that measure and frequently admire us for it. Add our vast resources plus the country's stunning natural beauty and it's easy to understand why Canada has long been the envy of much of the world.

It's not my intention to romanticize the country while expressing the feelings that grew within me while I was away. But that new swelling of pride marked a point of view I carried through my careers, in business and politics.

With two graduate degrees in hand, along with skills gained from working in other businesses in both the UK and Canada, in 1990 I joined the firm my father had launched, working closely with him to round out my academic studies with hands-on experience. We developed a close working relationship from the beginning. We didn't always agree, but we remained open to the other's point of view, weighing it against our own and finding a way to accommodate any differences.

There's nothing like grappling with real-life challenges to reveal abilities that weren't evident in the classroom. Among the things I discovered about myself in the business world was an interest in solving problems. I loved facing a challenge that demanded fresh thinking, or at least a new perspective, before determining and applying the best all-round solution. I also enjoyed working with others, finding ways to get the best out of them and out of myself in the process.

Those first few years we spent working together proved a whirlwind of growth. We expanded the firm into the U.S. and grew the company significantly in Quebec and across Canada through strategic acquisitions. In addition, we broadened our service offering to include not only advice on employee benefits and pensions, but also delivering them directly to employees, and providing counselling on their financial and psychological well-being through employee assistance programs.

As satisfying as the company's growth was to me, it opened my eyes to wider goals. I developed an interest in doing things beyond the business, especially if I could apply my knack for solving problems wherever the need was compelling. This led to volunteering my services to several organizations dealing with serious social problems.

It didn't take much effort for me to identify them. Sometimes all it took was a scan of the day's newspaper headlines, or a nudge from a colleague who was aware of, or already dealing with, various social crises. I worked on behalf of Covenant House, a non-profit organization dedicated to providing food, shelter and a variety of services to homeless youth between the ages of 16 and 24. Its Toronto location, the largest of its kind in Canada, depends on individual donors for 80 percent of its revenue. Part of me thrived in my volunteer work, and I soon found myself occupying the role of chair of Covenant House. This position kindled my interest in health care in inner-city Toronto, leading to a seat on the board of St. Michael's Hospital, where I eventually took on the position of board chair. In that role I helped govern an organization that had become a centre of excellence, critical to the delivery of health care to some of Toronto's most challenged citizens. I also became a board member of several others. My interest in public policy led me to becoming involved with a non-partisan public policy think tank, the C.D. Howe Institute. I joined the board of directors and served as chair from 2010 to 2014 — a role that would come into conflict with my move into partisan politics.

I enjoyed all my volunteer experiences, somehow finding time and energy away from my family and business obligations to deal with a new and often sharply contrasting array of problems. The term commonly used by those who devote portions of their lives to community services is to say they are "giving back," as though returning in some manner the privileges they earned or inherited. I'm fine with that, but it also suggests payment of a debt, or a sacrifice made as a form of penance.

I didn't see it that way. Of course, I could not disown the privilege I enjoyed of being a successful white male in a society that sometimes denied opportunity and equality to women, people of colour, single mothers and marginalized groups. But the work I chose to do, often on their behalf, was conducted because I believed I had the means — in training, experience and other measures — to make a difference, and I saw it as my way of making a positive impact on society. I suspect that others who engage in volunteer services would admit the same motive.[4] The skills you acquire and hone to achieve success in business are easily adapted for other applications, ones associated with your soul and personal satisfaction rather than your company's bottom line.

Our success at building the business resulted primarily from our ability to attract and work with exceptional people. It was they who deserved the accolades for achieving and often surpassing the company's targets for rate of growth, quality of service and level of client satisfaction. My focus, from my early days and through my time as chair and CEO, was on growth. I pushed both internal growth, doing more to serve existing clients and employees, and corporate expansion, by finding new clients and new acquisition targets. I was confident that profits would come later (and they did), generated by the quality of our delivery and our focus on people. I saw my primary duty as creating and maintaining an atmosphere that focused on and supported the people and the actions they took to reach our goals. In many situations, the most critical step involved understanding and responding to various concerns in an appropriate manner.

For example, when we acquired Sobeco,[5] a large Quebec-based pension and benefit business, we invested a good deal of effort in smoothly integrating their operations into the existing

---

4 I'm equally proud of the efforts I made on behalf of the United Nations High Commissioner for Refugees to open a secondary school for refugee girls in the Kakuma refugee camp in Kenya.

5 This was the business that advised the Quebec government on the establishment of the Quebec Pension Plan — an interesting precursor to my later work expanding the Canada Pension Plan.

organization. At the same time, we made a point of respecting their Quebecois roots while encouraging their key people to seek management positions offering greater authority, responsibility and remuneration. Many did just that, benefiting both the company and themselves in the process. This aided the integration process immeasurably; we were seen not as domineering outsiders but, to the degree possible after acquiring the company, as partners with shared goals and rewards. The move also helped us appreciate the culture of the market while preventing the potential loss of capable staff who might have sought employment elsewhere. All in all, a win-win experience, one that we would replicate frequently as we bought additional businesses and made them part of a larger, more vibrant whole.

I believed then, and still do today, that the best contribution leaders can make in business and government is to work with others to improve both their performance and the gratification they take from their job. It may be appropriate to hang the label *enabler* on me. Enablers achieve success by setting goals and achieving them while sharing fulfillment with the rest of the team. I wanted to practise this particular skill on a wider stage, which seemed a pretty good rationale for delving into politics.

—

The more I achieved at my business ventures, the more widely I searched for ways to build on them in the charitable–public service arena. Given my background, I gravitated toward tackling challenges related to financial security and health care, preparing me for addressing similar issues once I was in government. These were two major social concerns for Canadians, and both appeared in need of fresh assessment and practical new solutions. My experience with pensions provided me with the first major opportunity to make an impact on public policy, and on individual Canadians.

Employment patterns and the pace of change in the workforce accelerated through the 1980s and 1990s, with both employees and employers rethinking the post-war model of employment, when it was common to stay with a company for one's entire working life, or for most of it. Among the most critical concerns was the change in employment pension structure and its implications for working Canadians. My parents' generation had treasured the concept of long-term employment with firms whose benefits included an employee pension plan. The most desirable plans, from an employee standpoint, were defined benefit programs, whose beneficiaries could look forward to a guaranteed and often generous annual income throughout their retirement years. The level of income they could expect to receive was based on their number of years of employment and the income levels they earned. The formula varied, but the onus on calculating and delivering the benefit fell on the employer's shoulders.

This held great appeal for workers, who could direct their income almost exclusively toward daily living costs while employed. Saving for retirement was not a bad idea, but for those with a defined benefit pension it was not essential.

Employees of companies with defined benefit plans enjoyed an attractive level of security, and so to a degree did the companies themselves. The pensions fostered employee loyalty and, all else being equal, workers enrolled in the plans tended to remain with the employer, cutting both attrition and training costs. Even if smaller firms couldn't afford the long-term cost of providing retirement income for their employees, defined benefit pension plans were widespread in the corporate world, and they generated an interest in sticking with the same employer for the long term.

Toward the end of the 20th century, things in the workplace began changing drastically. Trade unions lost their bargaining power, and many industries underwent major restructuring. Globalization saw some firms move their operations offshore. In many cases, companies severely reduced or ceased operations in response to technological advances, straining their ability to fund their defined benefit pensions. Increasingly, the pace of change convinced many employers that the long-term financial commitment demanded by a defined benefit pension plan no longer made business sense. At my firm, we didn't waste much time trying to convince a technology start-up, for instance, to provide a defined benefit pension plan.

Pensions remained an important job benefit that helped attract and keep employees. But in an effort to manage their costs, many employers chose defined contribution programs over defined benefit plans. The difference is critical. In defined contribution plans the employer avoids responsibility for funding a defined level of pension. Instead, both the employer and participating employees share contributions to the employee's retirement account, eliminating the firm's long-term responsibility to fund the plans, and shifting responsibility and risk from the employer to the employee. Rather than being able to count on a predetermined amount of retirement income, employees found their retirement accounts and the income they would receive in retirement subject to the vagaries and volatility of the financial markets.

Government programs existed to assist Canadians in their post-employment years, helping to manage this increasing risk. Chief among them was the Canada Pension Plan, introduced in 1965. Well-structured and generally well-managed, the CPP represents a measure of guaranteed post-retirement income for employed citizens. But even with the addition of supplementary programs such as Old Age Security (OAS) and the Guaranteed Income Supplement (GIS) for those who qualified, middle-class retirees could look forward to receiving only about 25 percent of the income they had enjoyed during their working years from these sources, not enough to provide for a comfortable retirement.

Responsibility for funding and administering public pension programs is shared jointly by Ottawa and the provinces, with each province free to supplement their programs as they see fit. In 2015, when the Ontario Liberal Party announced its intention to launch a provincial pension plan, I felt this was one area where I could offer my expertise in helping them shape and operate it. Still busy with my duties as Executive Chair of what was now Morneau Shepell, I agreed to help design the program in response to then-Premier Kathleen Wynne's invitation. I had previously been an advisor to the provincial government on consolidating the asset management for pension plans sponsored by the provincial government — plans that were not already in a sector-wide plan like Teachers', OMERS or HOOPP. Familiar with key finance officials, I knew I could bring a perspective shaped by my experience of seeing fewer and fewer defined benefit pension plans.[6] The plan's purpose was to augment the benefits from the Canada Pension Plan; it would be cancelled should the federal government make appropriate enhancements to the CPP (which occurred the following year). In my view, this was an excellent way for the Ontario government to show commitment by enhancing the pensions of Ontarians while pressuring the federal government to recognize that, with the decline in workforce pensions, there was a need to supplement the Canada Pension Plan.

My experience in helping the Ontario government on pensions gave me a taste of public service and of the possibility of making an

6 I took part in an advisory panel assigned to recommend the means of providing pension benefits to the 3.5 million workers in the province who lacked adequate retirement pension benefits. The panel proposed the establishment of the Ontario Retirement Pension Plan. This was cancelled in 2016 when, as finance minister in Prime Minister Justin Trudeau's cabinet, I succeeded in revamping the CPP.

impact on issues that can fundamentally change lives. The idea of helping millions of people improve their financial security through public policy choices sparked my interest in government service, but the decision to seek a seat in Parliament didn't arrive like a jolt of insight into some sort of destiny. That would have made for a dramatic moment. But that's not how it happened at all.

I had achieved a satisfying level of success in building the business launched by my father to a substantial size, working closely with a team that I had helped assemble. And I still harboured the pride in Canada that had emerged when I was at school in France, and later in the UK, coupled with an awareness of the social needs I encountered during my stints at Covenant House, St. Michael's Hospital and elsewhere. Along with that, my time at the C.D. Howe Institute gave me a window into challenges we were facing as a country with slowing economic growth. Meanwhile, from the vantage point of my business I could see the increased stress facing workers and the widely varying outcomes for Canadians according to their education levels. The income gap among individuals was growing, even as the country was falling behind in terms of overall competitiveness.

At the same time, Prime Minister Stephen Harper's strident right-wing approach to various social issues was putting him and his Conservative Party on a collision course with many Canadians. The combination of success in the resources sector, the increasing awareness of climate change at all levels of society and the stagnant wages of middle-income Canadians spawned demands for a new way of addressing Canada's needs. If the Liberal Party could find a leader to inspire Canadians with a fresh approach to the country's economic, social and environmental problems, it could replace the Harper regime with ease.

Enter Justin Trudeau.

I knew little about him prior to his ascent as Liberal leader. We came from different backgrounds and moved in different circles.

It was clear, however, that he was positioned for success with the support of a team of savvy and experienced advisors — among them, Gerry Butts.

I had encountered Gerry a few years earlier when he was serving as president of World Wildlife Fund Canada. Full of vision and ambition, he had established impressive political credentials while working as an advisor and then as principal secretary to Premier Dalton McGuinty, Kathleen Wynne's predecessor. Disregarding my initial skepticism, Gerry convinced me that Trudeau had the capacity to win, adding there was a role for someone like me to help craft and execute the federal Liberal Party's economic policy.

I found myself drawn into the political process. Years before, when I first speculated about the potential of running for office in some distant future, my intensely private wife, Nancy, was not sure, to say the least. But that was before our marriage, the arrival of our children and the business goals I had yet to achieve. Now, though it wasn't her first choice, she could see the opportunity to make a difference. The timing was favourable. Our family was largely grown. Of our four children, two were about to head off to university and the next two were close to finishing high school. My father and I had taken our business public with an outstanding management team that was busy positioning the company to score even greater levels of success than previously, fulfilling a prime obligation to investors. With many of my personal and business goals achieved, I had acquired the experience, the vision and the desire to serve in the public arena. Now I had an opportunity to become involved at the federal level. Relocating or commuting to Ottawa would be minimally upsetting, and Nancy's concern about sharing a political life had generally dissolved over the years. Her family had been long-time Liberal supporters, so there were no loyalty lines to be crossed by my venture.[7]

---

7 Nancy's own Liberal leanings were well expressed when, as a youngster,

Timing, we are reminded, is everything — especially in politics. Gerry Butts had first raised the idea of my running for election in 2013. A by-election called to fill the vacancy created when Bob Rae stepped down to serve as First Nations negotiator in Ontario, would be held in the riding of Toronto Centre, a safe seat for Liberals. It was tempting, but family concerns were uppermost in my mind at that time. Nancy and I decided it would be wise to wait, and we did, watching Chrystia Freeland score a relatively easy win in November.

But the seed had been planted. When the riding of Toronto Centre was split ahead of the 2015 election, Chrystia transferred to the new riding of University-Rosedale, leaving a vacancy in Toronto Centre once again, the very same constituency where I had spent so much time with St. Michael's Hospital and Covenant House. My belief that Canadians were poised to discard Stephen Harper's government and many of its policies in the forthcoming election remained as strong as ever. When it was suggested that I represent the riding of Toronto Centre for the Liberal Party, with the expectation that I would be appointed to a cabinet position — no promises, just prospects — Nancy and I agreed to pursue the opportunity.

We made the decision knowing we would encounter three serious risks and concerns. First, it would be necessary to win the nomination. A low-risk venture to be sure, but a hurdle we needed to acknowledge. Then, having secured the nomination, we could expect to spend weeks campaigning for election. Going door to door and introducing myself to strangers before asking them to support me with their vote was not an experience I had undertaken before. Again, there was no assurance of success. And finally, even if I won the seat there would be no cabinet position unless the

---

she christened her dog Trudy as a symbol of her admiration for then–prime minister Pierre Trudeau.

Liberals secured a majority in Parliament. If this didn't occur, I could look forward to spending four years as a backbencher.

Every politician accepts this roll of the dice, of course. You cannot run for office without preparing to accept your lumps should you fail.

The other concern was the loss of our privacy once we chose to follow a path into politics. Up to that point I had managed to involve myself in public service free of media scrutiny. Whatever the future held for me as a member of Parliament and a cabinet minister, I could forget about that aspect of my life for the next few years.

We decided to take the risks — all of them.

Three

A Message on a Small Piece of Paper

My first public move was made early in 2014, when I became a member of the economic team working toward the 2015 election. I also agreed to speak on the topic at the Liberal convention in February which, along with marking my entry into politics, sparked my initial encounter with the realities of Ottawa media coverage.

Reflecting on my business career during my address at the convention, I spoke of the need to engage Canada's business community, a necessary move if we were going to address the need for economic growth. I proposed that the Party should focus on three areas that, in my opinion, needed attention and would help us win an election.

One was a need to encourage business investment by widening our efforts to assist enterprises of all sizes to succeed. This, I pointed out, was especially important for small and medium-sized organizations that represented engines of growth for the future and were in many cases not scaling up to the size required to compete effectively. Large corporations in Canada were less in need of government support, but also needed encouragement to increase investment. Tax policy would always be important as a means of increasing investment across the board, but direct efforts needed to be focused on smaller enterprises. We could do something, I proposed, to assist businesses of every size to reach their objectives, with benefits for all industries and in all regions.

Next, I mentioned the changing nature of pensions, drawing attention to the transfer of a major risk from employers to employees. This occurred when corporations abandoned defined benefit plans, leaving employees responsible for managing their own defined contribution plans. I linked this with the need to review the situation in health care, especially given the increasing burden on the system resulting from our aging population. Finally, I drew from another area of my business experience to speak of the mounting incidences of mental health issues arising from personal and financial distress.

From there I bridged to something new for me, but expected at a political convention — criticism of Stephen Harper and his Conservative government's approach to the issues. "Harper Conservatives," I stated, "turn a blind eye to these problems, their minds focused on partisan politics of the very worst kind."

There was nothing untoward or surprising about making such a statement at a Liberal convention. In this case, however, I made my speech in front of a large display screen highlighting my credentials, which identified me as *Chair of Morneau Shepell* and, unbeknownst to me, also as *Chair of the C.D. Howe Institute*. The latter organization, which carries the name of a former federal Liberal cabinet minister, had grown into a widely acknowledged non-partisan think tank since its inception in 1958. There is nothing inherently political about the organization, which publicly declares it is "an independent not-for-profit research institute whose mission is to raise living standards by fostering economically sound public policies" — an objective that I supported wholeheartedly — and defines its role as a source of trusted policy intelligence, distinguished by research that is non-partisan, evidence-based and subject to definitive expert review.

Almost as soon as I stepped off the stage, I was accosted by a reporter with the *Ottawa Citizen* who aggressively demanded to know if I was speaking for the institute and planning to move it in an openly anti-Harper, anti-Conservative direction. Nothing I had said even hinted at such a move, which would have been quickly rejected by the institute in any case. But the reporter kept insisting that it could be inferred from my comments, refusing to accept my repeated insistence that this was not the case. It was my first lesson in dealing with the realities of the Ottawa-based media, who play a much different game than the business press.

The following day I submitted my resignation to the institute, stating, "I believe I should stand aside before the end of my term ... to ensure that the institute's non-partisan reputation remains intact." The reporter's story on me, based on the belligerent interview, bore the headline "Bill Morneau Resigns from C.D. Howe Institute after Liberal Convention Speech."[8] No reference was made to my comments about the need for new policies to help companies, workers and the economy, nor to my work on behalf of St. Michael's Hospital, Covenant House and others. My instinct to protect the institute was, I believe, the right one. And this incident forced me to recognize that, while I might consider myself largely non-partisan, moving forward with my political ideals and ambitions had vaulted me into a new, aggressive environment.

My appearance at the convention was a bit of a curtain-raiser. Rumours were already circulating about my role in the upcoming election, and I quickly confirmed my intention.

Seeking public office — or more accurately at this stage, seeking the nomination to run for public office — was new and strange to me, so I fell back on the systematic approach I had used when aiming for a goal in business. My nomination depended on gaining

8 Glen McGregor, *Ottawa Citizen*, February 24, 2014.

the support of a majority of Party members in the riding. Step one was for me to get to know them and, in the process, to enable them to get to know me.

I took to the telephones, calling every member to introduce myself and ask about their concerns, then calling them again (and again) over the next several weeks to describe my response to their comments. I also kept a record of each member's stance on critical issues, identifying not just where and who each member was, but where they stood on key policies.

Step two in aiming for success at the nomination level: enticing individuals who support you to join the Party. This is where various machinations at the grassroots level can tip the scales. I and teams of my supporters went door to door in the riding, persuading residents to take part in the nomination process with a simple 10-dollar membership fee and their signature on a card. At this stage, of course, I had little name recognition, but my face-to-face approach, plus my directness in dealing with challenges that members identified as being of concern to them, proved successful in a large number of cases.

I mention these actions because at that stage my team and I were basically on our own. Neither Justin Trudeau nor any high-profile members of his entourage chose to "lean in" and offer to influence things in my favour. I wanted, and indeed expected, the Party leader's expressing of support for my nomination victory, but it never arrived. I presume he and his staff believed they had done enough by enticing me to run for a safe seat and identifying key organizers to assist me in winning the nomination. This was my first introduction to the loosely managed political process I would soon become well-acquainted with.

Trudeau and others at the top level of the Party could claim, with some justification, that they remained neutral not because they didn't care but because they wanted to avoid accusations of promoting a favoured individual to win the nomination. At its most extreme, this is known as "parachuting," and can generate deep resentment from constituency workers because it negates their local preferences and efforts. I understand how a move like that can generate ill feelings, but that happens only when the Party executive essentially dictates who will run for the nomination. In this case, there was no need to dictate anything beyond expressing confidence in me as a potential nominee.

Their decision to stand aside brings up a subject that can launch long and often emotional discussions among politicians and their supporters: Should party leaders take an interest in the capabilities and suitability of those seeking election, even openly expressing their preferences? Or should they remain adamantly neutral, leaving all the decisions up to those in the constituency?

In my opinion, it is critical for the Party leader to take an active role in alerting the riding constituencies to his or her preferences. The final selection is still in the hands of the constituency through the ballot process. But among the leader's earliest and most important post-election actions, should the Party win power, will be the selection of the cabinet. Elected candidates will represent the choices he or she will have in making the appointments and they in turn will (or should . . .) assume authority and responsibility for running the government.

We first needed a team of capable and dedicated nominees if we were to defeat the Harper Conservatives — not something that we considered a sure thing, by any means — and transform our proposals into reality. The things we planned to achieve as the ruling party would influence, to one degree or another, all Canadians for the better. This wasn't self-delusion; it was, I believed, the reason we all chose to move our lives in a different direction, one that would put enormous pressure on our privacy and our families. Or, to put it in a more specific context, we sought not to *be* something but to *do* something. We planned to deal with the vast number of challenges Canada faced — economic, social, environmental, Indigenous-related and more — many unique to our nation. To assume that one regime could handle all of these concerns successfully without actively recruiting a team of key candidates would be unrealistic. To not make an attempt — to not ensure that we sought and persuaded individuals able to best apply our collective wisdom and abilities to the task — would be unpardonable.

Good people, of course, come into the process on their own, with or without sponsorship from their party executives. Many superb MPs in every party managed to secure their own seat in Parliament. That's not a reason, however, for a party leader to avoid making his or her preferences felt regarding individuals who demonstrate the required talent and dedication in specific areas of responsibility.

That being the case, what kind of person should seek office, from the point of view of a Liberal supporter? I suggest someone who is pragmatic and adept at problem-solving and who seeks a middle path in search of win-win outcomes and continuous improvement. Underlying all of this is a socially liberal system of values, and guess who — or what — this sounds like? It sounds like Canada.

This country was built on a spirit of accommodation. The stumbles we made on our way to achieving shared goals over 150-plus years are regrettable. But that spirit of sharing and accommodation, flawed as it may be, continues to thrive. It remains one of the prime reasons for Canada's title, in many quarters, as one of the best countries in the world.

I didn't doubt then and I don't doubt now that Justin Trudeau and his team endorsed most if not all of these ideals, as did I. But being a Liberal, pragmatically seeking solutions to fulfill visions, risks forgetting that choosing the popular thing over the right thing can defeat the basic purpose of becoming involved in politics in the first place. Accommodating other ideas and working toward brokered solutions does not relieve you of the responsibility to accept that not everything is suitable to use in our efforts to win. The fixation on winning, an inevitable outcome of our democratic process, forces every thoughtful candidate to consider how far they will go to dilute or discard their basic principles. For me, it came down to wanting to make sure that we were making the right long-term decisions, even if it meant making some inevitable compromises along the way.

No matter how ambitious our goals and however lofty our ideas were, I knew we would never see them realized unless we won power. But finding balance is critical, and having the experience to choose the right path is essential to satisfying both electoral needs and economic goals.

I would confront this reality very early in my new role.

The Harper Conservatives made more than a few bad decisions during their term in office. It needs to be acknowledged, however, that along the way they took some steps that I supported on the basis that they were the right things to do. One of those steps, announced in 2012, was a proposal to raise the retirement age for Canadians from 65 to 67.

This change spoke to a subject I had dealt with over my entire business career, and a volume of statistics existed to justify serious consideration of the move. Between 2010 and 2030, the number of Canadians aged 65 and over will literally double from 4.7 million to 9.4 million. At the same time, a reduced number of full-time workers would be employed and, via their contributions to the country's tax revenue, be relied upon to support the menu of social benefits made available to retirees. This will place enormous strain on our economy through the loss of valuable workers who could still contribute to our economic success with their wealth of experience, and on such programs as OAS and GIS from which they would begin drawing. The numbers of recipients of those benefits and the number of employed workers were moving in opposite directions. Canadians were living longer and, thanks to the country's health care system and medical advances, these years tended to offer opportunities to seniors for more enjoyable years later in life, and a longer working career for greater financial reward if they chose it.

That was the human element. The economic element came down to this: How could demographic challenges and growing governmental financial obligations be balanced against a shrinking source of funding? Extending the retirement age by two years would be a logical response to an anticipated crisis, and something other countries such as the U.S., UK, Australia and most European nations were already committed to change.[9]

Harper's idea was a fiscally responsible action, but it played badly on many streets in the country. Age 65 was a traditional point to move from full-time employment to retirement. Most people planned to enter the next stage of their lives by that age, at least in theory, leaving them no longer dependent on wages or salary to finance their needs and lifestyle. Moving that date further into the distance sounded to them like a betrayal of sorts, whatever the rationale. (Ironically, I knew that the average retirement age in Canada was actually lower than 65, and timing of the government benefit could be managed to allow some retirees to start drawing benefits earlier, at a reduced amount, or to defer benefits past 65, receiving larger monthly payments in return for their patience. But that sort of nuance doesn't play well in electoral politics.)

In response to the negative groundswell against the Harper proposal, we pledged that if elected the Liberal Party would scrap the Conservative plan, maintaining 65 as the eligibility age to receive retirement benefits.[10] For this we were applauded by,

---

9 Andrew Allentuck, "Taking OAS Eligibility Back to Age 65 Makes Canada the Odd One Out When It Comes to Global Pensions," *Financial Post*, March 17, 2016.

10 CBC News, "Justin Trudeau Courts Seniors with Pension Pledge,"

among others, members of the Canadian Association of Retired Persons, which advocates benefits for seniors.

This reaction presented a problem for me. In my world, it's important that ends and means cohere. It should not be necessary to do something bad in order to achieve something good. Encouraging earlier retirement (seen by many as desirable) would have the unfortunate consequences of reducing the number of contributing workers and diminishing the overall cache of assets to fund these benefits for the following generations. But I was more worried about signalling that mature Canadians would no longer be part of our workforce than I was about the funding status of our government pension programs since, unlike several countries, many of our retirement commitments (most notably CPP) were sustainably funded by contributions from workers and businesses. I wanted to make sure Canadians understood that greater longevity could mean finding meaningful work past an arbitrary retirement age, helping them be more financially secure while supporting our collective economic future. In this case, the "something good" wasn't even a benefit for Canada as a whole; it was a way of improving the likelihood of our party winning the election, and one almost certain to reduce our economic growth and generate a future funding problem.[11]

Justin Trudeau recognized the value of Harper's proposal, but he appeared to have discarded it to reap extra votes and improve the chances for a Liberal victory. The move left me disconcerted. I was reminded of a quote attributed to a popular football coach in the U.S.: "Winning," he had preached, "isn't everything. It's the *only* thing." Whatever its impact on his players, the line left little room for principles within the coach's personal system of values.[12]

September 14, 2015, accessed online November 14, 2021.

11 I expand on this in chapter 18 when I deal with the need to dramatically improve Canada's productivity.

12 In an even more startling analogy, another U.S. football coach is reported

Federal politics isn't a football game, and Justin Trudeau isn't Vince Lombardi. A dedication to doing whatever it takes (and whatever you can get away with) to win in professional sports will meet the expectations of fans, who will cheer the attitude and the result with gusto. Doing the same thing in government may be increasingly common, but it is destructive to maintaining trust in government. Can you — should you — discard the very reasons you have for entering politics in order to win? That's not an academic question. It's a practical one. These are tough decisions that every aspiring politician has to make. I had to accept this unpleasant conclusion, which made me determined to find ways to deliver economically illiterate political promises with practical solutions.

—

In the run-up to the 2015 election, I managed to attract a large number of hard-working volunteers to my campaign, people of all ages and backgrounds who chose to donate their time and effort to send me to Ottawa and, in the wider picture, have the federal Liberals replace the Harper Conservatives. One of these campaign assistants was a charming 13-year-old Bangladeshi-Canadian girl. Along with a couple of her friends she had been handing out pamphlets and knocking on doors on my behalf.

One day at the end of a meeting she approached me and shyly asked if we could have a private moment. I agreed, and we headed for a quiet corner of our campaign headquarters. "I just wanted to give you this," she said, and handed me a small yellow piece of paper. On it she had written, in her neat schoolgirl handwriting, her name and the names of members of her family, six in all. Beneath this she had added the date they had applied for community housing in Toronto, their ranking on the list to receive

---

to have declared to his team, "Losing is even worse than dying, because when you lose a game, you still have to get up the next morning."

adequate accommodation, how long they had been waiting — a significant length of time — and that they were all currently living in a one-bedroom apartment.

There was nothing to suggest that this family was unique in Toronto. An untold number of immigrant families were no doubt living in similar situations. Her note opened my eyes not just to all the challenges we faced on the housing front, but to the wide contrast in living conditions across the country. If I succeeded in winning election, I could perhaps play a role in developing and applying policies to help people like this girl and her family. I could only do this if I were part of a team that made the right choices — choices that included deciding where to allocate precious resources, and how to spend those funds available to us to make a positive difference in others' lives. The choices, I knew, that would be tough but essential. I reminded myself that promises that thwarted our end goal, however expedient, came at a cost. This would prove to be the recurring frustration I had as finance minister, being constantly bombarded with politically popular, but expensive, ideas that sounded great when considered individually, but collectively added up to make it that much more difficult to properly steward the resources that would actually lead to a better long-term economic outcome for more Canadians.

I kept that small piece of paper through all five years I was in office, and I still have it to this day. It reminded me, while I was serving as finance minister, of three points to keep in mind. One was the need for us to offer assistance to new immigrants, helping them share in the wealth that attracted them here in the first place and assisting them in their search for success. These people, ambitious and determined, would help provide the engine for our future growth and enrich the cultural fabric of our nation. Another was the enormous challenge we faced in providing adequate housing. Given the vast range of issues associated with the crisis of limited affordable housing, our most immediate response was to apply Band-Aids here and there until it could be dealt with effectively. This was clearly not going to substantially improve our situation.

The note reminded me of a third point, and it kept echoing through the post-election period: we were not very effective managers in tackling and finding solutions for the vast range of serious issues we faced. We needed to find ways to come up with new policy options, a job that would be more complex than we expected because, as the federal government, we didn't own all the policy tools. Getting things done would mean, whether we liked it or not, working together with provincial and municipal levels of government, especially on issues like housing.

Against this background, depicted not by statistics and graphs but by real human conditions, I kept thinking about the unfairness of shifting values and principles for the sake of victory rather than with the aim of correcting the country's problems. Winning the majority would be celebrated with pats on the back, popping champagne corks and general hilarity. All well and good. Everyone loves to win. But how much would a win be celebrated among that young girl's family and others like them? How far would it go in improving their lives?

And what of our future collective success? That was the bar we needed to climb over. I was confident that we had the right plan in place, and a strong team to implement it, but I wanted to make sure we never lost perspective. I always wanted to remember the steps we took to ensure victory at the polls, and how our subsequent actions must lead to improvements in comfort, security and opportunity for all Canadians. If we neglected to keep that bigger goal in mind, there would be no purpose in my decision to enter public life.

—

Winning any contest is a source of pride. The amount of gratification enjoyed depends on the scope of the contest and the degree of the win.

All the effort that I and my team put into winning the Liberal nomination for Toronto Centre paid off, vaulting me into the ring as a serious participant in federal politics. I naturally felt a good deal of pride (and a smattering of concern about the change it would make in my and my family's lives), but it came with something of a cold realization.

To secure the nomination, I had run against some very good people, all long-time Liberal Party members. Uppermost among them was Diana Burke, who placed second to me. I had recognized Diana as a first-rate candidate and an asset to any organization in or out of government. She had proven this in her business career, rising to a senior executive position with Royal Bank Financial Group and being named to Microsoft's global advisory body on information security. She could also boast of a long history working on behalf of various organizations such as the International Women's Forum.

Had Diana sought a Liberal Party nomination in any other riding, I would have supported her without hesitation, which made my victory somewhat bittersweet. It was unfortunate that I had to defeat this valued and valuable member of our party in the process of launching my own political career. While Diana is very special, she was not the only excellent candidate to meet this fate. Canada is populated with talented, capable people who want and deserve a chance to serve in public office, and the more of them we can attract, the brighter the country's future will be. Which, I need to add here, is another good reason for a more managed process of attracting candidates for office.

—

Working to win the nomination had demanded one level of energy and commitment from me. Seeking votes from residents of the riding meant a different level of dedication.

I had been assured that Toronto Centre was a safe Liberal riding, but on my first foray into running for election I wasn't going to play it safe. I launched into the process of knocking on doors to introduce myself and ask about voters' concerns. Somewhat to my surprise, I enjoyed the experience. More than that, I learned much from it.

Whatever your occupation and whatever your abilities, there are things you cannot learn by sitting in an office while running a business. I knew this instinctively, but instincts can take you only so far when it comes to understanding people and the concerns that dominate their lives.

I believe my team and I knocked on every door in the riding. The range of opinions we heard was wide, but wider still was the assortment of residences and lifestyles we encountered in the inner-city riding. At one end of the scale was Cabbagetown, a neighbourhood of gentrified historic houses occupied, for the most part, by upper-middle-class mature couples and younger upwardly-mobile professionals. At the other end was Moss Park, where many residents lived in public housing facilities. Most were visible minorities and recent immigrants from all corners of the world. Many were extended families crowded into apartments so tiny I had difficulty imagining how a small nuclear family could deal with the conditions on their own, let alone with assorted grandparents and in-laws. It occurred to me that people living in smaller communities well beyond Toronto and its suburbs would find it difficult to believe these conditions exist in Canada. But they do.

The contrast between the concerns expressed to me by the two groups was not surprising. Cabbagetown residents wanted to speak about child care, taxation and retirement benefits legislation. In

Moss Park, the questions concerned limited housing and complex immigration policies. Surprising to me, but understandable from people who want more voice in government, I also heard many comments about the need to reform various elements in the current electoral process. I grew impressed by how savvy and perceptive many immigrants were about the election, especially about the positions of the various political parties on key issues. I had already noticed a substantial number of volunteers on my campaign were drawn from minority groups — as well as the sheer enthusiasm they demonstrated. Now I could see for myself the support for the federal Liberal Party that had developed among immigrants since WWII, thanks largely to its social policies. Surely much of their energy and enthusiasm also resulted from the opportunities Canada appeared to provide them, many linked to Liberal initiatives over the years. The dreams of these new Canadians, I felt, should be honoured and encouraged by government, not ignored.

The campaign experience reinforced my view that political parties should actively seek individuals possessing the skills, experience and qualities each party needs and values, and promote them as candidates. If we want people in public office who have the backbone, the capacity and the dedication to be effective in representing their community and governing the country, the parties should become more active in recruiting them. This would also provide the chance to confirm that candidates understand the political and parliamentary process before they arrive wide-eyed and wobbly-kneed in Ottawa. Great candidates are to be found in every riding of our country — it takes hard work to identify them and convince them to put themselves forward, but the country is certain to benefit from their presence and involvement.

Encouraging talented potential candidates to come forward with the assurance of support from senior party officials would do more than assist them through an unfamiliar process; it would produce better-prepared governments, with elected members groomed to get down to business free of an often confusing and lengthy familiarization period.

Both Chrystia Freeland and I were aggressively recruited to run in 2013 and 2015 respectively, and both of us assumed senior cabinet positions upon being elected in 2015. Our arrival, along with other MPs encouraged to pursue election, meant the Liberal team landed in Ottawa with an array of MPs whose well-matched talents equipped the new government to launch a program overwhelmingly approved by Canadian voters.

At this stage it's worth noting a key difference between the Canadian and American political systems. On a general level, I believe our parliamentary system is superior in many ways. But when it comes time for the senior figure in government — the prime minister in Canada and the president in the U.S. — to select members of his or her cabinet, he or she is faced with contrasting choices.

Members of an incoming federal cabinet in the U.S. can be chosen and appointed based on sharply defined talents and experience. The titles of the various cabinet members virtually dictate the qualifications of those to be appointed. Candidates for positions such as secretaries of agriculture, commerce, education and transportation, for example, are quite logically (and under normal circumstances) drawn from organizations and institutions actively engaged in those pursuits. In this way, newly elected presidents can launch their administration with the expectation that members of their cabinet are knowledgeable about operations and concerns within their sphere of responsibility. What's more, U.S. cabinet members literally walk into their positions without undergoing the drawn-out and often arduous process of running for election. It's not uncommon for an incoming president to be presented with an embarrassment of riches — multiple candidates, all possessing impressive credentials, to fill the same post with comparable qualifications.[13]

Meanwhile in Canada, incoming prime ministers must choose from a hodgepodge of candidates selected by party members in their local ridings rather than hand-picked by party leaders in accordance with their broader electoral platform. A prime minister fortunate enough to win a majority in the House may have as many as 170 candidates to fill perhaps 30 cabinet posts, but convention — and political reality — require the new PM to account for a range of criteria in his or her selection. Not only do cabinet members have to fill the specific requirements of the role for which they are chosen, the cabinet also needs to: a.) include representation from each province; b.) strike a balance in both linguistic and gender identity; and c.) reflect the wide diversity of the Canadian population.

Contrast that three-way balancing act with considerations for newly elected British prime ministers and U.S. presidents. The UK's House of Commons has 650 seats and nowhere near the demand for clear-cut geographical and linguistic concerns as a Canadian PM; and the U.S. Senate accounts for geographical representation in the country's Congress, removing this hurdle for the newly elected president.

Does this make the U.S. system for selecting cabinet members superior? Perhaps, but only if we don't manage our process well . . . because we have a key advantage. U.S. federal cabinet secretaries arrive at their jobs without having endured the nomination and election process that their Canadian counterparts must undergo. This often leaves them, in my view, unaware of the reality of people's situations, oblivious to the wide-ranging diversity of the

13 In reality, prime candidates for these posts are normally identified prior to the election process, but the premise holds true.

country and lacking a deep appreciation for the issues voiced by individual voters during the election period. Our process would have the best of both worlds if Canadian political leaders seized the opportunity to actively recruit potential candidates with specialized experience for specific cabinet positions.

The value of discussing a party's election platform with voters on a one-to-one basis cannot be overestimated. Sometimes it's hard to absorb information and provide answers for the serious dilemmas that people face. Earlier, I mentioned that I enjoyed the door-knocking experience of campaigning, and I did, primarily for the insight it provided me on the challenges I would be facing. The experience, while frequently troubling, prepared me in many ways to draft practical solutions to the issues we dealt with in cabinet. When it came time to tackle the housing crisis in Canada, formulating responses that were both focused and practical, my thinking was influenced by the experience I gained on the doorsteps of hundreds of constituents. Simplistic approaches intended to put more money into voters' pockets and enable them to buy a first house or condo would actually do more harm than good by raising prices, making their dream of home ownership even more unattainable. Real solutions to real problems, not quick-and-easy responses, carry more weight when you've actually met the people whom you are setting out to help.

There were other lessons as well. During the election campaign I encountered representatives of minority groups facing difficulties unique to them and easily overlooked by those focusing on "the big picture." They included leaders in the LGBTQ community, advocates for the legalization of marijuana, objectors to the challenges posed by China, and a host of other activists and concerned citizens. No one sincerely interested in finding solutions for social problems can remain unmoved by the kinds of real situations I encountered. If the goal of every elected representative in public service is to improve the society they represent, how can the logic of this idea be disregarded, especially by potential cabinet ministers? On its own, this one-on-one engagement with the electorate provides our Canadian system with an advantage over that of the U.S.

—

As the campaign unfolded, I was struck by both the frustration and general reasonableness of Canadians in my electoral riding and nationally. We have been famously labelled a *mosaic nation*. Neither a melting pot nor a homogeneous entity, Canada functions as a congregation of individuals with wide-ranging roots and contrasting customs who, while speaking multiple languages, consciously and defiantly choose to promote their own ideals *and* tolerate those of others. Adding more layers of complexity, much of our identity is hitched to the contrasting regional geography found within the world's second-largest sovereign nation.

Yet we make it work. Because we choose to. That determination embodies much of the Canadian exceptionalism whose existence I grasped during the university year I spent in France. It is admittedly shaken, or at least disturbed, during federal elections when our differences appear to grow in size and menace. And it is becoming more difficult to maintain when fierce partisanship and strident voices are amplified through social media, leaving little room for compromise or even, in many cases, rational consideration and response.

Overriding the widely varied issues in most regions of the country is a sense of reasonableness fostered by a general rejection of extremism and a coalescence around the centre — the traditional position of the Liberal Party.

Four

Political Personalities: New, Old and Hostile

On October 19, 2015, it all came together. The federal Liberal Party leapfrogged from the distressing loss of a few years earlier, when it was reduced to just 36 seats in the Commons, to 184 seats, providing us with a healthy majority. Two weeks later I was sworn in as finance minister, the first rookie MP in Canadian history to step into the job.

This was a significant day for Nancy and me and our family, a day when any concerns I may have had about succeeding in federal politics were dissolved by the passionate response of people who were deeply interested in smoothing the way for me with their advice and support.

The excitement of the party's victory was followed by a few days of silence and a veil of secrecy leading up to the swearing-in ceremony. I sensed that I was under consideration for the position of finance minister (and others had an even stronger perception), and an invitation to visit Ottawa shortly after the election made it even more likely. There I met Peter Harder, a former deputy minister of foreign affairs, soon to be appointed to the Senate, and Marc-André Blanchard, chair and CEO of McCarthy Tétrault, one of the country's leading law firms. Together, they were assigned the task of vetting potential cabinet ministers. Both men were excellent examples of outsiders who could add perspective and judgment to an essential process, a rare approach by the Trudeau government to reach practical conclusions. We quickly established an easy rapport, even while they probed for any possible skeletons in my closet. Happily, there were none.

Still, there was no declaration until a few days later when I was invited to attend a meeting with Prime Minister Trudeau, Principal Secretary Gerry Butts, and Chief of Staff to the Prime Minister Katie Telford. The formal offer was made, and I accepted. I remember returning to my hotel room, where I pondered how things were about to change and how prepared I was for it.

I had not been entirely surprised by the prime minister's decision. Nor were others.

A short time before election day, former prime minister Paul Martin had invited me to lunch. His sharp political instincts foresaw not only an impressive Liberal victory but my likely appointment as finance minister. I was immediately struck by the basic decency of the man and his interest in helping pave my way through the inevitable difficulties he knew I was about to encounter. He and I shared a business background, as well as a level of success and wealth that made us interesting targets for the media. Paul drew my attention to the international nature of the job, something not always obvious to Canadians, who assume that the finance minister's focus is largely fixed on internal matters. But Canada plays an important role in G7 and G20 conferences, and it's up to the finance minister to express our position on various matters clearly and effectively, without alienating countries whose partnership we depend upon.

The key, Paul explained, is language. He meant not just speaking competently in both official languages while avoiding a finance minister's lexicon, but carefully choosing words and phrasing for each specific audience and environment, including the press. "Think about the impact of your words and the confidence they express," he suggested, reminding me that every word I uttered would be weighed for its meaning, intended or otherwise. It would be my job, at times, to help Canadians understand what was going on with the economy, how it would affect Canada and what it all meant to them and their families. I should remember, he added, that I was "speaking from thirty thousand feet," rising above the issues of the day to cover things in a broad context.

He also mentioned, almost in passing, that I would have to put my business assets into a blind trust. I was already aware of this rule and later, as the newly appointed finance minister, I wrote the ethics commissioner to ask for detailed guidelines on following the regulation to the letter. I wanted to avoid any potential concern in this area, and I was prepared to arrange my affairs, with the commissioner's advice, to demonstrate with total certainty that I was free of conflicts. In response, the commissioner informed me in writing that there was no need for a blind trust in my case and that "the best measure of compliance" was a "Conflict of Interest Screen" that would ensure I had no awareness of issues coming before the government that could put me in conflict with my financial holdings. This practical solution was intended to isolate me specifically from government actions that potentially could benefit my holdings. It worked in practice but, according to the media and opposition, not in theory. I frequently had to withstand media and opposition attacks on my situation, despite the commissioner's recommendations, just as Paul Martin had experienced before me. Hindsight suggests that I might have sought more political counsel to confirm the best course of action on this, but after the federal ethics commissioner submits her ruling, would it really be necessary to confirm she was correct? It never occurred to me. I followed her explicit advice to the letter. *Not* following it seemed to me a much greater risk.

During my lunch with Paul, I was introduced to the unusual life of ex-politicians at the federal level — or at least former prime ministers. Our table had been set in a corner of the Royal

York hotel dining room, concealed for the most part from other diners by a private curtain. Despite the attempt at privacy, on at least three occasions people showed up at our table to greet Paul, shaking his hand and asking how he was doing. None knew him personally, but all wanted to acknowledge their admiration and thank him for his service, and Paul was unfailingly gracious to every one of them.

He was equally generous to me following my official appointment to cabinet, calling me that very day to offer his total support and promising to be available at any time to extend advice and guidance. This launched a careful mentorship for me, with Paul willingly sharing his experience of having to make tough judgment calls. He often called before and after important moments, usually to offer congratulations but sometimes to push and prod me to remember the reason I was in politics in the first place. I found his passionate concern for education among Indigenous youth especially inspiring. His personal contributions in this area, both in time and financial resources, are not familiar enough to Canadians, and I saw him as someone who never stopped thinking about how he could make a difference in matters important to him and our country.

I sought counsel from others as well, eager to learn from their experience and wisdom. I expected Bob Rae, whose depth of experience in Canadian politics ranged across both federal and provincial venues as well as the NDP and Liberal parties, to share his knowledge and advice frankly. And he did. He had been the Liberal member for Toronto Centre before Chrystia Freeland and was more than generous with his time. I was struck by the man's keen intellect and his very high standards and expectations for those following in his footsteps. To put it bluntly, he is a man who does not suffer fools easily. He remained patient with me throughout our discussion, even though I suspect my lack of political experience was obvious to him. Again, I noted the impact of celebrity, on a small but telling note. Despite having been out of office for some time, Bob was simply unable to pay for his own coffee — the operator of the café insisted that the drink was on him.

Jean Chrétien called to offer congratulations. I accepted an invitation to meet in his office, where I learned first-hand that there was no more wily fox in Canadian politics than the former PM. Here was a man who for decades had seen around every corner and peeked beneath every rock, assessing risks and opportunities better than any politician of his time. He was especially good at anticipating one of the most difficult aspects of my job as federal finance minister, a job he had also held.

His advice to me was direct and incisive: I should develop as cordial and effective a working relationship with the prime minister as possible — but there were limits to what was possible. "The more independent you are, the more effective you will be," he noted, then added, "but the more independent you are, the more you will be at risk."

He pointed out that I needed to understand that a healthy relationship between a prime minister and a finance minister involves tension. Our jobs were very different, he reminded me, so we often may have conflicting goals. Instead of trying to avoid tension as a result of this conflict, I should welcome it because it would provide a better outcome for the country.

They were wise words, drawn from the most experienced federal politician in the land, and they led to perhaps the most enduring takeaway I acquired from my years in Ottawa. As difficult as it may be at times, the tension between the two offices is essential to getting things done effectively. How else can you balance political objectives with fiscal responsibility?

Not all the guidance came from former Liberal finance ministers. In fact, the longest tutorial I absorbed was delivered by dyed-in-the-wool Conservative Michael Wilson, who served as finance minister during Brian Mulroney's tenure as PM. After that, he had carved out a career that would include his appointment as Canadian ambassador to the U.S. and serving as chair of Barclays bank in Canada.

Whether Michael Wilson's warm response to my request for a meeting was the result of his having been out of political office for many years or because he was basically a warm and decent man (I am in the camp that believes the latter), he welcomed my request and suggested a breakfast meeting. Breakfast became a two-and-a-half-hour session covering virtually every aspect of my new position. He had taken the time before our get-together to prepare pages (and pages) of notes covering a wide range of topics, including my working relationship with the prime minister, anticipating and reacting to challenges from across the aisle in the House, understanding the international issues I was about to face and working with the Bank of Canada (and the importance of central bank independence from politics).

It wasn't a lecture. There was no implication that he was talking down to a novice, although I clearly was one. Everything was positive and encouraging, delivered in a cordial manner. From time to time during my tenure as finance minister I took advantage of his offer to discuss some problem I had encountered. In every case he offered his opinion and shared his wisdom, playing the role of an ideal mentor and providing me with insight and understanding that might have taken years to absorb on my own.

I mention this not only to praise Michael Wilson's geniality and basic goodness, but to illustrate that although we were in different political parties, we shared similar views on how to manage things within the system. There were no points of disagreement between us on critical issues like housing, working with the central bank and handling international issues. Had we been sitting on opposite sides of the House as members, with one of us as the finance minister, I am quite sure our approach to each other would have been respectful, even if our points of view would surely have clashed here and there. I had the trusting belief that once the election campaign had passed, and excepting the catcalls exchanged during Question Period, things would be similarly amiable among members of the various parties. At times they were, and at other times I was surprised when my efforts to form working relationships with others of different political stripes were summarily rejected.

There's a good reason for the phrase *playing politics*. It's often seen as a game and, like in all games, each side will strive for victory, creating winners and losers. On the surface, that's not all that different from business. Through my business activities before arriving in Ottawa I had spent several years going head-to-head with competitors in pursuit of clients. We won more than our share of victories, but win or lose, when the game was over both sides moved on.

That's not how it works in Ottawa. Given the stakes and personalities involved, federal elections more closely resemble warfare than gameplay. Unlike in war, however, the battles don't end when a winner is declared.

I was far from naive when it came to recognizing that a victory in politics doesn't vanquish the losing side. They simply become the opposition. Fair enough. But I didn't fully appreciate the intensity of the perpetual battle to dominate Parliament, or at least public opinion, all intended to set the stage for the next election. Probably no one who hasn't directly experienced the process can understand the stress of the constant adversarial footing.

My response was to find ways of deflecting the sharper edges of exchanges with members of other parties by striking some sort of relationship beyond the political battleground. I began by initiating conversations with members of the opposition shadow cabinets assigned to monitor my decisions. Lisa Raitt of the Conservatives and Guy Caron of the NDP, both designated by their party leaders to criticize my policies and performance, proved to be bright, capable and genial personalities.

Lisa Raitt brought a good deal of expertise and experience to her position. With degrees in both chemistry and law, along with stints in the natural resources, labour and transport ministries in the Harper government, she initially displayed a warm manner, acknowledging me as a rookie in Parliament. Guy Caron, a former Quebec labour economist, was equally easy to engage in conversation. There was never any doubt, however, that we were on opposite sides not necessarily just on specific issues but on the entire playing field. Their job was to hold me to account, and they did it often and with some enthusiasm. There were days when I returned home with feelings of resentment when their comments were edgier than I might have expected, even while realizing that they had been doing their job with fervour and often with success.

Still, Lisa Raitt and most other members of the opposition were playing the game with a sense of decorum. This was not the case with Pierre Poilievre, who seemed to view the House of Commons not as a site for hard-nosed debating but as a gladiatorial arena where encounters were measured by the amount of blood spilled and the number of personal insults hurled.

He used his position as a member of Parliament to forge and deliver commentary on the floor of the House, where he was protected from legal action only by the parliamentary privilege that grants freedom of speech within the chamber and immunity from prosecution, even by those targeted with his baseless claims. He vaulted over the line on several occasions, at one point suggesting outrageously that I had employed my advance knowledge of financial policy to earn profits from insider trading on the stock market. It was a false claim, and he knew if he repeated it outside the Commons, it would lead to serious legal charges from me. He didn't, of course.

He may justify his actions and attitudes in any way he chooses, but collectively they are in conflict with almost every political value we have enjoyed as a nation for over 150 years. More to the point, they corrode the tolerant and centrist tradition behind Canada's historical success and international respect.

A seemingly endless antagonism sits at the core of parliamentary democracy, and to grumble about it would be futile. We should expect opposition parties to seek out and remark upon weaknesses in the actions of those across the floor of the House, but we should equally expect the criticism to be free of personal insults and outright false accusations. If nothing else, I believe that displaying a more courteous demeanour in both the House of Commons and the media would strengthen the confidence of Canadians in their federal government.

I realize that this is not a new observation; nevertheless, in my mind it remains valid.

A positive counterbalance to all of this arrived from across the border on the day of my appointment to cabinet when I received a telephone call from Jack Lew, the U.S. secretary of the treasury under President Barack Obama. He offered his congratulations and said he looked forward to working with me and the prime minister. I thanked him for his good wishes, we exchanged a few more words, and both moved on. His call reminded me that one of my most important duties, if I really wanted to make a difference for the Canadian economy, was to develop and nurture a strong relationship with my American counterpart. The call was important to both of us because it represented the first step in forming a relationship between the finance arms of our two countries, one that would ease future discussions that were certain to arise. I had no idea at that moment just how important those U.S.-Canada finance relationships would be when put under the stress of the next American president. Jack's call was a small step, to be sure. But I have never underestimated the value of small steps in building rapport with those who can influence your goals and responsibilities no matter which side of the border they are on.

Or which side of the aisle they sit.

—

The cabinet of the 2015 election can be described in many ways, including talented, enthusiastic, dedicated and, as noted earlier, gender-balanced. Many of the individual members lacked experience with the files assigned to them — not a surprise, perhaps, but something I couldn't help noting. Several of my new colleagues had interesting and varied backgrounds, but with very limited real experience in executive or leadership roles. Only a few, like Jim Carr, Scott Brison, Ralph Goodale and Navdeep Bains had had any prior business or economic experience.

It soon occurred to me that cabinet members came to Ottawa for many different reasons. Jane Philpott, for example, arrived with a distinct sense of government's place in establishing and maintaining an effective social policy. A highly capable family physician, she had spent several years in Niger, West Africa, providing medical care via a non-governmental organization and developing a training program for village health workers. During her participation in Médecins Sans Frontières (Doctors Without Borders) she helped develop an early training program for family medicine in Ethiopia. Not surprisingly, she saw Canada's place in the world as a country taking an active and engaged role in international issues, and she wanted to be a participant in that evolution. She was smart, sensible and an important contributor to cabinet views and agendas.

Jody Wilson-Raybould had invested much of her time before coming to Ottawa on Indigenous governance, focusing on what reconciliation and the federal government's role in it should look like. While she was wary to the point of being distant in our early personal encounters, her demeanour changed when trust built up between us, and she became a warm and friendly colleague. But her views and values remained fixed. At root, she is passionate about issues that matter to her. The government's financial obligations that emerged out of reconciliation efforts, for example, were understandably not her primary concern. As finance minister they were of major concern to me, of course, which created periodic flashpoints, yet we remained friendly and managed to work together well.

Chrystia Freeland's point of view had an international bent given her journalistic career prior to seeking elected office. As a result of her work with the *Globe and Mail*, the *Financial Times*, the World Economic Forum and others, she could boast an impressive network of contacts outside of Canada. Her Rolodex overflowed with names and numbers of influential people she could quickly access, an enormous asset in her initial positions, first as minister of international trade and later as minister of foreign affairs.

These were just three prominent and highly effective colleagues in a cabinet well-populated with other strong women boasting equally notable credentials. Patty Hajdu had overcome a difficult childhood to graduate with a master's degree in public administration and, prior to her election in 2015, rising to become executive director of Shelter House, the largest public shelter in Thunder Bay. Passionate and strong-willed, she brought a perspective that was far to the left of my own, yet I greatly admired her work, first as minister of status of women and later as minister of employment, workforce development and labour. She went headfirst into battle on behalf of social issues, which periodically put her at odds with the PMO.

Like so many other cabinet members whose agenda collided with my opinions, Patty Hajdu and I disagreed from time to time, but we always found ways to resolve things through an understanding and genuine respect for the other's point of view.

Others, most notably Catherine McKenna, proved more than capable in grasping and defining key issues within their ministry's area of responsibility. She embraced her role as minister of the environment with a compelling passion, but she also leaned in on other issues, bringing a realist perspective to the problems we faced.

I held special admiration for cabinet members who arrived well-equipped with international contacts and relationships they could employ virtually from day one. My initial parliamentary secretary, François-Philippe Champagne, for example, had held executive positions with ABB Group in Switzerland and Amec PLC in the UK, arming him with the means to tap sources of information among European businesses when he was appointed minister of international trade.

In contrast, while I may have lacked some depth of familiarity internationally, I had spent my career building a business in communities across Canada with offices in every major Canadian city, and even many smaller centres. When it came to domestic issues, especially those linked to social concerns, I started with an understanding at the grassroots level from my time at Covenant House and St. Michael's Hospital, but I clearly had more to learn.

Our firm delivered pensions and benefits directly to individuals and provided counselling to people undergoing personal stress. Thus, I was aware that average working Canadians were dealing with far more challenges than they appeared to be on the surface. I had seen the gaps in social services even more intimately when I had the chance to interact directly with kids seeking shelter at Covenant House in Downtown Toronto. I knew the hazards that working Canadians could encounter should their employers' retirement program run off the rails for one reason or another. And I understood the concerns and misgivings of Canadians who lacked access entirely to an adequate and well-managed retirement plan, funded in part by contributions from their employer. Knowledge, as we are often reminded, is the beginning of understanding, and I fully understood the need for a well-designed, well-managed Canada Pension Plan.

Lacking in many of Justin Trudeau's cabinet appointees, men and women alike, was managerial experience. That's at the heart of the job, after all. Making public statements or delivering sound bites to the media on a given subject may be the most visible actions by ministers, but they should not be the only measure of their performance. Each minister oversees a department that can comprise several hundred staff members — or thousands, depending on the ministry. Even with the assistance of the highly competent federal bureaucracy, the responsibilities of a federal minister weigh heavily on those who lack management experience.

It wasn't just novice cabinet ministers who needed an adjustment period. Those closest to the prime minister — operators like Gerry Butts and Katie Telford in the PMO, and Cyrus Reporter, chief of staff at the federal Liberal office — found themselves on a bigger, more brilliantly lit stage, playing more prominent leading roles and facing a larger, more aggressively critical audience. The decision not to rely on experienced insiders from previous governments may have satisfied the urge to demonstrate a new way of doing business, but it left open the possibility of rookie mistakes, an enduring problem for the Trudeau PMO.

I also had an enormous amount to learn, but I felt some attributes I brought to the job put me a step or two ahead of some others. I already knew many of the people I would be dealing with outside government, having consulted with or worked alongside them during my business career. My years at Morneau Shepell also had me actively involved in assessing and employing a range of government programs related to the financial file. Taxation, along with pension design and funding, were always factors in my decision-making as CEO of our business, and my time as a board member and chair of the C.D. Howe Institute involved me in thinking about fiscal policy and a raft of other policy matters.

I valued other experiences I had acquired prior to the election, many of them directly associated with the issues I and the ministry would be expected to address. Sitting on the board of AGF Management Ltd. had provided me with an inside look at the mortgage and housing markets, and, of course, I had spent my entire business career servicing the needs of companies across Canada in funding and managing employee retirement programs. I faced my own learning curve in government, but it was more closely linked to parliamentary procedures and practices than the nuts and bolts of my work at the finance department.

An early signal of some of the challenges I would encounter came from the prime minister's declaration to cabinet that all ministries would be considered equal in power and status. The driver for this statement was clearly to avoid hierarchies in the cabinet, including questions of gender parity. I saw this as completely unnecessary, since we had highly capable women in the roles of health, justice and international trade. In addition, clearly talented people like Carla Qualtrough, Mélanie Joly and Patty Hajdu, among others, played essential roles initially, and their influence would grow over time. Would acting on this general notion of equality, even if it was not really anything other than an empty statement, create other issues when it came to cabinet dynamics? For example, would it mean that each minister would be given equal time to speak in cabinet meetings? Would it require me to give equal weight to every request for funds? It all seemed an unnecessary effort to focus on the egalitarian aspect of Justin Trudeau's vision, which played well in some quarters but was, frankly, often impractical. Effective management was being sacrificed at the altar of image and presentation, and not for the last time.

The fiction of equality among ministries would have been workable to some degree had we agreed on an overall fiscal target. That way, each minister would seek to have her or his policy or objective agreed to as a government priority, generating competition for resources and stimulating a robust cabinet debate about ordering priorities. That was my goal, which would have allowed me to insert order in our cabinet deliberations and help my colleagues to coalesce around priorities; however, this approach to governance, and the need for necessary tension in search of reaching decisions, was not a consideration for the Trudeau government. I could not get agreement from the PM and the PMO to establish an overall target that would make the process subject to a framework, encouraging give-and-take when we considered policy options across multiple fronts. Instead, all proposals were listened to politely, with cabinet members approving them in principle, leaving the decision on whether to move forward to me, the finance minister, according to the financial merits of the proposal, then to be passed from me to the prime minister and his team. Rather than foster equality, this process had exactly the opposite effect of the original intention, creating a system in which decisions were punted to a higher authority. Savvy ministers would try to sidestep the process, creating unhealthy tension between the finance minister and the PM and PMO by going around me to plead their case directly to the PMO.

Alternatively, each ministry could have been given a fixed budget target, to be achieved through effective spending and department management. I wanted some means to provide a fiscal anchor and lend stability to the process. Without it, I was left trying to argue down every initiative. This meant the function of the prime minister and PMO when dealing with the cabinet came down to overruling me, disbursing funds according to pressure applied on behalf of the initiative rather than subject to any healthy debate to weigh alternatives in a transparent fashion. In effect, the traditional approach, with the prime minister and the finance minister playing good cop/bad cop, was made even worse, with the PM and PMO effectively encouraging a dysfunctional process. I understood and accepted the bad cop role, while nevertheless regularly arguing for targets that would bring some structure to the process. I had to rationalize every case, one by one, with the recognition that I couldn't assume fiscal responsibility and expect to win any popularity contests.

—

What I wanted and expected was a more effective approach to management. The prime minister introduces policies, and some of them will create conflict between cabinet ministers, generally as a result of competition for funding. This is where governance becomes key, and the responsibility to lay the groundwork for good governance rests on the shoulders of the prime minister, who must clearly state the government's main objectives. These need to be framed within financial limitations which are a crucial part of the overall agenda. This harkens back to my earlier point about the value of positive tension between the prime minister and cabinet members, the finance minister in particular. Such tension is not only inevitable — it's essential. The key is making it productive. The lack of understanding about this fundamental underpinning proved to be the source of many challenges to me over the next five years.

We began as a government with a well-developed but too expansive plan, essentially a blueprint for action once in office. Implementation in the early days was brisk. I delivered our fall economic statement within a month of assuming my role, meaning that some of our key promises on tax cuts for the middle class were in place by January 2016, less than two months after our swearing-in ceremony.

This early momentum, along with a busy PM and PMO, provided a good degree of autonomy to me and the finance department and was, I hoped, a positive bellwether for our term of office. The goal was to create a management structure that ensured the government's plans were evergreen, a function that the PMO could lead, with input and support from ministers. But a serious gap became evident. Action and execution were now required from the same planners and thinkers who had created our election strategy, calling upon two divergent skills that are rarely found in individuals, let alone an entire team. We soon fell back into the pattern of the previous Conservative government under Stephen Harper, with the PMO assuming increased authority over ministers and ministerial work. This involved a day-to-day management approach that was frustrating for ministers and ensured that neither the PM nor the PMO would realistically be able to allocate sufficient time to prepare for the future.

—

Recent years have seen momentum building toward centralization in federal government, resulting in fewer key roles played by cabinet members. The impact of this move has been to weaken the powers of cabinet and, as a result, diminish the process of selecting candidates. It's inevitable — if the prime minister and PMO expect little input from cabinet ministers and fail to encourage it, the talents and qualifications of candidates become less important. Why worry about how candidates can function on the job if little is expected of them in the first place?

And it cuts both ways. If people with the skills and enthusiasm to contribute to a party's agenda foresee themselves as, effectively, neutered in a potential role, they'll choose not to enter public life. This becomes a loss for everyone. Nobody of the calibre needed to run a government ministry will sacrifice so much of their time, privacy and often their income to become basically a figurehead, whose contribution is neither sought nor considered of value. I sensed that this was becoming more noticeable in the last decade or so, and I had hoped the Trudeau government would take the opportunity to reverse the trend. Two factors in 2015 were responsible, in my opinion, for inspiring candidates of a special calibre to run for office. One was widespread dissatisfaction with the Stephen Harper government. The other was the arrival of Justin Trudeau on the political scene as the new Liberal leader. Individuals who might have chosen to stay on the sidelines in other elections saw a remarkable opportunity to take part in a major change in style and values under Trudeau, which was enough to spur them forward. And the pitch was that the approach would be to entrust real responsibility to ministers in a cabinet-driven government.

It's difficult to imagine a cabinet group arriving on the scene in Ottawa with a more pronounced concentration of enthusiasm and vision than the team introduced by Prime Minister Trudeau at the swearing-in ceremony. The new faces and new energy represented more than a change from the Harper style. They held the promise of a substantial new agenda responding to pent-up demands among Canadians.

The swearing-in ceremony was and remains a historic event, introducing a group of primarily neophyte representatives with big things to consider, marked by the prime minister's equal distribution of cabinet posts to men and women. The steps to be taken — legalizing marijuana, medical assistance in dying and others — moved us into the vanguard of progressive nations on an international scale. We were young, fresh, urbane, enthusiastic . . . and untested, with not a little bit of hubris. (Moving from third place to first can do that.)

Much was achieved in the early going, thanks to pre-election planning. Clear objectives had been set and agreed upon as part of the pitch to voters. As a result of this clarity of vision, wheels began to turn and things got done from the first day cabinet members occupied their offices. The situation was enhanced by the PMO's attention being focused on acclimatizing itself to the new environment, leaving cabinet ministers and their staff to carry out their assignments unimpeded and largely free of second-guessing.

We had, in essence, a model that worked, initially, measured in the achievements being recorded. They include passage of legislation dealing with medical assistance in dying, shaped and largely shepherded by Jody Wilson-Raybould and Jane Philpott. Other programs got underway with promising results; revisions to the Canada Pension Plan, housing policy, Canada Child Benefit and the Advisory Council on Economic Growth were the beginning of a vast range of measures that marked the government as both energetic and productive.

It would be unreasonable to expect any government at any level to maintain this vibrant energy and output throughout its mandate. Things change, personalities evolve, events occur and the focus shifts. Nothing new there. Nothing new either about an awareness, with the passage of time, that another election date lurks somewhere beyond the horizon, and that re-election would depend on inserting new ingredients into the mix. But so much in life is determined by timing, and responding too early to an upcoming challenge may prove as injurious as responding too late. Which, as we'll see, is my view of what occurred within the first year of the government's mandate.

—

All of this became evident and disconcerting later. For the moment, still jubilant over our victory and the glamorous formality of the swearing-in ceremony, I had more practical matters in mind, including finalizing my personal staff and settling into my office.

Five

Travel and Revelations

The finance department was located in a sparkling new building on Elgin Street, just a few blocks from Parliament Hill. Named the James Michael Flaherty Building in honour of my predecessor, it had all the attributes you might expect for efficient offices, with clean lines and much glass. Jim might not have shared all of my views on social issues, but he displayed a commitment to fiscal prudence that I thought was important for the role. In any case, I can't imagine being finance minister to Stephen Harper was easy. Jim would have faced a challenge opposite to mine, as his boss had been engaged and directive while mine was less engaged and permitted his staff to take the lead.

The building's polished, contemporary design, reflecting 21st-century professionalism and productivity, began at the street-level entry and soared all the way up to the 14th floor, ending abruptly at my office door, where any suggestion that my staff and I were working in an age of computerization was non-existent.

The furniture was dowdy, the walls were bare and the environment suggested an aged hotel, not a modern office facility. I suspected the decor was the product of the Harper government's overly austere approach when it came to the public service.

I avoid spending money unwisely, but I know an attractive working environment generates energy for everyone who occupies it. Too busy with other duties to track down the protocol for requesting new furniture, I replaced the existing desks and chairs with attractive and comfortable items reflecting the building's style, paying for them out of my own pocket. They transformed the place into an inviting and efficient work area. To improve the cheerless blank walls, I wanted to rent some Canadian art from the Canada Council Art Bank, but Stephen Harper's people had applied a strict budget limit on the amount that could be spent for government facilities, including rental from the Art Bank. I understand and support the concept of setting upper limits on such outlays, but we were talking about an intra-government deal here. Money taken out of one government pocket to rent the artwork would flow back into another government pocket, after all.

My ministry lacked a budget to cover the art rental, so I hung some works from my own collection in the office.

This sounds like a small point, and of course it is. Pretty much every issue I faced during my term as a cabinet minister had more significant implications. But the symbolism was critical, in my opinion. Filling an otherwise contemporary workplace with dreary and outdated furniture suggested that neither the work nor those doing the work mattered very much.

My first meeting with the U.S. treasury secretary at his office in Washington, DC, later in my term was an experience in sharp contrast. Above the fireplace in what was then Steven Mnuchin's office hung a magnificent portrait of Alexander Hamilton, the country's first secretary of the treasury. The artwork and its prominent location said a great deal about the historical significance of Mnuchin's position and of the pride associated with the work performed there. The office furniture, while from another era, was well-maintained.

Visiting my counterparts in Mexico and France, I was similarly impressed by the elegant but practical decor. The rooms were not excessively lavish; they simply reflected an atmosphere in which serious discussions and major decisions were undertaken. I marvelled at our apparent inability to foster a mature approach to framing the critical work of government while practising judicious use of public funds. It was an extension of our attitude toward 24 Sussex Drive: we were fearful of investing funds on a public edifice befitting a G7 country in the 21st century.

—

Configuring my ministry's office space was, of course, not as important as choosing my staff. Four of the most critical positions were filled by individuals who brought exceptional abilities to their work and who stayed with me during my entire time in government. Ian Foucher served as a key policy advisor, Sharan Kaur became my key personal assistant and later my director of operations, Marion Pilon was a legislative assistant and later my director of parliamentary affairs or legislative leader, and Matt Barnes was a communications specialist who eventually assumed a lead communications role.

My biggest challenge was finding a chief of staff who could manage the office and handle the political challenges we would inevitably face. I also needed a director of policy, who would help develop key policy initiatives based on our publicly declared goals and translate objectives into specifics. I would also count on them to support my views and challenge me on blind spots.

Robert Asselin became my first director of policy. He brought a keen intellect and an academic insight from his time as a university professor, in addition to well-honed political instincts from years spent helping the Liberal Party in platform development.

Filling the chief of staff role was not as straightforward. The selection and appointment of a chief of staff would be key to the duties and the operation of the entire department. I needed someone whom I could trust implicitly and who boasted, first and foremost, keen political judgment. He or she would also need a good deal of experience in handling everything from ministry workflows and policy discussions to corporate communications and, importantly, hone my ability to function as minister of finance. They would also have to be capable of managing other staff members with skill and respect, earning my total confidence in handling every aspect of the job. Finally, I wanted someone with whom I could forge a close working relationship built on trust and a shared manner of getting things done.

The guy who met all of these qualifications was John Zerucelli, whose work on behalf of Liberal parliamentarians extended back to his university days. Smart and savvy, and a lawyer by background, he had been chief of staff to Ontario Treasury Board president Deb Matthews, and I looked forward to having him lead my team in the finance department. Most important to me, we had developed a strong bond through the election campaign, from my very first day in seeking the nomination in Toronto Centre. I knew he would have my back — and we had the personal connection to speak frankly to each other.

My selection was rejected by the prime minister and his embryonic PMO. I was informed that my chief of staff would be Richard Maksymetz. Richard had an almost encyclopedic brain on Liberal Party politics and a first-rate understanding of policy principles. He turned out to be exceptionally effective at the politics of the ministry of finance, knowing whom I needed to work with, and how. His keen intelligence meant that he could lean in on virtually any topic.

From the standpoint of Liberal Party politics, Richard was perfect. But over the two and a half years he served as my chief of staff, we didn't fully address a problem that accompanied me to Ottawa: my success in business and my private life made me an easy target for the opposition and the media. Both sought to characterize me as someone unappreciative of the concerns faced by average Canadians. This was a perceived weakness we were never able to overcome. It meant my value for personal privacy and my need to build the tough hide required to survive day-to-day media exposure and partisan battles did not become the priorities they should have been. Richard worked well with me, leading the team into policy deliberations, managing the department and supervising other important duties. But I needed to build new skills, especially political skills, to be fully successful at my job.

And I could not help wondering about the PMO's unbending insistence on Richard filling the position. Richard had long and close relationships with many within the PMO. Had he been selected for me because of his proven talents to perform a job that I felt should have been my choice to fill? Or had he been chosen to act as a link between day-to-day actions within my office and members of the prime minister's inner circle? In the end, I grew confident in Richard, and he helped manage the natural tension between the finance department and the Prime Minister's Office. But the micromanagement from the PMO was a sign of challenges to come.

Gerry Butts was not only the man who in a sense recruited me for the job, he was the person I knew best in the PMO. It was immediately clear to everyone that he, Katie Telford and the prime minister represented something of a troika.

As the base of the triangle of power, with the prime minister occupying the peak, Katie Telford and Gerry Butts represented contrasting and balanced skills. Gerry had the highest profile of anyone next to the prime minister, but in action he and Katie were seen to be on equal footing. Fiercely protective of the PM — they had been pals since their student days at McGill — Gerry could be combative with journalists and critics, shaping and shielding the government's narrative. In my view he was the backbone of the Trudeau operation; fiercely intelligent, and strategic to his core, he had been the architect of Trudeau's public profile and our policy priorities. He recognized the opportunity to break from the Harper days with a "sunny ways" image. He accompanied this with an understanding of the public's willingness to abandon the economic orthodoxy of balanced budgets and austerity in favour of a policy that spoke to the anxiety of middle-class Canadians.

Katie had earned her spurs serving as Trudeau's national campaign director, a job she carried out with obvious success. While Gerry focused his attention on Justin Trudeau's emotional connection with Canadians, Katie favoured data- and results-driven decision-making. I don't think it's an exaggeration to label her a political mastermind, someone whose instincts are constantly tuned to public opinion. Her management style included a strong emphasis on delegation, but, like Justin Trudeau, she favoured those with whom she had built trust in previous working relationships. This may have represented a source of comfort to her, but it became a problem for a government with an inevitable need to tap new talents. The major challenge she faced was getting decisions made. This had some benefit when working with Gerry, who is sometimes impulsive, but was a clear weakness when he stepped down.

One individual who impressed me from our first encounter was Cyrus Reporter, a lawyer with sharp instincts for managing political problems and a long-standing relationship with Justin Trudeau. As deputy chief of staff to the prime minister, he played the role of troubleshooter and project manager, skills acquired while serving first as chief of staff for Allan Rock in Jean Chrétien's government, and then as Justin Trudeau's chief of staff while in opposition. Cyrus had more high-level experience in federal politics than anyone else in the PMO, and it showed. Keeping talented operatives like him engaged would be critical to Trudeau's success, and Cyrus's early departure created a void that left political issues to languish.

—

It's expected that citizens of a democracy tend to grumble about workers in public service, hanging the unflattering label *bureaucrat* on them. Like many things in life, coming up against reality tends to shake up your rigid presuppositions.

I'm not prepared to say that every public service worker is a paragon of ability and energy, but almost without exception the people I encountered at the Department of Finance were as capable and dedicated as any at similar levels in private business. Paul Rochon, my deputy for my entire five years in finance, was not only experienced on a wide range of issues, he was highly intelligent, with the knack of quickly grasping the core of a problem. He was also adept at recognizing both the policy and the political objectives, locating an effective solution and finding the best way to get it done. Paul was especially valuable in the budgeting process, when he would marshal the talents of the broader team to help narrow the focus in response to the inclination of the PM and PMO to fund something on every file whether it made a positive impact or not.

The positive contribution of the public service was never more obvious than in times of crisis. During the COVID-19 pandemic, the department functioned like a well-oiled machine. As I explain later, all of us were faced with the need to find and apply effective solutions at breakneck speed. And we did, like delivering money directly to households through the Canada Revenue Agency, a concept that had never been applied before, and providing government-supported loans for businesses, which involved my negotiating with the banks to obtain their buy-in at administrative prices that were a fraction of those in the U.S.[14]

14 Gaining support from the banks was critical, as we needed them to administer the loans. It meant I had to negotiate directly with bank CEOs in securing their agreement to administer the loans at or less than their cost. With federal government guarantees on the loans, I argued, they could afford to cut their fees to the bone – and, after some cajoling, they did. In fact, the fees we paid were materially lower than the U.S. government was able to negotiate with their banks. I saw this as our banks leaning in appropriately in a time of crisis.

Whatever apprehensions I may have had before stepping into federal politics — and there had been many, as you can imagine — the one about working with the monolithic public service was soon swept away. When targets are set and the urgency is at hand, Canada's public service usually comes through.

The key difference between public service and private business isn't ability, in my experience. It's in necessary process.

In successful businesses, there is always an inclination to action. For publicly traded companies the action is driven by the demand for profit, expressed in quarterly reports, where a minor slip can make a major impact on share prices and shareholder confidence. In public service, however, the process involves getting it right by considering every angle and assessing the impact on every category of constituents. That's all fine and good, but it is also, by necessity, slow and meticulous.

—

My career in business and the resulting emphasis on action was only one of the contrasts between me and the prime minister. I had the sense that my focus on detail and my desire to get to the optimum policy outcome were both comforting — someone was managing the fiscal framework — and another potential source of discord. His near-singular focus on communication, which was his key strength, left it to the people behind the scenes to get the work done, and the various machinations were not his primary concern. His core team was the PMO, which meant that in practice, the rest of us were not his direct reports.

I didn't pay any of this much attention in the early days following the swearing-in ceremony. I was busy introducing myself to those who I knew would be watching and assessing me from the beginning, including the CEOs of major chartered banks and the finance ministers of the provinces and territories.

After about a week on the job I found myself in Turkey, attending the G20 summit. Most of the focus at this session was not on economics but on terrorism, driven by the horrific attacks that had taken place in Paris two days earlier. I added my comments to those of the prime minister, declaring that Canada would be resolute in combatting ISIS and all terrorism.

Two days later, I was back in Ottawa preparing the economic and fiscal update before introducing it in the House of Commons. I was barely two weeks into the job, and this would be the first opportunity for the opposition to judge my performance and for the media to focus attention on me.

The news was not good. Both the economic and fiscal outlooks had deteriorated since the Harper government's last budget, dropping the projected budgetary balance by about $6 billion and leaving a $3 billion deficit. Reviewing those figures two years into the COVID-19 crisis, and the measures taken to ride us through it, makes the financial problem seem small today, but it loomed large at the time. We had promised a budgetary deficit of no more than $10 billion in our campaign. Barely two months after our election it was clear we faced some tough decisions: Do we follow through on the platform commitments, including expensive promises on social issues and big infrastructure investments? Or do we maintain our "prudent" deficit spending approach, with a deficit less than one-half of 1 percent of GDP?

There was no appetite in the Trudeau team to constrain ourselves, and the economic argument to stick to $10 billion was not compelling. We could afford to maintain our campaign promises as long as we managed our expenditures carefully and set efficiency targets in other areas. I would have to face up to this decision while crafting my first budget.

We were still in the honeymoon phase of our mandate, enabling me to avoid intense early media exposure and deal with the pressing housing crisis. My department brought me what we agreed was our most urgent economic risk — the increasing reliance on the appreciation in housing values for overall growth, and the wealth imbalances it was causing among different generations of Canadians.

Earlier in the year, the Canada Mortgage and Housing Corporation (CMHC) had reported that housing demand in Canada was outpacing the construction of new housing units. This, together with low interest rates, generated a classic rising-prices scenario of low supply meeting high demand. It was made more critical by developers who were concentrating their energies on high-end condominiums, leaving low- and medium-income families facing a shortage of affordable homes.

The situation had not sprung up overnight. Earlier in the year, with the federal election approaching, the Conservative government chose to avoid dealing with the situation. In fact, the Harper government had largely put housing policy on the back burner over most of its mandate.[15] By not imposing tougher rules on mortgage insurance, the Harper government avoided the ire of first-time home buyers. They also chose not to support assisted housing programs.

Both of my predecessors, Jim Flaherty and Joe Oliver, were, I suspected, ideologically opposed to increasing government restrictions, even though taking serious steps to deal with the situation appeared necessary. But dealing with housing is always fraught with political risk. Existing homeowners are not upset by rising prices, while first-time home buyers want incentives and financial assistance to get into a rising market, fuelling demand for housing that raises prices even higher. The finance minister's job is to balance the situation by ensuring that houses are a little harder to buy, lowering prices and frustrating buyers at the same

15 To be fair, Jim Flaherty attempted to take early action on the problem, but he was politically constrained from doing so later in his tenure.

time, leaving neither side totally satisfied — which is a good reason to make things as apolitical as possible.

The steep and steady rise in house prices represents one of those situations whose influence extends well beyond immediate concerns. Yes, high prices make it difficult for first-time home buyers to enter the market; that's obviously distressing for younger Canadians, but the impact doesn't end there. High prices skew investment money toward residential development, especially for middle- and upper-level buyers, and away from more productive investments, like in growing companies and professional development. In addition, the supply of affordable rental housing declines when developers choose to upgrade existing rental units into higher-priced accommodation or owner-occupied units rather than accommodations for lower-income families. Finally, it becomes a source of dissatisfaction between generations; younger Canadians watch in envy as older generations bask in the wealth of existing homes priced well out of their range.

The Harper government's most significant response to the housing crisis during their tenure had been an attempt to manage homelessness without tackling the root cause. The Homelessness Partnering Strategy represented one effort. Unfortunately, along with severely reduced funding in 2015, the program bypassed provincial governments to engage directly with municipal governments and community organizations. This may have been a well-meaning effort to streamline the delivery of benefits, but it did little to develop a partnership between the country's top two layers of government. More realistic, perhaps, was the Harper government's decision to revise regulations on insured mortgages, reducing the maximum amortization period from 35 to 30 years in 2011, and then to 25 the following year.

More had to be done. Unfortunately, the most efficient steps would have the effect of making it difficult for first-time home buyers to enter the market. This sounded like bitter medicine, but it was the only reasonable cure given the circumstances. Within a month of taking office, I announced that the minimum down payment for an insured mortgage would rise from 5 percent to 10 percent on the portion of the loan exceeding $500,000.

I saw this as a demonstration of both the wisdom and the risk of pursuing what was clearly good policy but (possibly) bad politics. Despite that, I took some pride in seeing the regulations enacted, because I was able to get it done on my own early in my ministerial career, avoiding political interference from other quarters. Much of the credit should go to my finance team, who were well prepared to assist me on our first venture into an important policy decision.

At the time I didn't understand that my ability to get this done was a product of fortuitous timing. I was riding our post-election tailwind, and the prime minister and his team were focused on their own learning curve, keeping them too busy to micromanage me and my team. The only way to continue the policy independence would be to create distance from, and tension with, the centre, meaning both finance and the PMO would have to accept some degree of internal conflict, with all of its risks and rewards. But that was not in keeping with "sunny ways," so we didn't develop the hard edge necessary to fight for economically reasonable decisions as the PMO took greater control.

All of this turmoil underlined my belief that good economics and good politics are tightly linked. Unfortunately, their timelines are different. Good economics assumes and demands prolonged deadlines to achieve success; good politics is too often scheduled according to the next news cycle. In my opinion, the best way to solve this disconnect is to seek broader institutional support for decisions as a means of ensuring long-term economic health and to limit the appeal of short-term decision making. Placing more decision-making authority in the hands of OSFI (Office of the Superintendent of Financial Institutions) or the CMHC on the housing file might ensure that decisions on mortgage insurance regulations are made by professionals with the skill to effectively manage the market dynamics. While the politics of getting governance changes like this across the finish line are challenging, the advantage to our long-term economic health would likely be significant. It would also create continuity through inevitable changes in government leadership and, from a political standpoint, establish the ownership of projects and policies whose value extends well beyond election cycles.

—

By year's end I had achieved or was on my way toward meeting some worthwhile goals. I had also gained valuable insight into the world of federal politics in Canada, a view every newcomer acquires according to his or her previous experience. I had been worldly enough to know that the business of politics and the politics of business were notably different, but I didn't appreciate how significant those differences are.

Overriding it all were two lessons on making the adjustment from managing a business to entering public life as a federal cabinet minister.

First lesson: politics is hard. So is succeeding in business. Nobody built an international publicly traded corporation while sitting around with their feet up. But this was different. Of course, enormous time and energy are demanded by both business and politics; the difference is in the way those precious resources are allocated, and the intensity of the spotlight focused on them. In business, I had spent more than 80 percent of my efforts on policy, management and client issues — where do we want to go and how are we to get there? — and maybe up to 20 percent on external communication concerns, including giving speeches, handling press releases, dealing with shareholder interactions and so on.

Politics reversed the balance. As much as 80 percent of my time was spent on a range of activities with no direct linkage to the task of discussing, formulating and executing policies that dealt with serious national concerns. Substantial amounts of time were devoted to preparing for Question Period; participating in Question Period itself; crafting and delivering speeches; dealing with the press; and so on. This is not to belittle these activities; they constitute the core of the term *public* in public office. But understanding how much time, energy and preparation this part of the job demanded took a period of adjustment, plus a recognition of the cultural differences between business and politics. Failure in business can be viewed as an accepted element in the risk-reward equation. Failure in politics is more likely to be fatal and unforgiven — like walking a tightrope with no net.

Question Period is a startling event, almost a sideshow addendum to the serious business of governing the country. It is also the most visible aspect of what can only be categorized as a form of warfare between groups of people whose supposed goal is to grapple with the challenges facing the nation. There is little opportunity for truce between political parties, an event that rarely seems possible in the public eye.

As I mentioned earlier, among the first things I did after arriving in Ottawa was to contact opposition critics. I planned to sit down and, in a genteel manner, discuss the differences between us in search of mutually beneficial solutions. If nothing else, I hoped I could establish a respectful attitude, one that acknowledged our differences but confirmed that we had the best interests of Canada at heart.

I failed to realize that the other side's job was to find ways to thwart me at every turn, with virtually no limits on the means at hand. This doesn't make them bad people (or at least not all of them), but neither were they benign actors. The practice represented an entirely new reality to me and my new colleagues. It made an already demanding job even harder to carry out.

Second lesson: operators are essential. Anyone who harbours the idea that he or she can step from private life into politics, especially at the federal level, as easily as changing their shoes is badly mistaken. Experience in dealing with the machinery and protocol is essential, and it cannot be purchased on the open market.

I learned this lesson first-hand, but its importance was reinforced by watching Prime Minister Trudeau wrestle with various challenges toward the end of his first term. When experienced staff began to leave, problems developed. For many replacements, it was their first encounter with federal politics, forcing them to deal with the same getting-acquainted process that newly elected members of his cabinet had dealt with. We had all faced an expected learning curve, but the new hands-on operatives needed to hit the ground running, and many couldn't.

In sports vernacular, the prime minister lacked bench strength in the PMO — a corps of individuals who, through highly competitive seasons of play, acquired both the knowledge to get the job done and the tough hide to fend off criticism while doing it. Things were made even more complex by the prerequisite for partisan loyalty. Your CV might list all the years spent in the political fray, but if they were under a Conservative or NDP banner, or even during a less cherished era or level of the Liberal Party, you could not expect doors in Trudeau's Liberal regime to swing wide, which limited the choice of replacement players. None of these concerns was immediately debilitating. Their impact came later.

To the surprise of some and the delight of others, the Justin Trudeau government scored some impressive early victories that produced major benefits for substantial numbers of Canadians. Many of them, I'm proud to say, sprang from or were enabled by the Department of Finance.

Six

Policies and Promises

The Party's rise from the depths of the 2011 election was a stunning achievement, but there was no resting on our laurels, no sense that we were sitting atop some metaphorical mountain, bathing in the glow of victory. Everyone began formulating the steps needed to execute the plans that had been responsible for our success in the election.

I was among that group, but I was almost instantly diverted by other demands that took the prime minister and me away from Ottawa-based obligations and into the drama of global events at the G20 conference in Antalya, Turkey. Aside from the predictable mechanics of scheduling travel and making accommodation arrangements, the prime minister and I needed guidance on dealing with representatives of other nations, most of them having attended a number of similar meetings in the past. What was the protocol? How should we deal with difficult situations? What challenges could we expect to encounter? A skilled and effective federal bureaucracy anticipated these questions and provided answers and guidance, enabling us to fit in smoothly and function effectively. I was grateful for their experience and talents, which eased the stress of an early challenge.

Prime Minister Trudeau found himself in the spotlight at the G20, as he soon would elsewhere. His promise to take action on climate change stood in stark contrast to the laggard attitude of the previous Canadian prime minister. Our resources sector, anchored by Alberta oil sands production, had thrived under the Harper regime, creating a substantial lift to Canada's economy and deep concern among countries alarmed at the long-term impact of fossil fuel consumption. They were particularly concerned about the oil sands because, along with filling pipelines with petroleum, the process of extracting oil from these reserves was seen as a major polluter.

The prime minister could not condemn the oil sands outright. They represented a massive contribution to Canada's economy, and while some environmentalists insisted they be closed down, our approach was to introduce policies that would reduce our carbon emissions in the short term and support a transition toward a net-zero carbon footprint in the longer term. This was a more aggressive stance than that taken by our predecessors, and with more ambitious targets, although we were too early in our mandate to have actually accomplished anything.

To me, the issue could only be addressed by balancing environmental concerns and economic reality. Canada's recent economic growth had been fuelled by increases in our oil production during the Harper years, yielding substantial and badly needed improvements to our overall economic picture, given the Harper government's ineffective response to the financial crisis of 2007–08. Following a heroic and coordinated G7 response to the immediate period of crisis, the most serious event of its kind since the Great Depression of the 1930s, Harper became an advocate for austerity at the 2010 G8 meeting held in Canada at Deerhurst Resort. His goal, reflecting the Conservative Party's traditional posture, was to avoid a continuing deficit position.

That's a reasonable point to make, but timing is everything, even in managing fiscal policy. The Conservative policy produced an anemic growth period for Canada, one I felt could potentially have been avoided had the federal government continued to prop up the economy until the recovery was assured. Hindsight is 20/20, and I wasn't there at the time, but there is no arguing that the resources sector was relied upon as the primary driver of our economic engine coming out of the financial crisis. This put us in an extremely difficult position while we grappled with the problem of addressing our role in the climate change debate. Although the slogan of the Trudeau government stated that "protecting the environment and growing the economy go hand in hand," there was no getting around the fact that the energy transition would be a central challenge for our government, much more than we could have imagined at the time.

—

Back to the G20.

The first G20 meeting I attended was an eye-opener. My initial response was to view it primarily as a venue to launch and foster relationships, laying the groundwork for future discussions or weathering future crises; with strong relationships in place, positions can be quickly understood and partnerships can be established. Even at the geopolitical level, it's far easier and more productive to ask a friend for assistance or support than to ask a stranger. Attendance at G20 sessions can pave the way for cooperation and collaboration within the group, often facilitating and resolving major international issues.

Beyond that, I had to wonder about the practical results these meetings generate. Do they lead to meaningful action? Or are we all seated around a talking table, where the only thing that gets produced is a long and dense communiqué from member countries with every word laboriously negotiated, but with little movement on critical issues from one meeting to the next?

Some have dismissed G20 meetings as a waste of time. I came to agree with Paul Martin, who told me at our first meeting that there was real value to the sessions, something that became more obvious to me the longer I was in office. We were able to tackle issues of global importance at the G20 meetings and advance our common understanding, much of the progress resulting from mutually beneficial relationships developed in admittedly excruciatingly boring sessions where each country explained its position on the issue of the day.

High-level international meetings like the G20 act as a form of insurance policy, generating goodwill that can become decisive in times of crisis. This became evident within six months of the first G20 meeting I attended, when Brexit occurred, and the G20 members most affected by the move prepared to deal with the impact on capital markets. The G7 sessions included more like-minded nations with action-oriented colleagues around the table, but they didn't include important allies like Australia and Mexico. Meanwhile, the International Monetary Fund (IMF) and World Bank meetings were too big and orchestrated to leave much time for side discussions. Whatever the event, the cultivated goodwill paid dividends when I found myself a couple of years later in a complicated negotiation with the finance minister of Saudi Arabia on an important file, something that would have been infinitely more difficult had I not had the opportunity to meet him earlier.

The G20 meetings also provide insight into challenges facing other countries; having grasped the extent of these issues, it becomes easier to understand the difficulties their leaders deal with. It is one thing to read about the internal politics of another nation. It is another thing entirely when you can discuss directly with your counterpart the actions they're taking to accomplish goals similar to the ones you're working on, or to hear first-hand about the challenges they are grappling with.

I experienced this when we began to consider taking an aggressive approach in our push for a new trade agreement with India, a country that is not easy to work with. Boasting a population of 1.4 billion, and grappling with a wide range of economic, political and social concerns, many issues discussed with the country's representatives while seated at a G20 table are dwarfed by larger concerns they face back home. We may have been frustrated by India's often contentious interventions at G20 meetings, but managing the world's largest democracy presented them daily with concerns that made our own challenges look like child's play.

The overriding benefit of G20 meetings is the recognition that most meaningful actions between member countries occur elsewhere. The meetings create the foundation to make them happen.

—

Media coverage of our electoral win and early performance was glowing, positive and personal over the opening months of our first term. This was hardly unusual for an incoming government, especially one scoring a major victory like ours. With so many new faces for the media to cover, many of us were selected for special focus. I tried not to pay attention to the media hoopla. In the early days of our mandate, the momentum of our electoral victory may have propelled us through the steps we had outlined in our plan, but it became clear that we were working within an informal management structure. The tone and objectives set by Gerry Butts were based, we assumed, on discussions with the prime minister. We were expected to work closely with the inner-circle PMO team to get things done.

This wasn't quite the Chrétien system of management, which was marked by ministerial freedom practised at the end of a short leash. It meant we were in constant discussion with the centre — that is, the PMO. This was appropriate given the limited background of many novice cabinet members. Some, including myself, had gathered extensive outside experience in the fields to which we had been assigned, but we had limited experience dealing with all the unique aspects of politics at the upper level of government. Guidance from the centre enabled the government to move forward effectively, generating a good deal of confidence in the future. We had a plan, a management structure and a system to keep us on track, we thought.

We quickly scored successes on many fronts — improving parental benefits, increasing aid for lower-income workers and seniors, legalizing marijuana and reducing taxes on the middle class — and brought a new focus on science and a continued emphasis on immigration.

But as critical as all these priorities were, none spoke to economic expansion; they were not sufficient to lay the groundwork needed to overcome our extended low-growth trajectory. Moreover, a couple of early challenges, including rolling the retirement age back to 65, placed extra long-term stresses on our economy and defied my attempts to see them shelved or slow-walked, which I regretted.

I championed more specific action to address the slow economy: assembling a blue-chip panel to develop strategies leading to specific targets for long-term growth that would produce higher living standards and greater opportunity for the middle class, drawing upon the best thinking available from business, academia and government. With this, we could ensure that our plans would produce a growing economy, essential to our agenda of recalibrating benefits to low- and middle-income Canadians.

At a speech to the Toronto Region Board of Trade on December 14, 2015, I announced plans for the formation of the Advisory Council on Economic Growth. I summed up the council's role by explaining that the government's top priority was to produce strategies designed to elevate our productivity and growth, adding that the council "will inform our work as we develop and implement a strategy that will build on the foundation we will set with Budget 2016 and restore hope for Canada's middle class."

A month later I revealed that Dominic Barton, one of Canada's most insightful and successful international businesspeople, would serve as chair of the council. The council itself would be made up of 14 Canadian and international leaders from business and academia, including Mark Wiseman, Suzanne Fortier, Michael Sabia, Elyse Allan and Chris Ragan. Thanks to Dominic's role as CEO of McKinsey & Company, the global management consulting firm would assist the council in assessing our current situation and future scenarios, as well as in drafting recommendations. I also noted that all the members of council would perform their services for an annual salary of $1 each. McKinsey committed to supporting us on a *probono* basis, working closely with the Department of Finance in what turned out to be a particularly effective partnership.

The reliance on third-party and private sector experts to broaden our expertise was not new for the finance department. Outside advice had been sought by past governments, but our approach was unique in that we had the outside experts work closely with our team at finance in developing new policy objectives. In this case, the goal was straightforward and, in my view, critical to the country's future: crafting a strategic plan to enhance the long-term growth of our economy.

We developed a number of good ideas and concepts. They included setting immigration targets and expanding the number of scientists available to work on new developments that could either support existing economic activities or inspire new ones. One of the most exciting concepts, to me, was the proposal to identify superclusters — focused investments in key areas of current and emerging growth, ranging from our agricultural sector to the digital economy. These were places where Canada enjoyed an existing or potential differential advantage versus other countries. We also developed a new institution, the Canada Infrastructure Bank, to increase investment and attract private sector financial resources into important public projects.

The council's first report, released on October 20, 2016, took an approach entirely in keeping with my private sector experience: set a goal and develop a plan to achieve it. Our objective of increasing Canada's real pre-tax median household income by $15,000 above the previously forecasted baseline of $90,000 for the year 2030 would be an impressive jump. We identified three high-level tactics consistent with our government platform and which promised to make a huge impact. We proposed to increase productivity via smart, strategic investment in infrastructure; to bring more foreign investment to Canada to turbo-charge Canadian businesses, which would drive innovation and expand our trading capacity; and to attract more exceptional talent to Canada through immigration.

The challenge, as is always the case, lay more in execution than in articulation. Two more reports were made by the council, all directed toward reaching the defined goal. The third and final report was released December 1, 2017.

The council's recommendations stirred a good deal of discussion about how we could secure Canada's financial future. But the fundamental question was how we could continuously come up with the best approaches to improve our collective well-being. The council was equipped with the right people and was addressing the right problems, but without a consensus within our government that action was required, and lacking the means to garner support across party lines and in provincial capitals, its key recommendations were unlikely to have the desired impact.

By the end of 2016, we could justifiably claim a good deal of success at fulfilling our promises to voters, neatly rounding off the first year of our government. We had completed or set in motion policies that represented the bulk of our election platform. Many were major advances on the social and financial fronts. I'm especially proud of our enhancement of the Canada Pension Plan, raising the benefits to reflect the contributors' average income, and the increase of the Canada Child Benefit, which lifted an estimated 300,000 children out of poverty. Both of these represent major milestones in assisting low- and middle-income families, and I believe they will represent two of Prime Minister Trudeau's most important legacies.

These early steps were material achievements, not just conceptual proposals — they were real steps forward, making genuine and measurable differences to Canadians. We were making solid progress. One group of independent academics concluded we managed to keep 92 percent of the promises made during the 2015 election campaign.[16] I don't know where that stands in terms of political history — does anyone track these achievements like batting averages in baseball? In any case, keeping better than nine out of ten promises in any field is a source of pride. In politics it may be record-setting.

We were able to deliver on the pledges we had made in the election campaign because the plan had been well-developed. Practical goals had been set and clearly defined; everyone understood what we intended to do as well as the rationale and the means of doing it.

Nothing, of course, is carved in stone. Politics involves moving targets, which means last year's or last month's assumptions no longer apply. For example, while we were executing our plan with considerable success, the economy was not proving as robust as we anticipated, leading to slower growth and a bigger deficit. This was not a development to be ignored — it was an issue to be managed,

16 Andrew Cardozo, "The Trudeau Record: Promises Kept and Broken," *the Hill Times*, October 14, 2019.

meaning the original plan needed rethinking and adjustment. We had gone from planning to execution rather smoothly in the early stages. Now we needed a managerial mindset to keep governing effectively, making improvements and adjusting to changing conditions. Unfortunately, it wasn't there. The same team that had shaped the plan before the election was now asked, in the post-election period, to take the helm and steer us on a different course, a role that demanded an entirely different set of skills.

The PMO had a plan to deliver in a changing reality by keeping us on track and measuring results. Gerry Butts had become enamoured with British political advisor Sir Michael Barber and his teachings on deliverology. Sir Michael explained his ideas in his book *How to Run a Government: So That Citizens Benefit and Taxpayers Don't Go Crazy.*[17] Cabinet retreats were held for him to discuss his approach with us in person, and copies of his presentations were circulated among various departments. The setting of measurable targets and the development of a management process to get the desired results or recalibrate efforts when necessary were familiar to me.

I considered several of Sir Michael's ideas valuable and thought-provoking. For some time they were considered the best way of making inevitable adjustments, starting with transitioning from generating ideas to applying a management mindset. Unfortunately, management is about more than tactics and strategies; it is also about execution. We lacked not only the staff and the conviction to carry through while adjusting to changing circumstances; we were also without experienced management at the top to make sure that focus and discipline were maintained as we adapted to evolving conditions.

Nothing in the political arena remains static. By our second year it became apparent to me that we no longer possessed the three

17 London: Penguin Books, June 2016.

basic components of our earlier success. During our first year we had followed an established plan, provided the ministries with power to execute their programs and operated with an appropriate level of oversight from the PMO. We were largely able to develop the complex policy necessary to deliver on our agenda without the PMO micromanaging the process.

These key elements felt like a distant memory by our second year, when we were no longer riding high on our electoral success and the broadly based goodwill it had generated. Without these guiding principles, the seeds were planted for problems and failures that could otherwise have been avoided.

Seven

Adventures in Budgeting

To many Canadians, the most visible function of a federal finance minister is to present the budget for the coming year to Parliament. It's done with great fanfare, wide media coverage, high secrecy and, traditionally, new shoes for the finance minister. On every other day when Parliament is in session, the spotlight is on the prime minister. On Budget Day it swings to the finance minister, who must stand and speak to a long and complex document that will face detailed analysis from economists, accountants, media pundits and the Parliamentary Budget Officer, plus extensive criticism from the opposition.

The process of developing the budget is enormously complex, as you might imagine. It also throws into focus the inherent tension between the finance minister and other members of cabinet, and between the finance minister and the prime minister. Whatever goals and ambitions cabinet ministers may have for their portfolios, the money needed to make it all happen rests in the hands of the finance minister, subject to the PM's approval. Should some objective favoured by a cabinet minister be shelved or drastically cut back in the budget, the bad guy is inevitably the finance minister. The prime minister's goals and his response to cabinet ministers' pleas for funds often come into conflict with the finance minister and the finance department, who both consider fiscal caution a necessary hedge against unknown future crises. Budget 2016 is when I became the bad cop in the minds of many colleagues.

I understood and accepted the job and the label. Somebody needed to say "Stop!" or at least "Slow down!" when needed. My prudent approach to finance and economics was well known when it came time to craft the 2016 federal budget. (I recall being advised by my political team to cease using the term "prudent" in cabinet meetings because it was driving some people in the PMO crazy.) I knew there was certain to be some disappointment among ministers who anticipated substantial expenditures for their pet projects. And until then I had neither crafted a budget nor spoken for an hour to Parliament and the country. Now, like it or not, I was about to become the target for either applause or condemnation, depending on the source.

Yet, when I stood to deliver the government's 2016 budget on March 22, I was less nervous than might be expected. Our campaign platform, overwhelmingly supported via our massive win in the election a few months earlier, had incorporated all of the measures I would be covering, so there would be few if any surprises along the way. Moreover, members of the finance department, from deputy minister on down, had years of experience in shaping budgets, and I drew upon their expertise and assistance to avoid any major faux pas in its construction. In addition, my warm and energetic parliamentary secretary, François-Philippe Champagne, and I had hosted a series of pre-budget discussions in various locations across the country, seeking ideas and comments on ways of supporting middle-class Canadians through budget proposals.

Crafting the budget document proved an educational process for me and the new cabinet. As finance minister, I was required to sign off on each decision relating to the budget. The process of getting to that stage proved both complex and alien to me. The sheer volume of the work meant that I was often brought in late in the process of deciding on individual proposals that were not central to our plan. I wanted to read more than the "two-pagers" the department provided me on each topic, but there was no way I could read more than 10 to 15 pages per budget request. To do so would have meant addressing hundreds of asks while I was already going deeper still on especially important or complex subjects.

We had provided broad direction to the public service with our campaign platform, along with an overview of the priorities to be considered early in our mandate. Every cabinet member, however, wanted their measure to be in that first budget, and every department claimed it had for years been starved of funding for important projects by the Harper government. So, every single budget request came to me, and somehow I had to understand, consider and decide them one by one. Performing a similar task in business would instead be handled as a collaboration, launched with the establishment of overall goals and an exchange of viewpoints to arrive at agreement on a limited set of measures to pursue.

There was no such agreement on priorities within our new cabinet. Finance assessed budget alternatives for each department, endlessly reviewing and debating them among political operatives and experienced bureaucrats until we had a document to submit to the prime minister and PMO for sign-off. The end result was a process bogged down in a huge volume of analyses and deliberations. Setting clear priorities beforehand, either in the total amount of investment we wanted to make (a fiscal target, which was my obvious and repeated demand) or in key departmental initiatives we wanted to consider, would have been far more efficient. The failure to do so left cabinet ministers often disappointed with our response to their asks. We advised them to make the asks and do all the supporting work, even when it was clear that their request would not be a priority. In my world, it would be far superior to tell people in advance that they weren't likely to make it on the list, producing less frustration later. That approach would also have reduced the incentive for cabinet ministers to bypass the finance minister and plead their case directly to the PMO and eventually the PM. In some cases, this workaround resulted in expenditures being committed according to who was a favourite rather than which priority was right for the country. It took some time to get used to this convoluted process and find a comfortable compromise.

—

Early on in my tenure as finance minister, it became clear that there were some systemic issues that would challenge the traditional approach to budgeting. For example, our government wanted to ensure that opportunities for women were considered in every budget request. It wasn't only about increased workforce participation by women, as important as that is to our economy and equal rights. We wanted to deal with persistent inequities through a gender-based analysis, systematically ensuring our expenditures advanced the cause of women's equality in the workforce and society more generally. I know there were those who, because of this approach, which included addressing issues like pay equity, called us *woke*. But it always seemed to me that you had to tackle the tough, apparently intractable problems, like the gap in men's and women's earnings, with new and direct action.

Indeed, even small actions speak louder than words. In 2018, when I chose the iconic Black activist Viola Desmond to appear on the 10-dollar bill — the first Canadian woman ever to be portrayed on a banknote — the decision proclaimed her heroic status in a manner that no PR release, House of Commons speech or other public declaration could match. It was a celebration, a universal and unmistakable signal of the importance of gender and racial equality, that could not be ignored.

—

As important and difficult as dealing with gender issues is, I had an even steeper learning curve in addressing financial issues to help improve the situation of Indigenous people in Canada. Their appalling treatment throughout our country's history presented an enormous challenge to our government. We were simultaneously looking backward to acknowledge past wrongs and looking forward to search for effective corrections to be applied today, trying to ensure we invested wisely to make the biggest improvement possible.

The basics may be well known by the bulk of Canadian society, but the scope of the problem remains underappreciated, involving infrastructure, education, social obligations, health concerns and a string of other factors related to living conditions that needed attention by the federal government. Underlying the issue was the question of racism too often encountered by Indigenous citizens and too often overlooked by mainstream Canadians.

The racism factor, as deplorable as it may be, was beyond my mandate, but we worked hard to find the most effective way to tackle concerns like living conditions and education. I was assisted in this area by Indigenous leaders who opened my eyes to the lives of the people they represented and provided guidance on reaching decisions regarding priorities and budgets. Every budget cycle would include meetings with Perry Bellegarde, National Chief of the Assembly of First Nations; David Chartrand, president of the Manitoba Métis Federation; and Natan Obed, president of Inuit Tapiriit Kanatami. All were impressive in their perception and assessment of the needs while being appropriately persistent advocates.

The effort to deal with the legitimate concerns and demands of Indigenous people will continue well into the future. Major multi-faceted challenges tend to thwart many well-meaning measures. Providing housing, installing effective water systems, grappling with the remoteness of many communities from major centres and tackling the effects of climate change exemplify the scope of the problem.

Progress is being made. Not as quickly nor as broadly as Indigenous people want to see, no doubt. But I believe a new model has been set to produce lasting improvements and that future federal governments will continue moving toward the goal of equal funding and opportunities that Indigenous people expect and deserve.

—

In the 2016 budget, other challenges urgently needed to be dealt with and overcome. The Canada Child Benefit (CCB) program and the middle-class tax cut, two key features of our campaign platform, were proving more expensive than estimated. We had planned to finance both moves through an increase in income tax for the upper 1 percent of income earners, along with the elimination of universal child benefits (which were being distributed even to the wealthiest of Canadians).

Our immediate problem was the math behind this promise: it didn't work. The CCB was proving more expensive than we had modelled, and the increase in the upper-level tax rate brought in less money than expected because, as my department pointed out, when you tell people you are going to raise their taxes, they react in a way that reduces their exposure to your new measure.[18]

---

18 In hindsight, I regret supporting the idea of a tax increase on the 1 percent in that manner. It was a populist approach to signal that we would focus our attention on middle-income Canadians by going after the rich. A talking point for the prime minister in Parliament, it hugely frustrated the business community. It worked initially from a purely political standpoint, because it was our most popular election promise. But it began a narrative that made it difficult to have a constructive dialogue with the people prepared to invest in research and development to benefit the country. Many top-level taxpayers assumed we were going after them as an easy solution to our funding problem. They were among the country's most successful and influential group, and our proposal's

—

I searched for a way of managing our platform commitment without increasing the deficit. This was a difficult task that I frankly relished because the balancing act and problem-solving challenge were reminiscent of my business experience. Working closely with Jean-Yves Duclos, minister of families, children and social development, secured us an early win with the CCB. Though the PMO was involved, the leadership remained with the finance department.

I had been directed by the prime minister to work with Jean-Yves. Initially frustrated by the suggestion, I expected a laborious process with no real advantage to be gained by including my colleague. I was wrong. Jean-Yves, an academic economist and, like me, a new politician, brought a willingness to work through the options and an analytic rigour that pushed us in directions we might not have otherwise gone. We found a way to make the program more cost-efficient while creating what I believe to have been the most important economic win for families in our first term. If this was a model for how our government would function and work together in the future, I recall thinking, it was a good one. We were able to apply discipline to the business of governing, finding ways to balance the cost of doing the job effectively. And it kept control of the process within the Department of Finance, where it belonged. With a clearly defined objective we were able to focus on our goals — Jean-Yves from the perspective of ensuring that the benefit met our aim of supporting lower- and middle-income Canadians, and me paying attention to fiscal concerns.

---

biggest impact was to reduce business confidence in us. There were other, more nuanced ways to deal with the growing divide between the 99 percent and the 1 percent. Our idea might have succeeded had we not gone for a high-profile but largely symbolic attack on the most successful — not necessarily the most wealthy — Canadian taxpayers.

All in all, it illustrated, in my mind, how things could and should be done in government.

The Canada Child Benefit was criticized during our election campaign by the Conservatives. They favoured Harper's approach, which offered tax credits to families for specific activities such as children's fitness programs, claiming this allowed them to target key support groups. Our program, they declared, might discourage parents from working, creating what some Conservatives labelled a "nightmare scenario."

In reality, our program built on an existing child tax credit, employing an income-tested formula and producing a more targeted approach while adding additional resources to the pot. Lower- and middle-income families saw their child benefits rise by $2,300, a significant step in protecting many of our youngsters from the debilitating effect of poverty.

I continue to hear from people who tell me how the CCB changed their lives. A taxi driver told me he was able to meet his family's needs by working only six days a week instead of seven. While driving me home from a constituency event, he actually called his wife and had her dig up all of their family financial records to let me know their situation pre- and post-CCB. Syrian refugee parents said they were able to take English classes alongside their jobs, enabling them to communicate with their children's teachers. Poor families in Canada were able to buy more and better food, leading to a drop in food insecurity and to better eating habits. The development of the CCB marked an excellent moment in our first budget process. It stands as testimony to the power of the analysis and planning that went into our election campaign, and our ability to adapt and deliver in the face of new constraints.

—

While I was still riding an incredibly steep learning curve, the professionalism and preparedness of people in the Department of Finance ensured that things played out with logic and smooth efficiency. Budget Day itself, however, saw the rational approach transformed into a multi-ringed circus.

The process of delivering the budget was a mundane event. It consisted of my reading a frequently rewritten and reviewed script without the opportunity to insert ad lib comments. Given the highly partisan audience, I expected the usual caustic commentary from the opposition scattered among waves of approval from the Liberal benches. I was, however, unprepared for the media response, with every print and broadcast vehicle racing to dredge up some unique angle or tidbit for their audience, although drawn from exactly the same content.

We had titled the budget "Growing the Middle Class," noting that strong economies are built on a foundation of economically secure middle-class families, representing a primary goal of the budget. Two of its prime elements were the middle-class tax cut, with its bigger paycheques for an estimated nine million Canadians, and the CCB. Along with these initiatives, we committed to invest more than $120 billion over the next decade on much-needed infrastructure. We stayed true to our spending commitments in our first budget, so the projected deficit, greater than expected because of falling oil prices and lower economic growth, was not my primary concern — yet.

This most important economic promise of infrastructure investment was intended to help grow the economy directly while making Canada more efficient and productive in the future. I didn't understand at the time just how arduous it would be to get provinces and municipalities to accept money for projects that Canadians desperately needed. Committing to this large budgetary investment was the simple task; the hard work would come later.

There was more, of course — investments in education and infrastructure on behalf of First Nations, Inuit and the Métis, plus financial assistance for veterans, among other measures. Beneath it all was our oft-repeated talking point about revitalizing the economy, "over the years and decades to come, so that it works for the middle class and helps those working hard to join it."

Criticism of the budget was predictable but somewhat muted from the opposition parties. The biggest headline-grabber came from the Parliamentary Budget Office (PBO), which accused us of not having been sufficiently transparent about budget details, a claim I disputed.

The PBO is an institution installed by the previous Harper government to effectively scrutinize government accounts, advocating maximum transparency. Its function is to provide independent analysis on trends in the national economy and the state of the nation's finances. On request, it estimates the financial cost of any proposal for matters within Parliament's jurisdiction. The problem their comment raised, which persisted throughout my time as finance minister, was that it put the PBO in an adversarial position, constantly complaining that it didn't have the resources to fully understand and dig into the government books. Stephen Harper may have seen the advantage of this additional layer of scrutiny, and our 2015 platform actually proposed to broaden the PBO role, but I didn't see many benefits from the body. I suspect that every future Liberal or Conservative finance minister will feel the same way.

All in all, I considered my first budget a relative success given our collective inexperience in government. Too bad we were unable to replicate its success in future budgets and other endeavours. Our later efforts lacked the discipline of the campaign blueprint and fiscal restrictions I was able to apply to the 2016 version, and the response they received and their effectiveness suffered as a result.

Things were complicated by that concept of cabinet equality advocated by the prime minister. Cabinet ministers logically assumed that "equality" provided them with identical rights to whatever portion of available funding they might choose to claim.

The concept of priority when it came to allocating funds did not seem to enter into the picture, and interpreting "equality" meant that every advocate for a government expenditure felt obligated to plump for new funds, or at least justified in doing so, in as loud a voice and with as much passion as everyone else.

Managing this situation was something of a challenge to me, one that became more complex when the PMO's response was "Let's give them something to keep them happy," a line that became common as time passed. This was at best a makeshift solution to a growing problem, one that shattered any pretense of fiscal restraint.

In essence, money became a means for the PMO to manage egos and relationships between cabinet members, something I was unable to overrule. Dispensing money to make a problem go away is easy. Defining and enforcing spending guidelines, with limited and justified exceptions, is difficult, but it's a key measurement of management competence. That was the tool I wanted, one that in my estimation would have been fundamental to fostering a more robust and productive process of cabinet deliberation. This, however, would have weakened the power of the PMO and acknowledged limits on our stated goal of crafting policy that favoured middle-class Canadians. It would also have pitted cabinet members against each other, which was inconsistent with the early and naive Trudeau goal of cultivating harmonious relationships among cabinet members.

That first budget launched suspicion among the media that I was working in a box, leaving little for them to explore where I and the finance department were concerned. I tended to stick to my script, avoiding ad libs and controversial statements. I didn't see any advantage in being controversial, and I still don't. As a former and very successful Conservative premier[19] claimed, "bland

19 Premier of Ontario William Davis.

works." I didn't aim to be bland, just to keep my head down and do my job. But there was a price to pay for my approach.

The media thrive on stories, especially inside stuff not covered in news releases and formal interviews. Not surprisingly, they treasure contacts with people who are potential sources of such tales or who can at least be counted on to deliver an eyebrow-raising quote.

That wasn't me. Not because I resented or rejected the media and their role, but because I was naive about how different the relationship is between private and public entities where the press was concerned. CEOs and other senior businesspeople are always aware of the various parties — shareholders, employees, vendors, community leaders — whose interests deserve careful consideration before they make any public comment. I used to leave it to communications specialists in our firm to handle press coverage. But in government, one way or another I was viewed as a prime source of commentary, a role I didn't want to accept, and this made a few people uneasy. Certainly, my lack of interest in seeking out the press and getting my name in print made me an anomaly among the political class.

But I learned that I didn't have a choice — I had to be a key voice in government. I may not have become the media's leading source of behind-the-scenes stories — in fact, I know I wasn't — but my effectiveness in dealing with the press was a whole lot better at the end of my time in politics than it was at the beginning.

One aspect that limited the scope of the comments I made to the media was my focus on both delivering statements in French and understanding the responses back to me in that language. I was in the uncomfortable position of being "good enough" in the language that I was expected to deliver speeches and answer journalists' questions in French, even though I hadn't spoken it much over the previous 20 years. So I tended to craft my words in a manner that, translated into French, I could deliver with a sufficient level of clarity and confidence. This technique didn't lend itself to making me comfortable onstage in front of French journalists. It would take a couple of years before I mastered the subject matter in both official languages with enough confidence to speak "outside the box."

Some members of the press, I suspect, understood and perhaps even sympathized with my position. But I didn't help their task of finding and reporting the uncovered and unacknowledged angle of a story by sticking to the script, so in my earliest days on the job there was little opportunity to forge close relationships with them.

Budgeting formalities aside, my work as finance minister involved three main categories. The most critical was department work, which entailed collaborating with teams of people to come up with ideas and reach decisions that would carry our policies forward. Then there were activities I labelled *outside* work, where I acted as spokesperson in response to questions and concerns from media outlets. Third was parliamentary work, involving protocol and procedures associated with the governing process. Of the three, I enjoyed the department work most because it was familiar to me, although the scale of the decisions to be made was obviously different from anything I had experienced in the private sector. Instead of dealing with a single corporation or industry, we were concerned with an entire nation's financial status and economic future. We were also, I discovered from the earliest stages of preparing the budget and, indeed, throughout my time as finance minister, dealing with serious management complexities.

The usual procedure in business was to meet and collaborate in small groups whose members were closely attuned to the objective being discussed. Each person brought a different perspective and clearly defined role according to their expertise and area of responsibility.

In government, I would enter a room prepared to evaluate progress and exchange ideas not with a relative handful of participants, but with a dozen or more people who had been involved in the file since its inception. Having an immense degree of expertise around the table with long experience on each issue is invariably helpful in reaching a decision, but it put new cabinet ministers (or even experienced ministers who hadn't the time or inclination to do their homework) on the spot when it came to managing the meeting and retaining control over its progress. I needed to apply a range of skills to manage the process and the people, trying to keep them engaged and enthusiastic while fostering the cohesiveness that I knew was so important to maintain.

I was always impressed with the quality of the work the finance team turned out. Their attention to detail, their thoughtful evaluation of options and the reasoning behind their proposals were all performed with more care and consideration than almost any business decision I had seen. We were, after all, overseeing the entire national economy.

I came to value the working sessions with my finance team, despite their size and unwieldiness, because they led to well-considered decision-making and tight teamwork. Some time later I was surprised to discover that the prime minister and some senior cabinet ministers chose not to take part in similar sessions with their teams. For me, these meetings were essential, and an important part of my decision-making process. I couldn't have done without them.

In spite of the outstanding work being done, challenges kept arising. Increasingly, the PMO chose to view our proposals through a communication lens rather than a policy lens, playing to the media rather than assessing whether something was a good policy to achieve our goals. I wasn't the only one to deal with this challenge. Other ministers encountered the same or similar difficulties in rationalizing well-researched and well-structured proposals, too often sidetracked over essentially trivial concerns that dealt almost exclusively with politics rather than content.

This, of course, is the way of government. It's a natural tension between the practical and the political, and between two entities, the PMO and the finance minister. However, without both the tension *and* the rigorous debate needed to address and resolve issues, you cannot have a government that functions well.

Eight

Pensions and Health Care: A Study in Contrasts

I'm not sure who coined the phrase about politics being the art of the possible,[20] but at least one achievement during the first term of Justin Trudeau's government confirmed it for me.

It involved the refiguration of the Canada Pension Plan (CPP), a subject with which I was obviously very familiar. The CPP had been launched in 1965 to provide guaranteed income to retired Canadians. At the time it was seen as a worthwhile benefit, especially for lower-income people, but not critically necessary for all. That's because more than half of workers were employed by large industrial companies, such as automotive manufacturers and steelmakers, that provided attractive employee pension plans. These were generally defined benefit plans that guaranteed the specific amount to be paid for life.[21]

By the arrival of the 21st century the picture had changed. The number of private firms providing defined benefit pension plans declined dramatically until by 2011 fewer than 25 percent of male employees enjoyed that benefit. At the same time, income levels for top-tier executives had escalated significantly while entry-level

20 Most sources credit Otto von Bismarck, the 19th-century unifier of Germany.

21 I referred to these in some detail in chapter 2.

employee incomes remained almost stagnant in real terms over the same period.

Female employees were hit by a similar decline in pension coverage, but, in an interesting (and unusual) contrast, they suffered somewhat less because more women worked in the public sector, where defined benefit plans remained the norm.

During my career building a business that helped organizations with the management of pension and benefit plans, I was directly involved in the movement away from defined benefit pension plans. Employers increasingly came to see them as too expensive in an era of declining interest rates (low interest rates mean you have to put more money aside to invest for the future pension benefit). Meanwhile, many employees no longer saw themselves staying with one employer for their entire career. They preferred a portable pension benefit that allowed them to move among companies or even industry sectors.

With those dynamics, defined benefit plans in private industry became rare, exacerbated by the burgeoning gig economy that employed a growing number of young Canadians. Instead, companies offering pension benefits began relying on defined contribution programs in which employees had to gauge their own contributions according to how much they could afford. They were also left to manage the funds on their own or with guidance from their employer.

Saving for retirement is hard to do for someone who is simultaneously trying to raise a family or buy a house. None of us knows exactly how much we need to save for retirement (we don't know how long we will live, let alone how much we will need as income in our declining years) or how the volatility of the investment markets will affect our nest egg. The obvious way to help lower- and middle-income Canadians invest for retirement would be to introduce an enhancement to the CPP — a sort of forced retirement savings plan for the entire working population. This was an idea easy to grasp but difficult to execute.

The perfect solution would be a portable benefit providing better coverage for seniors and managed by the Canada Pension Plan Investment Board (CPPIB), one of the world's most sophisticated investment managers. The major obstacles would be getting the provinces and the federal government to agree and redesigning the plan to make sure it provided better coverage for the people who needed it. These would not be easy tasks. Generating increased CPP benefits would require an increase in payroll-based contributions from both employers and workers, a step easily (and likely) construed as a tax increase even though, in reality, it was an investment in future security. Even when the benefits were pointed out to taxpayers, the rewards would not flow into their hands for decades — not an easy sales pitch, but an important one.

Other means of accruing money for retirement income were available, notably the Registered Retirement Savings Plan (RRSP) and Tax-Free Savings Account (TFSA). These were widely used by middle- and upper-income individuals who earned sufficient income to divert funds to the plans. With RRSPs, contributors could enjoy immediate tax benefits (annual contributions may be deducted from taxable income), a strong incentive to save for the future. TFSAs didn't offer the immediate tax break of RRSPs but brought the bonus of withdrawals, including investment earnings, free of income tax. Both were generally supported by Canadians with sufficiently high incomes, but too many Canadians risked being poorly underfunded during their retirement years.

None of this was news to political leaders across Canada. Unfortunately, enacting legislation to divert money into the hands of government, no matter how reasonable the amount and how convincing the rationale, is rarely a popular step for elected representatives to take. It's worth noting at this point that CPP contributions had been raised just once in the previous 20 years.

Only one provincial government — Ontario — had taken steps toward providing sustainable retirement income for its citizens and hang the consequences. I had a history on this file. In 2012 I had been asked by Premier Kathleen Wynne to serve as investment advisor to Ontario's minister of finance, Dwight Duncan, who had been assigned the task of reviewing and facilitating the pooling of public sector pension fund assets. Working together, Dwight and I laid the groundwork for the eventual establishment of the Investment Management Corporation of Ontario, which resulted in lower costs for the funds thanks to the economies of scale.

This was a modest first step toward improving the pension picture for Ontario residents working in the public sector, but more was needed. Two years later Premier Wynne tapped me to serve on a panel created to advise the province about supporting the 3.5 million Ontario workers whose projected retirement income would likely be inadequate without adjustments. In response, the panel crafted the Ontario Retirement Pension Plan (ORPP) to supplement the CPP. The ORPP included a provision to cancel the proposed program should benefits from the Canada Pension Plan be enhanced.

It's difficult to imagine any goal in federal politics more suited to my background and interest than revamping the CPP, and I tackled it with enthusiasm. Along the way I gathered a full understanding of "the art of the possible" line. I also managed to apply, with some success, my mantra on the importance of building relationships in life, business and politics.

—

Defining the steps to be taken on this major file was easy. Figuring out how to take those steps without a stumble would prove a challenge.

Enhancing the CPP to sufficiently raise the annual payments level would begin with raising both the level of savings made by employees (meaning higher deductions from their paycheques) and the level of contributions from their employers (meaning higher employment costs). The actual increases would be based on negotiations to determine the ideal enhancement to the Canada Pension Plan. We aimed for an income replacement of one-third of pre-retirement earnings, up from one-quarter of earnings in 2016, to a maximum level of $79,500 in 2025.

It's worth pausing to note that our goal was to ensure these enhancements would follow the CPP's original financing structure, with funds accruing in each year of employment. We intended to make sure the enhancements were fully funded by employee and employer contributions. No pension payments would be paid out of current cash flow, and no government deficits would be created or drawn upon to make the payments. The increase in CPP contributions would be phased in over five years, beginning in 2019, and employee contributions would be tax-deductible.

While I had confidence in the professionalism and investment expertise of the CPPIB, I wanted to immunize this increase in benefits from criticism that we were creating a future risk. At the end of the 2021 fiscal year the amount of money within the CPP coffers exceeded $550 billion. The plan is sustainable for the long term, making the CPP an incredible asset for our country and the envy of many finance ministers I met at G20, IMF and World Bank meetings. Even in an era of trillion-dollar balances, it's a staggering amount of money to draw upon, made even more impressive by the success of the CPPIB. The Canada Pension Plan Investment Board is one of the largest pension fund managers in the world, with a global reputation for its asset management skills. More than half of the reserves in the CPP were generated by the CPPIB's investment policies.

Designing the program demanded a point of view on what constituted a base level of retirement income support. It also took more than a little cold, hard estimating of the size of the burden we could reasonably place on employees and employers, both of whom were about to be asked to contribute more. We did not want employer contributions to place undue financial burden on start-up companies, whose cash flow was often strained in the first few years of operation.

I focused a good deal of attention on measuring the level of increased payments that would elevate CPP contributions without imposing a heavy burden on employees and employers alike. This led to some practical decisions regarding the amount of retirement income to be paid.

Most of our efforts were directed to assisting low- and medium-income Canadians, bringing their CPP benefits measurably closer to the income earned while they were employed. Since the CPP would continue to be fully funded by contributions, substantially raising pension income in the retirement years would require a significant increase in money paid into the employee's plan during their working years. But there was a limit to the increase. It simply made no sense to ask lower-income workers to salt away money they couldn't easily spare on the basis of a promise of receiving higher income upon retirement. Let's remember that the same group would be collecting Old Age Security and Guaranteed Income Supplements in addition to their CPP income. With this in mind, the maximum CPP annual income was set at $20,600. To achieve this level, the contribution increase was set at 2 percent on earnings up to the 2016 cap of $54,900 and 8 percent on earnings between $54,900 and $62,500 (in 2016 dollars), to be shared equally between employers and employees.

Reviewing the proposed program, I was confident in its fairness and in the positive improvement it would make for lower- and middle-income families. The CPP was a joint federal-provincial program, so all I had to do was sell it to the provinces. I needed all provinces on board because we didn't want an outcome that reduced labour mobility. For all eligible Canadians to benefit from enhanced CPP payments, someone working in New Brunswick, for example, needn't be concerned about losing any pension benefits should they relocate to Saskatchewan or any other province in Canada. This was a particular problem with Quebec, which theoretically could go its own way and not agree to the enhancement because the Quebec Pension Plan functioned separately from the CPP.

Selling the idea wouldn't be easy. We and the provinces would be asking employees for a little more pain today, in the form of increased withdrawals from their earnings, for the promise of rewards "tomorrow"— tomorrow being as many as 30 or 40 years in the future.

Ontario was on board from the beginning. Premier Kathleen Wynne and her cabinet responded with enthusiasm, providing a pressure tactic for me to apply on other provincial governments. Alberta's NDP premier Rachel Notley was similarly responsive. Both provinces gave us a good starting point.

With Quebec operating its own pension plan, its response was not as critical as other partners, although we needed them on board to provide the national labour mobility that I considered essential. Quebec kept an open mind on the idea, as did British Columbia and Manitoba. With Liberal governments in power across Atlantic Canada, I was optimistic that I could anticipate positive feedback from them as well.

Only Saskatchewan was neither on board nor inclining that way. The Conservative government there did not consider CPP enhancement an important policy objective for their province. They also expressed legitimate concerns about the plan's affordability for businesses and lower-income Saskatchewan citizens.

My approach to negotiating with the provinces and factions opposing the idea was based on one overriding strategy: I would not dismiss their point of view nor minimize their concerns. I focused on listening carefully to their comments and responding with answers recognizing that not all of their objections were without merit, nor were they necessarily rooted in strictly partisan views. Their opposition was often linked to very real concerns that needed to be addressed, and I insisted on showing respect to them, a position I have always favoured in both business and political negotiations.

I approached my counterpart in Saskatchewan, Minister of Finance Kevin Doherty, by accepting that his concerns were legitimate. He was dealing with a set of issues I had to assume could be addressed. Kevin was both smart and civic-minded, and it became evident that he was to some degree reflecting Saskatchewan Premier Brad Wall's political views more than his own. Besides being a savvy premier, Wall was experienced and popular. He knew installing a program that would cost money today for a benefit many years in the future would be a hard sell to small businesses and people trying to get by on low incomes. Kevin understood both the immediate economic issues and the longer-term problem of ensuring that people can retire comfortably and with dignity. He wanted to be helpful, but he also needed a solution that his boss could agree with, giving both of us the common goal of coming up with an answer to Premier Wall's concerns.

Carlos Leitão and Mike de Jong, finance ministers at the time for Quebec and British Columbia respectively, were focused on unique situations in their own provinces. Mike, who had headed a number of BC ministries over his political career, was experienced, wily and effective in explaining his problems with the plan as submitted. Carlos's background included serving as chief economist for a bank, providing him with a deep appreciation for many facets of our pension proposal.

Harking back to my intention to take each province's position seriously and accept their concerns, I approached them accordingly. Mike's objection was primarily political in nature: he needed a solution to the problem of charging people more money through increased contribution levels, a matter all provinces needed to deal with, whatever the degree of their support. Kevin Doherty, who shared this concern, pointed out the irony that by asking lower-income Canadians to save more, they potentially could be better off in retirement than in their working years. This may not sound so bad until you remember that the expenses incurred in working years — kids, mortgages, commuting to work — are inevitably higher than in retirement years. Both Mike and Kevin also were uneasy about the costs to be borne by businesses, especially small businesses, and I shared that concern.

Reducing the contribution amounts in order to soften political misgivings was a non-starter to me. I was convinced that the CPP expansion must be a fully funded program, financed by contributions from participants and their employers plus investment returns, with no potential to be drawn from general tax revenue. Any rise in benefits must be linked to a similar rise in contributions.[22] To get around objections resulting from this point, I proposed raising the level of the Working Income Tax Benefit or WITB. Now known as the Canada Workers Benefit, this program provides refundable tax relief for working low-income Canadians. Having this in place softened anticipated objections to raising CPP contributions, making it more palatable to Saskatchewan and BC.

At first, Carlos Leitão announced that Quebec would abstain from the changes. While I was initially worried about this, I understood that he needed time to work with his colleagues in Quebec City, who were not anticipating the need to have a final decision at our negotiating sessions. I also knew, from my experience working on pensions in Quebec, that their astute policy-makers would come to the same conclusion that I did: having a Quebec

22 This in contrast with the U.S. system, where Social Security payments are covered by payroll taxes without accumulated funds — in other words, money paid to citizens collecting Social Security payments is being earned over the same period by employed persons without an existing (and profitably invested) fund.

Pension Plan that was not aligned with the Canada Pension Plan would put employers in Quebec at a disadvantage when trying to recruit people from other parts of Canada. I chose to set aside the question of Quebec for the moment, expecting Carlos and his government to come around in their own time and in their own way, which is what happened.

Success was achieved, and the fruits of that success will become obvious many years in the future. That's when today's lower-income Canadians will face their retirement years with confidence, knowing that their new status will not trigger a dramatic drop-off in funds to threaten their comfort and security.

I have two key points to make about the experience.

First, my decision to increase the WITB benefit level as a means of soothing the provinces' political concerns was made on my own, without prior approval from the prime minister. We based the amount of the increase on detailed calculations to make the maximum impact at a reasonable cost. Still in the early days of our first term, I had the trust of the prime minister and his office. This permitted me to apply my judgment in the best interests of the country, and he agreed with the decision I made after the fact. That's probably not the best way to do things, and I don't propose that it become standard procedure across the board. I made this move only because I had the PM's confidence to do so. Any time we can take an important step forward in an area of joint federal-provincial jurisdiction, supported by unanimous agreement from the provinces, we should not pass up the opportunity to do so.

My second point is one I made earlier: never underestimate the power of working relationships. Too often we Canadians, along with much of the rest of the world, assume that progress is a by-product of power alone. That needn't be the case. Many aspects of negotiation depend on one side understanding the other's perspective and values and finding ways to accommodate them. I chose to view those who did not agree with our proposals not as opponents but as partners. Every session began by getting to know both the individual and the premise behind their concerns, working from there. The strategy ran through every stage of our efforts to enhance the Canada Pension Plan for the people who counted on it most. And it worked.

A *Globe and Mail* columnist may have said it best when he noted, "A bigger CPP retirement benefit is huge in a world where a majority of workers have no company pension plan to rely on," later adding, "The CPP is a great equalizer. It's a pension for the masses, and it's getting a little better."[23]

The ability to look ahead and not only anticipate future needs but take steps to see them acknowledged and accommodated is an element of politics that needs to be valued and respected. Very often, changes in policy will generate long-term benefits but lack short-term understanding and appreciation. The ultimate value of their introduction and implementation may not be realized until well beyond the tenure of those wishing to see them enacted. Prime Minister Paul Martin's CPP reforms, controversial at the time and now recognized as wise and beneficial, are a good example. So are the GST/HST and free trade agreement with the U.S.

As much as any democracy, we in Canada need to be able to adjust our focus sufficiently to see the long-term gain that will prove to be a bargain at the cost of short-term pain.

—

Pensions for working Canadians remains a vital concern for both levels of government to deal with, but it pales in comparison with the importance — and the cost and complexities — of providing the universal health care coverage that gives so many Canadians security and comfort. Like the CPP, our health care is dependent

---

23 Rob Carrick, "The Reality of CPP Reform: We Can't Afford Not to Make these Changes," *the Globe and Mail*, June 21, 2016.

upon a federal-provincial partnership, but the terms and conditions of the partnership are not so straightforward in this case.

Early in our mandate Jane Philpott and I hosted a meeting in Ottawa with provincial and territorial health and finance ministers to introduce ourselves and listen to their concerns. To no one's surprise their needs centred almost exclusively around money — they wanted more of it.

Our national health care system is provincially focused; each province and territory is responsible for managing and maintaining health care facilities and programs for its residents. The federal government lends support, and ensures health care availability for all Canadians, by funding about 22 percent of the cost. At just over $43 billion in 2021–22, this makes health care financing the country's largest federal-provincial-territorial transfer. Those numbers tell almost the whole story of provincial and federal positions on health care: the provinces see a program that should be jointly funded by provinces and the federal government, protesting that the federal contribution is too small; and the federal government sees a $43 billion contribution that provides it with limited ability to drive a more effective and cost-efficient system, a huge contribution to the provinces with no joint governance.

As much as or more than other government expenses, health care costs in Canada keep rising in response to population growth, technology advances, pharmaceutical costs and other developments, plus political pressure from powerful interest groups that include physicians and other care providers.

It's hardly a surprise that the provincial and territorial governments turn to federal coffers to relieve them of financial pressures caused by higher health care costs. They argue that the federal government generates more total income than they do, which is true. What is never discussed is the ability of each province, on its own, to increase funds by raising its sales tax (or other taxes, for that matter). They have total control over this, as illustrated by Alberta, which chooses to impose no provincial sales tax at all. It's not constitutional guidelines or precedent that prevents provinces from exploring this route. It's optics. The provinces won't look good to their electorate by seeking more money from sales taxes or other taxes, but they can appear near-heroic by demanding that the federal government provide more funding for health care.

From Ottawa's point of view, the federal treasury should not be viewed as a form of piggy bank to be raided whenever health cost increases plunge the provinces and territories into the red. Larger federal transfers are basically stopgaps. They serve as a more attractive method of improving finances in the health care system than searching for ways to improve efficiency and reduce waste. Such steps are not easy to take, but constant demands for a bigger share of finite federal income are not a solution either.

Moreover, little proof exists to suggest that increased federal funding leads to better performance in provincial health care systems. Tracking the impressive 6 percent annual increases in federal transfers to the provinces and territories that evolved from the 2004 Health Accord suggests the biggest impact was to raise incomes for health providers, especially physicians. No one, including me, is going to claim that the majority of Canada's health care providers are overcompensated, especially in light of their largely unselfish response to the COVID-19 pandemic and its demands. But there is some evidence that an increase in physicians' income has the perverse effect of reducing patient access to them because some medical staff respond by reducing their hours of availability. Whether this is indeed the case is yet to be confirmed and measured. Nevertheless it appears to suggest that as with many recipes for improving efficiency and equitable response to social concerns, the popular solution of spending more money to fix the problem is both overly simplistic and underwhelming in its impact.

Speaking of COVID-19, the impact of the pandemic laid bare a number of deficiencies in Canada's health care system. Hospitals and staff surged to capacity thanks to support, financial and otherwise, from wide-ranging sources. Among the effects was an inability of the system to provide non-COVID-related care, particularly for patients suffering from severe threats such as cancer. One authoritative paper indicated that more than half of surveyed cancer patients reported that their appointments had been cancelled, postponed or rescheduled as a result of COVID-19.[24] Delaying cancer treatment is a traumatic experience measured in potentially higher deaths due to the disease, and equally high levels of stress and anxiety among suffering patients. The global impact of COVID-19 may have been unique, but various sources suggest that it may also be a harbinger of future waves of viral and other diseases. How well will Canada be able to cope, and will the step of increasing available funds from Ottawa represent the sole solution?

It's a difficult question to answer, and should be considered in light of our performance compared with 11 similar health care systems elsewhere in the world. A 2021 study by the Commonwealth Fund was not encouraging.[25] The study's results measured Canada's spending on health care as a percentage of GDP at 10.8 percent, placing it roughly in the middle of 10 surveyed countries who spent from 9.1 to 11.7 percent. (The exception was the U.S. expenditure, where costs soared far above other nations at 16.8 percent of GDP.)

Despite our spending level, the overall rating of our health care quality, evaluating items like access to care, administrative

---

24 Sherene Chen-See, "Disruption of Cancer Care in Canada During Covid-19," *the Lancet*, July 23, 2021.

25 Martina Dolan, "Commonwealth Fund: Health Care in the U.S. Compared to Other High-Income Countries," AboutHealthTransparency.org, August 4, 2021, accessed online January 6, 2022.

efficiency and health care outcomes, placed us tenth — well below all the other nations except the U.S.

—

Recognizing the importance of our health care system to Canadians, we noted with some misplaced pride that in 2017 the federal and provincial and territorial governments reached new funding agreements for Ottawa to provide more and better home care and mental health support for Canadian families. We considered the negotiations successful for two reasons: I had managed our federal expenditure and commitment down from the previous level of spending increases, creating room for our other agenda items; and we addressed what we thought were the most compelling issues in our health care system, or at least those that were attracting the most interest from a polling standpoint — home care and mental health care.

Saying that the provinces were to spend a portion of the increased federal funding on these priorities meant taking a leap of faith that we could actually tell the provinces what to do and monitor their responses. Based on my experience as chair at St. Michael's Hospital, I knew that directing health care dollars to a specific area didn't always have the expected outcome. The responsibility for determining where health care dollars are spent should ideally be placed close to the action. As my team at finance told me repeatedly, "Money is fungible" — meaning that the provinces could move their resources around to satisfy our demands while not fundamentally changing their health care strategy. Specifying where and how the money was to be spent would be, we believed, evidence of our governing ability and our relationship with the provinces; but in reality, this simplistic approach left many long-term challenges unaddressed.

Beyond the perennial fiscal challenges, our system was still deeply flawed and unfair because it did not include access to pharmaceuticals closely linked with health care.

While many employers provide coverage for a wide range of prescribed medications, about one-third do not. That leaves a substantial number of people on their own when it comes to paying for often expensive medications prescribed by their physicians. As a result, millions of our citizens do not take the pharmaceuticals needed to maintain their health because they cannot afford to purchase them. Although an effective drug program would represent a large drain on the federal and provincial governments, it would reduce costs for individual Canadians by an equally impressive amount thanks to a range of benefits such as bulk-buying and national policies to obtain better deals. This would replace a patchwork of provincial plans with a consistent national approach. Other price reductions could be expected from harmonized programs.

The potential annual savings varied from a ballpark estimate from the Parliamentary Budget Office of $4 billion, based on a Quebec formula, to an impressive $7.3 billion published by the *Canadian Medical Association Journal* in 2015.[26] There was a good deal of evidence to indicate that drug prices paid by Canadians were about 25 percent higher than the median price paid by other nations in the Organisation for Economic Co-operation and Development, so there was room to economize.

There would be further dollar savings to be had with many more Canadians avoiding serious and costly health issues by taking prescribed medications rather than neglecting to because

---

26 Steven G. Morgan, Michael Law, Jamie R. Daw, Liza Abraham and Danielle Martin, "Estimated Cost of Universal Public Coverage of Prescription Drugs in Canada," *CMAJ* 187, no. 7 (April 21, 2015): 491–497.

they couldn't afford the cost. Of course, this work was done on the assumption that Canadians would agree to abandon an approach that worked for most of them, even if deeply flawed, and move to a new system offering comprehensive coverage for less well-off Canadians.

I don't know of any complex problem that can be solved merely by adding signatures to a document, and certainly none that affects virtually everyone and represents a substantial cost to the public purse. To explore all the ramifications of launching a program that would provide pharmaceuticals within our national health care plan, we launched an advisory council headed by Dr. Eric Hoskins. Along with being a qualified and practising physician, Dr. Hoskins had served as minister of health in Premier Kathleen Wynne's provincial government, a post he resigned to assume duties on the council.

I didn't have a role in choosing Eric, whom I knew personally and liked, but I did have the strong sense that he favoured a wholesale change to our system. I saw this as highly expensive; difficult to implement because we would be changing benefit plans for the majority of Canadians (and more so, given all the other initiatives we had committed to); and fraught with huge complexities for the federal-provincial relationship in health care funding. My experience at the helm of the country's largest corporate authority on employee benefit plans told me this effort could eat up all of our government's time — and then some.

Unsure of what the council's recommendations might be, I became aware of the problems we could anticipate in introducing a national pharmacare program. More than half of all Canadians already enjoyed an employer-based system to fund prescribed medicines. How would they react to a major change? Pharmacare would represent the largest single modification to our national health program since its inception. Installing a new plan to provide prescribed medications could generate serious opposition from families happy with their current employer-funded arrangement. Added to the challenges, I suspected, would be the response of insurance companies in the business of selling the employee prescription drug plans and anyone else who might be unsure of their status under a new arrangement. Such a massive change would require a lengthy period of negotiation and persuasion, one that risked having the concept die on the vine. It would be better, I believed, to do things incrementally.

I didn't have to look far for confirmation. In the U.S., Bill and Hillary Clinton had tried to introduce a national health care system to provide universal coverage similar to Canada's and every other industrialized nation in the world. Despite its clear benefits, the idea was condemned by a broad swath of groups who were unhappy and uncomfortable about such a revolutionary idea. It took President Barack Obama to make headway not by insisting on a total makeover, but by introducing the concept in stages.

A similar approach sounded better to me. I did not believe that a stroke of a pen could swing all of Canada into universal coverage of prescription costs, as attractive as this might be to many people. Pharmacare might have been an ideal solution (and I agreed it was the unfinished business of our health care system), but it would have encountered enough stiff resistance to derail the whole concept.

I made a public comment to express my preference for a "fill the gaps" approach that would make progress on a pharmacare plan without prompting a knee-jerk negative reaction from those who questioned its need. One gap we might cover was the number of firms not offering prescription drug payments as part of their employee benefits package. It would be relatively easy for government to mandate this coverage among firms with a sufficiently high number of employees.

At an annual cost of $3 billion, I judged we could provide pharmaceuticals for the Canadians currently without coverage, reflecting a system employed in Quebec. In this way, I suggested, we could extend coverage to those who needed it without ditching the existing system.

The reaction to my comment was swift and harsh from proponents of universal coverage, especially labour and medical professional groups. In the political arena, those on the left rejected the notion that we couldn't leapfrog directly into 100 percent coverage, claiming we would break an election promise by not instituting full payment of prescription medicine costs. Some interpreted the idea as evidence that I was proposing a makeshift patch job instead of taking a firm step toward universal coverage.

Things didn't get any better when the advisory council released its findings, recommending a universal single-payer program with an annual price tag of $15 billion introduced over an eight-year timeframe. This proposal unleashed criticism from the usual quarters; Conservative leader Andrew Scheer labelled the $15 billion a veiled tax grab, and Jagmeet Singh of the NDP demanded that we match his party's promise of implementing universal coverage immediately, which I considered implausible. Unfortunately, I lacked the opportunity to deal directly with the issue and, in any case, shaping health care programs was not my role.

Hindsight revealed a couple of errors. One was our lack of attention to the subject, which prevented us from focusing on the idea closely enough to bring it to fruition. This was regrettable, but not really surprising. In government, as in any other endeavour, there is a limit to the number of things you can permit to seize your full attention. Pharmacare was important, and we perhaps needed to elevate it on the scale of our goals as a government dedicated to improving the country's social programs. But where did this issue fall, for instance, relative to dealing with climate change or cross-border trade with the U.S., or a dozen other concerns?

Being a responsive government does not involve boiling the ocean. It demands that, faced with 20 or so items on your to-do list, you prioritize with accuracy and concern, identify those items that are most critical or most likely to achieve the most good for the most people and find ways to get them done. Most importantly, the work to solve the unfinished business of health care can't be done unilaterally by the federal government, and it can't be a second or third priority. It sits at the top of the list of Canadians' concerns, it is fundamental to the fiscal health of the provinces and it demands the combined focused attention of the provinces and the federal government. There is no shortcut.

—

Canada's failure to recognize and correct the various weaknesses in our health care system over the years has not been due to a lack of effort. Released in February 2012, the Drummond Commission Report laid out a road map for health reform in Ontario. Its 362 recommendations targeted a variety of provincial programs and services, offering proposals to improve the system without resorting to unfettered spending. There is little evidence that meaningful progress has been made in addressing issues identified in the report.

We are the proverbial frog in the pot of water heated on the stove where funding for our health care system is concerned. We need to recognize that steadily rising health care costs are unsustainable. The causes are many, but one of the core problems is the belief that our current method of delivering health care is somehow sacrosanct. It is not. Fresh thinking is desperately needed to improve both the quality of the care and our long-term ability to finance it.

Constant demands from provinces and territories for more federal money are not the solution, or have we forgotten that governments don't have money as such? Federal governments are no exception to that rule. Their sole source of money remains taxes paid by citizens, who understandably resist the implication that they represent an infinite source of cash for government programs.

Our health care system needs new realistic, wide-awake and effective management at both the provincial and federal levels. Without them, things are going to get worse in the coming years, despite increasing amounts of money applied as an ever-growing Band-Aid. All of this must be viewed against the hard-nosed reality that an increasing number of elderly Canadians are about to make new demands on our health care system – demands that can be expected to increase year by year.

The challenge is clear and, in my view, urgent. Ways must be found to improve the performance of provincial health care systems. Pensions are pretty complicated, and we figured that out. We cannot avoid the difficult topics. We must begin with leadership and with a new model of federal-provincial collaboration.

How? Here are two basic steps:

1. *Resist depending on larger federal transfers as a response to changing conditions and rising costs.* Provincial freedom and responsibility in tailoring and managing health care should include the obligation to explore every means of improving quality of care while maintaining high levels of effective patient diagnosis and treatment. This will not be an easy task, given the importance of controlling excessive health care costs. If successful, however, it will prove more permanent and productive than leaning upon the federal government for greater (and ultimately limited) support.
2. *Examine ways to structure constructive debate and build consensus around the need for reforms.* Rising health costs are not an exclusively Canadian problem. Other countries have dealt with the issue and reached varying degrees of success. We can explore the steps they have taken and, where practical, adapt them for our own needs. We can also, I am

> confident, develop our own solutions to the problem not just by spending money but by investing more effort, ingenuity and dedication.

Time and again, Canada's health care system ranks at or near the top of all of the country's qualities that its people treasure. Many of its challenges spring from design flaws and from our unique situation with vast distances between communities that expect consistent services. We should not consider these insurmountable problems, preventing us from reaching and maintaining world-class status in caring for the well-being of every Canadian.

I share the pride in the attention and investment we pay to caring for every Canadian, regardless of their financial or social status. I also believe there is substantial room for improvement in our hands to find and apply the steps needed to make the system even better.

Unfortunately, for too long our approach to solving our health care crisis has consisted of shutting our eyes, pointing our fingers, applying Band-Aids and generally assuming that things will work somehow, all of it reminiscent of the joke about the doctor telling a patient, "Take two Aspirin and call me in the morning."

At some point, without leadership that places all the issues on the table and obtains agreement from the provinces on steps to be taken, no one will be there to answer the call in the morning.

Nine

Dealing with Debt

The question of debt is a significant challenge to deal with, especially for a government committed to progressive policies. Even for those who don't focus on financial issues, there is an expectation that efforts will be made to avoid deficits and reduce debt within an elected government's term or somewhere in the foreseeable future, despite the investment and spending commitments made in an election campaign. This is the magic trick expected of every government.

As finance minister, dealing with government debt was one of the most fundamental parts of my job. In the public eye, it basically defined my job. Whatever demands I encountered from the prime minister and cabinet members, on Budget Day I was the one who stood on the floor of the House for as long as it took to describe how, where and why we would be spending public funds, and what kind of shortfall we might encounter.

In our first year in Ottawa, I saw the need to make investments as a step toward improving our productivity and growing the economy. Our rate of growth had been declining, which represented our most serious concern; succeeding at every other initiative would depend on our financial ability to address it. We needed to stop the decline and reverse the trend, which meant doing some things differently. This was the consensus among those of us who developed the economic plan that had been the basis of our campaign platform, and making it work would demand we take bold steps. Since Paul Martin's second budget as Prime Minister Jean Chrétien's finance minister, Canada had been clinging to the gospel of balanced budgets, maintaining forecast deficit levels as relatively minuscule percentages of the GDP.

This made many voters comfortable, especially those who equated public debt with household debt. Stephen Harper didn't garner many expressions of approval during his years as prime minister, but his austere spending record was one aspect of his government that struck a positive note with some Canadians. Were we prepared to break the mantra that kept repeating "Balanced budgets are good"? Our strategy for the 2015 election campaign insisted on it, which made explaining our position on debt one of the biggest issues I faced.

—

No matter how much we could — and did — justify and promote the menu of programs we planned to introduce, we could expect pushback from the opposition and large numbers of Canadians who consider any kind of debt, but especially public debt, to be bad news. To them, *debt* is a four-letter word as obscene in its own way as any other, especially when preceded by *government*. That's understandable. Most of us are taught from childhood that debt is to be avoided. Unfortunately, many people make the error of equating household debt with government or public debt and — just to reiterate — it's always better to have less of both, but that's one of the few things they have in common.

Public debt applied as an investment, with expectations of widespread benefits in the future, should not within reason be avoided. Good business management policies accept this, as do the vast majority of economists. Building and restoring infrastructure is one example where debt is more than justified as a major step to increase productivity. Both of these are feasible within a low interest rate environment, such as the one we had in 2015.

Even with low interest rates, it's not always reasonable to use debt financing because it carries two risks: having sufficient funds to pay it back, and the potential for increases in rates. When I ran a small business, I wanted to avoid debt on our balance sheet for the same reason I wanted to avoid personal and household debt as a citizen. In those instances, debt is definitely a four-letter word rarely spoken aloud.

But things occur when the scale changes. Running a large business, it became clear that the debt I carried was cheaper than the equity I had to raise. Using debt as a lower cost alternative to accessing funds made sense. Debt that can be serviced without major sacrifice can serve as a key element in managing and growing a business.

So, there are two different dynamics when dealing with debt. On one side is the citizen dynamic, which is opposed to debt of almost any kind. The mantra repeats "Debt is bad," and it certainly is if an individual or household is carrying several thousand dollars in credit card debt bearing an annual interest rate of 20 percent or higher. No one, including me, could possibly justify that level of financial liability. But that's not a sophisticated way of understanding government finances.

The other dynamic looks at debt the way well-managed businesses, especially large expanding operations, evaluate it. Financing investments in that manner is more than justified; sometimes it's necessary as long as the investments are going to be productive. Whether investing in bridges or in people, these decisions have to be made with an eye to enhancing productivity.[27]

---

27 I offer a more detailed view on Canada's debt position in the wake of the COVID pandemic in chapter 14.

—

Assuming office in November 2015 provided us with an opportunity too good to pass up. The basis of much of Stephen Harper and his government's appeal during their tenure had been cost-cutting, an approach that I for one have no problem supporting when pursued judiciously. Unfortunately, Harper and his team had swung the pendulum too far in response to some steps taken many years before by the governments of Pierre Trudeau and Brian Mulroney. When Mulroney and the Progressive Conservatives took office in 1984, they faced a $37.2 billion deficit. Ten years later the deficit for fiscal year 1993–94 stood at $38.4 billion. (In fairness, as a percentage of GDP the deficit had dropped from 8.3 percent to 5.6 percent in that period. This was still much more than we were considering on a deficit-to-GDP basis when we came into office in 2015.) Getting the deficit back to a more acceptable dollar level had required severe steps be taken by Jean Chrétien and Paul Martin, beginning with their budget of 1994–95. Taking over from Paul Martin and the Liberals in 2006, Harper's Conservatives maintained and, in some cases, extended the austerity policy, carving into various programs much too deeply.

Our view was that the stagnant growth of middle-class incomes revealed a need to rethink the federal government's approach to social issues. I was already familiar with challenges facing society thanks to my work on behalf of St. Michael's Hospital and Covenant House, along with recent experiences seeing the housing and poverty problems in the downtown core of my riding of Toronto Centre. We wanted to avoid the levels of inequality and polarization we were seeing in the U.S. by providing more support to low- and middle-income Canadians through lower taxes and additional family benefits, and reinforcing the importance of a progressive tax system. Our aim would be for a roughly balanced budget with a small deficit, as long as we didn't create long-term problems. A declining net-debt-to-GDP ratio, by definition, does not create a bigger long-term debt problem. We could certainly use a fiscal anchor — a budget rule that covers all spending decisions — to help in managing my colleagues' requests, but when you're moving in a positive direction, the need for an anchor is not the biggest concern you face. What was most needed was discipline in maintaining our modest spending targets, plus constant vigilance in considering the risks associated with the debt, based on costs or potential economic events.

The plan made sense by any measure. It would be my job to persuade Canadians to see it that way.

—

An obvious move would be to lock in rates while we were in a low-interest environment. We did this to the extent possible, given the federal government's role in making sure that markets existed for all debt terms. I also strived to maintain — or lower — the percentage of the GDP represented by the debt. This would give us an opportunity to launch and fund some items that the prime minister and I considered worthwhile, within a framework that didn't create undue future risk.

Raising government debt without an overwhelmingly necessary justification is not a popular move in Canada or, for that matter, in any other economically developed country. Under the correct conditions, however, it needn't be considered a questionable move. Borrowing to invest can deliver major long-term payoffs under some conditions. Suppose your retirement fund is valued at $600,000 and you have total debts of $250,000, at reasonable interest rates. That being the case, how would you feel if you borrowed money to invest in your retirement fund and it grew to $850,000 with a higher debt load of $300,000? The debt has increased by $50,000 but the value of the investments in your retirement fund has jumped by $250,000. On that basis, you are actually in better financial shape.

The parallel works for government in a similar fashion. You have to carry the debt, but in an environment where interest rates are both low and steady, this is not an overwhelming problem. Canada in 2015 was in a good position relative to other countries, with low interest rates for the foreseeable future and a large GDP relative to the debt.

But this was no reason to stop being careful, which was the challenge I faced as finance minister. We couldn't expect substantially lower interest rates than we had because they were holding at historically low levels already. And I had to defend against excessive spending sprees on unnecessary programs in response to the acceptable debt-to-GDP ratios we were enjoying. What we needed was managerial discipline, along with vigorous debates on priorities to determine the things we needed to do most, and how much we were able and prepared to invest in them.

We determined to direct funds toward restoring Canada's infrastructure, an expense that many people, economists or not, do not place in the same category as social programs. Infrastructure spending buys practical bricks-and-mortar edifices, structures that are visible, roads that provide transit, broadband capacity to enable communications — all practical and reasonably permanent enhancements to productivity. Each represents an investment rather than an expense, something that can be put to use to deliver more prosperity. Blending infrastructure renewal with social programs gave us an attractive recipe that many Canadians, including debt detractors, would find palatable.

Putting everything together for the 2015 election campaign, we were upfront about our fiscal commitments, which, we calculated, would result in a $10 billion deficit. Measured against GDP, this was a reasonable figure based on the state of the economy at the time. But remember that comment I made earlier about planning for change? Between the announcement of our election platform and the day we officially took office, things changed — most notably the economy. We could not unfurl the program that got us elected and keep to our promised deficit level.

During our early days in government, I was encouraged by what seemed to be an appreciation of the need for fiscal discipline among my colleagues. We had worked very hard, for example, to control costs associated with our Canada Child Benefit and remain within our initial budget deficit number. From that point forward, however, I began lobbying for a deficit target, even internally, to manage the requests flowing from cabinet ministers wanting to fulfill needs in their areas of responsibility, and from a federal bureaucracy starved of funds during the nine years of the Harper government.

Without a realistic revised deficit target we were in effect flying by the seat of our pants. In an organization as large and multifaceted as the federal government, setting and maintaining a target on debt, backed by periodic reviews on spending, is essential. My requests for both struck no chords with the prime minister or the PMO. Both rejected constraints on spending to avoid being seen as replicating the austerity moves of the Harper years. I was left to manage the finance portfolio without tools.

Things were relatively straightforward in 2017, a year of economic growth that reduced the ratio of our debt to the GDP substantially. But I continued wrestling with demands from cabinet members to fund projects they deemed essential. Interest rates remained low, which was reassuring, but we were still without a plan in the event that our growth rate slowed and interest rates climbed.

In response, I began a mini-mantra of my own, a series of conclusions and requests intended to deal with the situation in a rational manner. What I sought was obvious, and should represent the foundation of any federal government:

- Set a target for debt, which would serve as a guardrail to prevent us from drifting toward fiscal disaster.
- Set a similar target for departments, embedding limits in their budget requests.
- Restrict increases in transfers to other levels of government without deep discussions on the outcome.
- Control fiscal costs by restricting the launch of new programs unless full discussions regarding long-term costs are held with other levels of government.

These ideas, I believed, would have generated head-nodding approval from any previous minister of finance in the country's history. That was not, however, the response from either the prime minister or the PMO, where my proposals were perceived to be totally offside.

Their response wasn't as surprising or disturbing as it might first appear. I saw it as a natural product of the anticipated tension that develops between a finance minister and the prime minister. But it soon became clear that we were functioning within a demanding economic environment with no long-term framework to guide us before embarking on new policies, and no agreement with the provinces to ensure they could afford to launch new spending programs. We were drifting with neither a compass nor a rudder.

And then COVID arrived.

—

The COVID-19 pandemic represented a unique crisis of enormous impact, requiring a massive increase in debt levels versus GDP.

But here was the question I posed from the outset: *Since someone is going to take on debt during this pandemic, who should it be?* The answer was either individual Canadians who lost income and would have to borrow substantially to pay for groceries and rent; or businesses that would have to borrow to cover their overhead; or provincial governments, with their responsibility for current and future health care costs; or the federal government, which boasted the lowest debt levels of all and had access to the lowest cost of debt.

Step back and look at all the players in the drama and it becomes clear that, to help individuals and the businesses that employ them emerge from the pandemic with minimal losses, the federal government would have to take on the debt.

And that's what we did. The broad picture made enormous sense when seen from that perspective. The primary challenge in situations like this is to design and implement steps to provide maximum productivity and positive impact, working together to ensure that all of the government's potential tools are employed judiciously. With that goal in mind, I worked closely with Stephen Poloz, then governor of the Bank of Canada, and Superintendent Jeremy Rudin at the OSFI. We were something of a triumvirate working cooperatively but separately: me focused on the overall economy, Stephen Poloz on monetary policy (independently), and Jeremy Rudin as our source of expertise on banking regulation. When COVID arrived, we had an established working relationship, built over the previous four years. We had confidence and trust in one another, knowing that each area would play its appropriate role. This was critical in dealing with the crisis. Fast action was needed, with little time available for get-acquainted sessions. We and our teams all knew our roles and got down to them immediately.

It paid off. For me, one of the most memorable moments occurred early in the pandemic when the three of us, working independently, developed complementary measures, fitting each into the others smoothly and effectively. It was a testament to our emphasis on teamwork and demonstrated to me the strength of our long-established government institutions.

As I write this, the COVID-19 pandemic continues to unfold, with new variants and new challenges arriving randomly. The pandemic, we hope, will eventually run its course with the price measured in both human and financial costs. Canada has, in my opinion, scored a good level of success in dealing with the human side by investing the funds needed for services, equipment and vaccines.

Every death from COVID has been a tragedy, and nothing would excuse any government's hesitation about spending money to lower the toll because of a reluctance to raise the deficit. When the impact of COVID-19 is finally behind us, however, the deficit will remain and our country's economic achievements will hinge greatly on our ability to manage our fiscal policy.

We had the fiscal capacity to respond decisively and effectively to the financial crisis of 2008, emerging from it in better shape than almost every other nation, the U.S. in particular.[28] How well will we maneuver our way with the COVID pandemic in the rear-view mirror?

Let's put things in perspective from the top: according to the 2021 budget, Canada's federal debt was predicted to chart at 51.2 percent of GDP in 2022, and things were not expected to fall back to historically normal levels until 2055. That's pretty sobering. Reducing the debt level will be essential to provide us with the capacity to deal with inevitable and unpredictable future shocks. (Could anyone in 2018 have seriously predicted not only the advent of COVID-19 but the extent of its impact on the world?)

---

28 Stephen Gordon, "Recession of 2008–09 in Canada: Turning Point and Recovery," *The Canadian Encyclopedia*, October 24, 2017, accessed online January 7, 2022.

Where do we go from here in our thinking on debt and deficits?

As a starting point, we need to consider the sustainability of Canada's fiscal policy. The 2021 Fiscal Sustainability Report issued by the Parliamentary Budget Office determined that the current fiscal trajectory was not sustainable for the general government sector, which includes the federal government, provincial and territorial governments and public pension plans. The report assumed annual real GDP growth of 1.7 percent; real per capita GDP growth of 1.0 percent; an assumed long-term inflation rate of 2.0 percent; and a three-month treasury bill rate of 2.2 percent over the long term. On that basis, only the provinces of Ontario, Quebec and Nova Scotia are financially sustainable.

Many astute commentators take an appropriately cautious view on national debt. In 2020 former Bank of Canada governor David Dodge pointed out that if growth levels and interest rates through the 2020s track those of the previous decade, interest rates on the accumulated debt would be in the neighbourhood of 7 percent, not much higher than they had been in 2017. But if growth weakens or interest rates climb higher, and the debt level approaches 60 percent of GDP, charges for servicing the debt would rise enough to put pressure on other government spending.

I have always had enormous respect for David Dodge, who preceded me as chair of the C.D. Howe Institute; his legacy as central bank governor and former deputy minister of finance looms large. His reminder that the future is unknowable should be easy to accept after we have endured a totally unpredictable global pandemic. I consider his prudence in the face of the unknown as the only reasonable course of action to take when managing a national budget.

To return to the household debt analogy I mentioned earlier, if the size of your debt remains fixed while the interest you pay on it rises and your income level falls, you are in serious trouble.

Reverse the two — interest levels fall and your income goes up — and all is sunshine.

But of course, no one knows if those events or any others will occur in the future, which is one reason Thomas Carlyle labelled economics "a dismal science." Predicting the future levels of interest rates and productivity levels over several years is at least as risky as betting this month's income on weather forecasts or some other random event. Budgeting forces us to plan for the most likely future (with contingencies), not the one we hope will arrive based on our policy initiatives. In our case, the lamentable lack of systematic approaches to increasing productivity meant I needed to face the likelihood that we would not change our growth trajectory.

Facing the hard truth that we could not assume growth would produce economic results and allow us to spend without increasing our deficit was not my only problem. I knew focus and discipline in our budgeting were essential because we had to consider the broader context and the inevitable challenges we are facing as a nation. We can identify the things over the medium and long term that will influence our capacity to spend and invest. They include:

- *Our energy transition.* This will inevitably impact domestic petroleum and natural gas production, lowering the income we earn from export markets. Done right, we may see an upside if we remain aware of the possible monetary return to be earned from developing and exporting technologies, expertise and products related to clean energy, but it's not something to bank on while setting budget targets.
- *Our growing, aging society.* It's good news that Canadians are generally living longer, but this raises concerns. Will they extend their working years, mitigating to a degree the anticipated decline in the working population? Will

they retire at the same age as the current average, thanks to good planning and progressive policies such as the enhanced CPP and other support programs? What effect will a growing portion of aged residents and a shrinking sector of younger employed workers have on government income?

- *Indigenous reconciliation:* This is one example of substantial, unavoidable and obligatory debits to be dealt with. We will need to continue to invest in Canada's Indigenous Peoples to right past wrongs while ensuring they have access to the same opportunities and levels of public service enjoyed by other Canadians. Considerable uncertainties exist regarding the levels of funding required to support policies that will achieve this objective.
- *Assistance to provinces and territories in fiscal strife.* Crises of varying magnitude are likely to evolve among the provinces and territories, many the result of ongoing demographic changes. Ottawa needs to continue playing its vital role in providing Canadians everywhere with comparable levels of service at comparable rates of taxation.

For those who believed we could find money for these and other inevitable pressures, my job was to remind them that our source of funds — taxes — was not likely to produce more federal income without economic growth. Raising taxes in a period of low growth is rarely productive, and, frankly, there is limited room in general for increasing revenue from moves on taxes. Compared with some other OECD countries our tax revenue as a proportion of GDP sits in the comfortable middle, providing us in many cases with a competitive advantage. At 40.2 percent in 2020, it was lower than that of France, Germany and Italy (52.1, 45.9 and 47.0 percent respectively) but significantly higher than our neighbour and largest trading partner, the U.S. (32.4 percent).

That low U.S. rate ties our hands somewhat where taxation policy is concerned. Thanks to our geographical proximity and our integrated industries and markets, the U.S. is a direct competitor for talent and business investment. Higher taxation rates between two competing regions need to be assessed carefully. Do they, for example, reflect widely allocated benefits such as universal health care and others? If not, how much of a differential is sustainable if we want to keep our best and brightest in Canada? There is an upper limit to tax levels when investors look at Canada in comparison to the U.S., and in the interests of attracting people, business and investors to Canada, I believe we're near or at the limit. (I'll have much more to say about this later in the book.)

With an already large debt plus headwinds from demographics, the price of energy transition and limited ability to increase the take from taxes, we have no choice but to exercise fiscal prudence. After dealing with crises of historic proportions through the past decade, this should not be a controversial matter. As difficult as the shocks of 2008 and 2020 were, they taught us the importance of disciplined budgetary decision-making. That's what it takes to avoid financing current consumption through excessive deficit spending, while investing in policies to support long-term growth.

Here are my three essential guidelines to assist Canada in moving forward and maintaining our strong financial position:

1. *Understand that disciplined spending requires adherence to a meaningful fiscal anchor.* David Dodge has suggested that deficits should represent no more than 1 percent of GDP in the near term.[29] He also proposed replacing the debt-percentage-of-GDP as a fiscal anchor with one based on debt servicing costs, reflecting the impact of varying interest rates. Every government needs to articulate an anchor and

29 David Dodge, "Two Mountains to Climb: Canada's Twin Deficits and How to Scale Them," in *Rebuild Canada*, Public Policy Forum, September 14, 2020.

maintain transparency about its adherence to the target.

2. *Improve management of direct program spending.* There are various ways of implementing this approach. Here are two:

    - Employ a structured review of government program spending. This is hardly revolutionary — most large organizations continually review their allocation of resources not only to gauge their current status but to prepare themselves for unexpected demands on funding.
    - Focus clearly on the cost-benefit assessment of new program proposals. Key to this step would be a review of how the government will exit a program once its objectives have been achieved or if it is unable to demonstrate a program's effectiveness. This would apply equally to tax expenditures.

3. *Resist pressure to increase transfers to the provinces without a robust discussion and negotiation on outcomes.* On health care, the most important file, it is clear that without meaningful reforms to improve efficiencies and patient care generally, increased federal transfers alone will not substantially improve the system.

Debt need not be a bad word — Canadians just need to be assured that it's employed to support enduring investments or in response to crises, and that it's kept at sustainable levels.

Ten

The Collaboration Challenge

As I noted earlier, my first budget was relatively easy to craft because it was constructed on the foundation of the platform that got us elected. A year and a half later, on the first day of spring 2017, I presented a second budget that, instead of being built on a planned and structured approach, was composed of a number of new ideas based on a year of down-to-earth experience.

Even though many of our 2017 budget policies were based on our 2015 election campaign promises as well, enough time had passed since then that we had to defend each idea on its own merits rather than resting on the laurels of our strong mandate, which is the way it should be. In shaping the 2017 budget, I labelled it an economic inclusion agenda. I sought to maintain our philosophy of investing in the future while keeping the scale of the investments at a reasonable level. We proposed increasing our defence spending to purchase search and rescue vehicles, along with an 11-year plan to generate more affordable housing. We also proposed extending health resources for First Nations people, and other socially responsive programs. The budget also provided for an increase in immigration, supported by investments in learning and development to hasten the integration of new Canadians. These moves could be construed as logical extensions of our election platform and, all things considered, I expected them to roll out smoothly. But there were lessons to be learned and applied.

More importantly, I was trying to pivot to policies that would help us address our longer-term challenge of inadequate investment in our future. I knew that if we kept doing things the same way, we were unlikely to have better results, and there was really no arguing with the fact that our results were subpar and likely to get worse because of our demographic reality. I anticipated that the most important element of my second budget would be the growth agenda. It certainly was to me, but not to those intent on finding fault with our plans.

Anytime a government proposes something new, it risks criticism or even rejection from almost every direction, beginning with the opposition. We anticipated this response to some aspects of the 2017–18 budget. Looking back, however, it's clear to me that many items we proposed did not stir controversy because of their content, but rather because of the political environment and the challenges of collaborating effectively with provinces and the private sector.

Probably the best example of the collaboration challenge is the introduction of the Canada Infrastructure Bank, a signature policy in our second year in office. Not only did we not get grudging acceptance from the opposition benches, we didn't even get strong support from the intended beneficiaries at the provincial and municipal levels. Even powerful ideas intended to generate future prosperity are fodder for political discord.

The background here is important.

In 2012, I was asked by Ontario finance minister Dwight Duncan to complete a study on behalf of his government on the potential of forming a new Ontario pension fund, to bring together the smaller public sector pension plans in the province, in the hopes that they would have better fund returns — and more secure pension plans — due to economies of scale. It was, at heart, a pretty simple idea: the biggest pension plans in the province — OMERS for municipal employees, Teachers' for employees in the K–12 education sector and HOOPP for the employees in the health care sector — all had huge pension assets, and they each had the capacity to invest globally, while still being cost-efficient.

What I found, when I went out to talk to all of the smaller pension funds, was real frustration that they weren't large enough to invest in some asset classes that had been enormously successful for the larger funds. The most-cited example was infrastructure. Our large pension funds had all realized that investing in infrastructure assets like roads, bridges and airports was perfect for their plans. The assets were long lived and created excellent inflation-protected long-term returns with generally low rates of risk. Perfect for a pension plan that is looking for stable returns to ensure that their assets will be significant enough to pay pensioners far into the future.

From this study, I concluded that we could do better by bringing these smaller Ontario public sector pension plans together. Following my report (with an extended delay after its submission — often the case in the public sector) the Investment Management Corporation of Ontario (IMCO) was born, not exactly as envisaged but with the right intent. Now there would be more opportunity to invest in assets that could help to make the smaller pension plans more secure.

But I didn't just learn the benefits of consolidating our pension plans through the study. I also found out something that was of more importance for the long-term future of Canada. The large Canadian pension funds were among the most sophisticated investors in the world when it came to investing in infrastructure, yet they spent most of their time and money on investments that weren't actually in Canada. They couldn't invest at home nearly as much as they would have liked, because the infrastructure assets in our country were less open to investments from the private sector. We weren't effective at bringing private sector money into our plans, meaning that most of our infrastructure investments had to be made by the public sector. There were exceptions to this, but clearly this was an area where we could do better.

So, I came into office with this perspective, that there was an opportunity to ramp up investment in Canada by our very own pension funds, increasing our capacity to build our infrastructure while addressing some of our long-term challenge of insufficient levels of investment in our country — a huge win-win. Wouldn't it be great if we could bulk up pension funds — like we did with IMCO — and then find projects they could invest in here in Canada?

—

Enter my Advisory Council on Economic Growth. We were searching for ways to put Canada on a better growth trajectory, and increasing our level of investment was job one. Here was a good, obvious idea: find a way to get pension funds into long-term Canadian infrastructure assets to support pensioners while stimulating more public-private collaboration.

We knew that the logic was sound. And there was no reason for it to be partisan.

Like many other industrialized nations, where much of the infrastructure was built in the early post-war period, Canada must deal with upgrading and improving major structures and systems virtually everywhere in the country. The work done by my Advisory Council on Economic Growth identified this as a critical issue to be considered as we examined ways to deal with Canada's slowing economic progress and lagging productivity. An obvious response to at least one aspect of the situation would be to upgrade our infrastructure. We don't want critical infrastructure to fall into disrepair or to drift toward obsolescence, and there is much more to be done to ensure that we have the infrastructure necessary to provide wider digital communication and broadband access. Addressing the need with funding would be an important, cost-effective government investment, especially since public infrastructure investments are not likely to crowd out private sector investing. A general rule of thumb on the benefits of investment in infrastructure is that each dollar invested in modernizing a country's infrastructure returns about $1.40 or more in long-term growth.

The term *infrastructure* encompasses a vast range of projects, from concrete examples like roads and bridges to sophisticated electronic systems, to broadband coverage. It's difficult to argue against the significance of these investments as a means of generating growth and productivity in a global economy that grows ever more fiercely competitive. The problem we faced wasn't finding a justification for infrastructure improvements; it was locating the funds needed to get the job done without crippling other projects or placing excessive demands on the federal and provincial budgets. It would also mean agreeing with the various levels of government on what would be the most appropriate investments. Not surprisingly, every level of government has its own perspective. Subways are less attractive to governments supported by rural ridings, and superhighways hold less appeal to urban dwellers who use public transit.

I quickly realized that funding for infrastructure projects brought me back to worrying about federal-provincial cooperation, in this case complicated by the addition of municipal concerns. Much of what we might want to fund, especially roads and public transit, would involve municipal participation to some degree. This, I knew, would create considerable debate about the merits of different investments.

My hope was that by introducing the potential of more funding into the picture, we could use the carrot of new sources of capital to get all parties to agree on important projects. I proposed introducing the Canada Infrastructure Bank as a way of leveraging public spending by bringing private sector investments into the picture with revenue-generating projects. From my 2012 work, *The Morneau Report*, I knew there would be no problem finding pension funds that were looking for infrastructure investments to generate long-term financial returns. Creating a new approach to funding infrastructure projects had the potential to yield four or five private dollars for every dollar of federal funds spent on new infrastructure. This was a prize worth aiming for.

We knew some government infrastructure investments were never going to attract private funding because they had no way of generating income, the primary goal of private investors. Some existing infrastructure could be sold, in whole or in part, to pension funds and other investors. In other cases, we could develop new projects that would produce revenue streams, making them attractive for private investors. We could also use the government capital allocated to the Canada Infrastructure Bank to help finance projects that might not otherwise get off the ground. I saw this as a huge potential win: this strategy would inject money into the economy to stimulate growth and would create new infrastructure more quickly to enhance our future productivity. We had a potential win for municipalities and provinces (more funding, quicker project realization), for pension funds (more investment opportunities with good risk-adjusted returns) and for the federal government (more investment in our economy, and better future productivity).

But first I had to explain the idea to a skeptical public and communicate it in the aggressively partisan environment of Parliament. The logic was sound: once a government commits to and completes major infrastructure projects, public money has been pulled out of the revenue stream for good. So why not develop a means of generating cash flow from previous capital investments in infrastructure, producing an income stream that becomes a source of cash to fund future projects? In addition to new projects, some existing public facilities could be sold to private interests in an agreement that ensured necessary renovation and maintenance procedures were followed and, where appropriate, public access was maintained. The proceeds of the sale would be used to support new developments. We would, quite simply, get more done with fewer taxpayer funds.

We could privatize airports or expand the nation's network of toll roads and bridges, recycling assets and earnings into the CIB. Modern airports are capital-intensive infrastructures involving extensive areas of open land, sophisticated communication systems, complex road configurations, customs and immigration facilities, and on and on. Given the scale of these projects and the critical role they play, governments traditionally provide planning and funding for airports and similar structures and are likely to continue to do so in the foreseeable future. But is it necessary for governments to maintain the operation of the facilities once completed, even through arm's-length organizations? What if airports, once operational, were transferred to qualified private sector operators, with governments receiving a lump sum payment or ongoing payments negotiated via a share of earnings or a leasing agreement? The payments would be recycled through the CIB to fund new infrastructure projects on a similar scale and with a similar shared income agreement.

The idea of handing over publicly funded large-scale projects to private operators may sound outrageous to many Canadians, but the rationale has been proven elsewhere. I'm a believer in employing public funds to initiate major developments that fill critical roles for society. I also recognize enterprises under private management are inevitably more successful at generating customer satisfaction and efficiency than government-managed operations at almost every level and in almost every endeavour. Selected projects, by the way, needn't be as complex and sophisticated as airports. We're not as familiar with toll roads and bridges in Canada as people across Europe and the U.S. are, but once in place, the tolls, which then go to a private operator, are generally accepted as a worthwhile fee in exchange for better infrastructure (and, by the way, an effective means of encouraging reduced energy consumption).

The concept of public-private enterprise had been proven. What we needed in 2017 was a tool to apply it efficiently in Canada, and an infrastructure bank was the answer.

Bringing the idea to fruition would require negotiating our way around significant hurdles. One, embedded in the Canadian psyche, distinguishes between operations that appear innately governmental in nature versus those where Canadians feel comfortable dealing with private enterprise. It's a picture of two solitudes, one defined as government interests exclusively and the other relegated to entrepreneurs and investors. The prejudice is fading with time. For example, I recall when Air Canada was a Crown corporation, along with the Canadian National Railway and Petro-Canada (now part of Suncor). Despite serious concerns expressed by left-wing politicians at the time, all three operations became privately owned, publicly traded corporations. They managed not only to achieve high levels of efficiency but generated impressive returns to shareholders, including several pension funds investing on behalf of future retirees.

Beyond the perceived public-private chasm, I anticipated other obstacles. Employees in government operations were likely to express concern about job security, fearing that private operators would be more prone than government to reducing staff during economic downturns. I understand the concern, but the reality was different. The move to private from public ownership in the three examples above did not result in significant job losses, nor has it occurred widely in other cases.

An even bigger challenge would be the necessary collaboration with provincial and municipal governments I mentioned earlier. The federal government would demand that provincial funding be included for projects falling under provincial jurisdiction; projects relying on private sector contributions would also require provincial approval. Discussions about who pays how much and for what inevitably become highly politicized and complex. Would an infrastructure bank ease this step or complicate it?

We had floated the idea of a Canada Infrastructure Bank during our 2015 election campaign, and it all came to fruition in June 2017 with royal assent to the act creating the bank. Janice Fukakusa, former chief financial officer of the Royal Bank, was appointed inaugural chair with Pierre Lavallée as president and CEO. But obtaining the agreement necessary to get projects up and running would prove extremely challenging. It was difficult to make it a priority in our provincial discussions when we were already busy on multiple fronts with the provinces, ranging from health care to the taxation of marijuana and negotiations on internal trade.

Consequently, CIB leadership could not count on focused government support while they pursued potential projects. Only when the politics proved irresistible was success guaranteed. This happened with the first major project assumed by the CIB: the Réseau express métropolitain, a light rapid transit system in Greater Montreal. Linking several suburbs with a connection to Montreal-Pierre Elliott Trudeau International Airport, when completed it will be the world's fifth-longest fully automated transit system, relieving traffic congestion throughout the Montreal region.

Elsewhere, the CIB encountered various obstacles, many rooted in general unfamiliarity with this new organization and its way of operating. Others grew out of biases unrelated to the CIB concept, including Ontario's then-premier Kathleen Wynne's response to rethinking the Gardiner Expressway, an essential artery and a constant headache for Toronto over several decades.

Year after year the Gardiner is the target of complaints about its ugly appearance, poor design and expensive upkeep. Instead of accepting endless stopgap maintenance on the highway, we had a better idea. "What if sufficient funding were provided from the federal level to dramatically improve its operation," we asked, "in return for collecting a portion of tolls from vehicles using the road?" I saw it as a highly visible and practical example of the infrastructure bank concept, one that could lead to wide acceptance of similar projects once the bank was established.

Premier Wynne was not only a fellow Liberal but something of a hero of mine thanks to her efforts to launch the Ontario Retirement Pension Plan as a supplement to CPP benefits. This time she disappointed me. Her response was fast and firm: no more toll roads in Ontario.[30] End of story — and the resumption of continuous grumbling about the Gardiner Expressway.

Airports, as I noted earlier, were good examples of ways to employ the infrastructure bank idea. Looking into them, Toronto Pearson International Airport appeared an attractive choice. But the politics were a problem, a reality I encountered immediately.

My Liberal colleagues had concerns about this opportunity for Pearson airport almost as soon as the idea became a topic of discussion. People who worked at the airport, as well as taxi drivers, were immediately worried that any change in ownership structure would leave them vulnerable. This reasonable concern is one that has been dealt with in other airports around the world, and certainly was a problem that I saw as solvable. But the hard truth is that political will is needed to get these kinds of initiatives

---

30 Wynne's negative response to toll roads in the province was undoubtedly linked in some manner to the experience with Ontario's Highway 407. Initially created as a toll road, the plan had been to charge tolls only until the capital investment had been recovered, estimated to take 35 years, at which point it would function toll-free like other superhighways in the province. In 1999 then-premier Mike Harris, a Conservative, granted a 99-year lease to a Quebec consortium, which sold the lease at a substantial profit to Cintra Global S.E., a subsidiary of Spanish firm Ferrovial S.A. Although Premier Harris promised there would be no increase in toll rates, they have risen steadily. The rise in tolls could have been handled with a better contractual agreement, but, with its automatic tracking of traffic and absence of toll booths, the 407 has proven the mechanics are feasible and beneficial.

across the finish line, and I just didn't have the support of my colleagues or the PMO.

The challenge I faced was the result of too many things going on in our government. With so many competing projects and programs, many ideas that would generate the biggest long-term positive impact on our economic picture were left at the altar because of more immediate concerns. With as many as 50 high-priority projects on the table, it's a challenge to focus sharply enough to give them all the attention they deserve and the start-up momentum they need to succeed. Understandable? Yes, but also, in my view, evidence of bad management.

In the end, I'm happy to note that the CIB continues to hold great promise, and I hope sufficient political will can be found to make it a long-term success. I'm encouraged by the current leadership and board at the Canada Infrastructure Bank. I hope their stewardship leads to an institution that depoliticizes, as much as possible, the inclusion of private sector funds as a means of renewing our infrastructure.

Canada is an ideal place for this concept of public-private partnership thanks to our history of providing government seed money and support for major developments by private enterprise, all the way back to construction of the national railroad that helped create this country. What's more, Canadian pension funds have proven outstandingly successful thanks to their participation in large-scale ventures all over the world involving public and private funding, and we could tap that potential ourselves. The money, the expertise and the opportunities are right here at home, with the added attraction of lower political risk than in many other countries.

The challenge in getting the Canada Infrastructure Bank up and running was a clear demonstration to me of the need for focus and management in our government. Unfortunately, we were not able or willing to invest the political capital needed to maximize its potential. If we weren't able to get agreement from other levels of government when we were committing to send them funds, then we should realize that the level of trust and ability to collaborate was truly a problem to be addressed.

Certainly, I was not yet necessarily the best advocate for our growth-enhancing policies. I may have been in the second year of my job, but I hadn't yet mastered the art of communicating our ideas effectively in the combative world of Ottawa. My lack of experience gave our opponents some pretty large targets to shoot at, including our efforts on private corporation tax policies and my clumsiness at communicating important measures to make our system more equitable.

But the lessons from that second budget are clear: we will not create a stronger economy without the willingness to embrace new ideas and new ways of getting things done. Like other advanced economies, we've found ourselves in a position where it's harder than ever to achieve stated goals. Even good ideas, non-partisan ideas, meet with disapproval because they come from the other team. And that's before we get to the federal-provincial negotiating table.

Eleven

NAFTA and a Wedding Invitation

By middle age, we've learned the kinds of lessons that life hands us. One is to never assume you know what is about to happen next, which holds doubly true where politics is concerned.

Our relationship with the U.S. began well. Prime Minister Trudeau and President Obama formed an almost immediate bond, based on the similarity of our policy objectives and the contrast with the previous Harper government. From my perspective, Jack Lew's call of congratulations to me in October 2015 was a good beginning, leaving us all believing we were starting off on the right foot. And we were. Connections made at the G7 and G20 sessions strengthened our relationship, although we were realistic enough to realize that Canada was not at the top of the U.S. priorities list. Nor were we likely to be, unless we said or did something to severely annoy them. To his credit, Brian Mulroney recognized this early in his years as prime minister and brilliantly circumvented any issues by fostering a strong personal connection with President Reagan. We might have achieved similar success with President Obama, but we had barely a year to establish a relationship with him before the 2016 election brought Donald Trump into the White House.

The feelings between us and the Obama government were warm at all levels, and we were well aligned on key issues. I recall a lunch at the National Gallery in Ottawa when the prime minister, International Trade Minister Freeland and I hosted President Obama and his national security advisor, Susan Rice. It was generally enjoyable, but we soon became aware that they had other things on their mind besides talking about hockey. They were, of course, hard-nosed and experienced, nearing the end of President Obama's second term, and we were the new kids on the block. Still, we enjoyed an immediate rapport and looked forward to a generally smooth association with the U.S.

Then came November 8, 2016.

Nancy and I and our daughter, Clare, were at an election-watching party that evening, hosted by U.S. ambassador Bruce Heyman and his wife, Vicki, a lovely couple interested in all things Canadian. Nancy and I had come to know them well in the brief period since our election. Their interest in art coincided with Nancy's, which cemented the relationship, and the evening went well — until it was clear that Trump was going to win. Several media representatives were present, and I knew they would seek my opinion of the event, something I did not choose to comment on.

I suspected the world was about to change, and I was correct. The repercussions of Donald Trump's victory basically hijacked our agenda when it came to Canada-U.S. relations. We had incorporated several items on our list of issues to address with the new administration. None of them had anything to do with renegotiating the North American Free Trade Agreement (NAFTA) or, if Trump's threats were to be taken seriously, rescuing it from the trash can. And there were threats of collateral damage as well. We had been about to explore the goal of developing a free trade agreement with China, but the new U.S. president's sabre-rattling about China's trade policies put that plan in jeopardy as well.

The prime minister and I agreed that our first goal should be to develop a closer relationship with top officials in Washington. If we were going to be forced to renegotiate the terms or even the continued existence of NAFTA, we had better find some friends in the administration. My new counterpart in Washington would be Treasury Secretary Steven Mnuchin, and I sought him out at the March 2017 G20 finance ministers' meeting in Baden-Baden, Germany. We established a rapport rather quickly, built on shared respect and our business backgrounds, if not on our respective policy agendas. He agreed to come to Ottawa, where we hosted him with a list of events and engagements that almost rivalled a state visit.

Things went well between us — so well, in fact, that Steven invited Nancy and me to his wedding in June of that year. The wedding ceremony and reception took place at the historic Andrew W. Mellon Auditorium in Washington, DC, with Vice President Mike Pence officiating and President Trump dominating the room. The reception was as opulent as you can imagine. Nancy and I shared a table with President Trump's daughter Ivanka and her husband, Jared Kushner. Michael Milken was also at our table. He had gained notoriety during the 1980s, first for his development and promotion of high-interest debt instruments known as junk bonds, and later for his conviction and sentencing on a range of criminal charges. During a conversation with Jared Kushner, I commented on his father-in-law's surprising electoral victory. "We have a very low ceiling," he commented, suggesting that a large percentage of the population would never vote for them, "but a very solid floor." By that he referred to the large segment of steadfast supporters responsible for the president's electoral success. He knew he couldn't raise the ceiling, so he was focused on raising the floor.

One of my clearest memories of the event was marvelling at the number of billionaires I saw in one location that day. I was also reminded that the Donald Trump whom I and the rest of the world had observed in public was no different than the man I encountered in private settings. He was very much the same person.

Nancy and I left Washington feeling very good about my relationship with the U.S. treasury secretary. I had gone from first handshake to wedding guest with him within barely six months, which made me feel optimistic about the NAFTA negotiations that were scheduled to get started in a few weeks' time.

The renegotiations of NAFTA stretched for almost a year. We knew it would be a long game, and we expected that President Trump was likely to decry almost every aspect of the existing agreement with few positive observations on the progress of the new talks.

Many issues were strenuously debated, and at great length. It often seemed that we slipped two steps backward after taking one small step toward resolution on a specific point. Then, on June 1, 2018, almost a year into the process, the president slapped totally unjustified tariffs on our steel and aluminum exports into the U.S., claiming it was a matter of U.S. security. I immediately contacted Steven Mnuchin, pointing out the absurdity of this rationale and trying to broker a deal that would halt the tariffs, to no avail.

Back in Ottawa, we reached the only conclusion we could: we would put reciprocal tariffs on the U.S. With the benefit of excellent strategic insights from David MacNaughton, our ambassador to the U.S., we were careful to make sure that our tariff list would be politically difficult for Trump's base, intensifying the pressure on them to remove the unjustified levies.

On the day we were set to announce our tariffs, which also happened to be the first day of my family vacation, I got an irate call from Steven Mnuchin, who implored us not to go forward. This was the first of dozens of calls between us over a five- or six-hour period. He made several trips in and out of the Oval Office, where I'm pretty sure he was dealing with an even more irate president. I was away from my office, so my activity consisted of calls to the prime minister and PMO, informing them how upset the president was at our proposed actions — which, of course, was the point of our strategy. We went forward with our tariffs, which put the pressure on Steven and me to solve the problem. It took us until May 2019 to have the tariffs removed, which opened the door to finally getting an agreement on the new NAFTA.

I learned several lessons from my interactions with the Trump administration. Whatever the contrast between our political systems and cultural values, Canada and the U.S. share an economy that grows more tightly integrated year by year. Both countries benefit from this arrangement, but we Canadians need to remind ourselves that this is not an equal partnership by any means.

No two economies in the world are more tightly connected economically. Each day of the year, cross-border traffic of products and services between Canada and the U.S. averages about Cdn$2.5 billion. This gives us about the same trade balance with the U.S. as they have with China, whose population is 38 times Canada's.[31]

That's impressive. And let's remember that Canada is very much a trading nation, as we have been since the Hudson's Bay Company shipped beaver pelts overseas a hundred years before Confederation. But closer examination of the numbers reveals the core of many problems we encounter with the U.S., measured by both economic and political standards. Those hundreds of billions of dollars on our side of the border account for less than one-fifth of total U.S. international trade yet represent about three-quarters of our international trade. Perhaps we should think of our trade balance with the U.S. more as a trade imbalance. Commerce with them may be incredibly important to our economy, but from their side of the border our trade volume with them appears much less significant compared with the rest of the world, including China, Mexico, Germany, Japan and dozens of other nations.[32]

---

31 Statistics Canada, Top Canada Trade Partners, 2020.
32 U.S. Census Bureau, Foreign Trade: U.S. International Trade Data 2021 (Accessed July 18/22).

Breaking down the annual volume of trade between Canada and the U.S. is both impressive and revealing. In 2019, when the renegotiated NAFTA was signed, two-way trade totalled US$718.4 billion, almost exactly balanced in total dollars on each side. U.S. exports to Canada were US$360.4 billion, and we sent an almost equal amount — US$358.0 billion — the other way. This balanced equation was not important to Trump. He had a political agenda, not an economic one. The fact remained that we were second only to Mexico as their largest overall trading partner. Look a little more closely at the figures and you'll note that we were the largest goods export market for the U.S. that year, well ahead of both Mexico and China. No country spends more money to purchase U.S.-manufactured goods than Canada.

Things have been shifting in recent years. We may be purchasing a growing volume of U.S. goods, but the U.S. is importing smaller relative volumes of ours. Canada's share of goods imported into the U.S. dropped from about 18 percent in the year 2000 to barely 12 percent in 2020. Meanwhile, over the same period, China's share of goods jumped from about 8 percent in 2000 to about 18 percent in 2020, an almost equal reversal.

The more you drill down to examine our trade, the more you can uncover some surprising facts, like the 1,500 nurses who crossed the Ambassador Bridge from Windsor to Detroit each day during the COVID-19 pandemic to care for American patients.

In a speech I made in February 2022 to the Center for Canadian Studies at Johns Hopkins University[33] I addressed many of these topics, suggesting at one point that "after spending decades trying to be less reliant on U.S. trade, and expanding to China, we are now in a place where that strategy looks problematic. We need to think more about how we expand our U.S.-Canada relationship,

33 A Thomas O. Enders Memorial Lecture, named for the U.S. ambassador to Canada from 1976 to 1979.

and take up slack there and in other places from what will likely be a decelerating relationship with China."

—

Having close access to the world's largest and most dynamic market makes it worth the risk of suffering collateral damage from shifts in U.S. trade policy. We can never forget the old adage that when the U.S. sneezes, Canada catches a cold. The second decade of the 21st century, however, brought new realities to bear not just on our trade with the U.S. but on that country's international relationships generally. We disagreed vehemently with many U.S. trade policies and their impact on Canada, but we couldn't ignore them. Our best move would have been to avoid annoying U.S. leaders, yet that's exactly what occurred during our term in office.

The need for Canada to tread carefully in economic and other matters with the U.S. has varied over the years. Few instances of serious disagreement arose between us for some time following the end of WWII. Now and then some hostility flared up — like President Lyndon Johnson's infamous tantrum over Prime Minister Lester Pearson's criticism of U.S. policy in Vietnam — usually triggered as much by personality as by politics.

Over the past two decades, however, Canada-U.S. relations have been strained by political polarization in the U.S. To some degree this has strengthened the bond between major political parties on both sides of the border — U.S. Democrats and Canadian Liberals can find much to agree on when discussing topics such as climate change, energy consumption and social programs, and U.S. Republicans and Canadian Conservatives stand together in reasonable comfort on the other side of the chasm.

Personalities intrude, as they always will. It was difficult to observe any encounter between Prime Minister Harper and President Obama without being aware of the discomfort between them. On the other hand, Justin Trudeau and Barack Obama looked to the outside world as though they had bonded like frat brothers almost from the beginning. In stark contrast, Trump and Trudeau appeared to be circling each other like wrestlers in a ring. The growing antagonism between the two leaders became sharp-edged under the influence of combative media outlets which serve primarily as reinforcement mechanisms for established political views rather than unbiased news outlets.

—

The North American Free Trade Agreement dated back to 1980 when Ronald Reagan floated the idea as part of his successful presidential campaign. It was finally signed in 1988 as the Canada–United States Free Trade Agreement, which expanded into NAFTA with the addition of Mexico as a free-trading partner. Despite some overheated rhetoric from the right wing of U.S. politics — Ross Perot, the 1992 independent candidate for the presidency, warned against signing a North American trade agreement, saying the U.S. would hear "a giant sucking sound" indicating U.S. jobs being drawn into Mexico — NAFTA was signed by President Bill Clinton in 1994.

From the moment the Trump White House announced that the newly elected U.S. president considered NAFTA "the worst trade deal ever negotiated," most of Canada held its breath. You didn't have to be an economist to know that cancelling the agreement, which President Trump threatened to do, would cripple many sectors of business in Canada. At its heart, the decision to radically alter the terms of the agreement, or revoke it entirely, hinged not on hard economic realities but on one man's personality. In comparison with Canada, the U.S. economy would have felt only a minor impact from blowing up the pact. Throwing NAFTA out would, however, generate approval among Trump supporters who, for the most part, disagreed with the principle of free trade, among other values. I suspect our entire nation collectively exhaled only on November 30, 2018, when all three parties signed the newly named Canada–United States–Mexico Agreement, or CUSMA.[34]

Getting there was a harrowing journey, made amidst President Trump's bluster and threats, although perhaps not quite as excruciating as many Canadian media outlets portrayed it. Nonetheless, the process taught us a number of lessons about fostering good international relations generally and tracing a future path for our dealings with the U.S. specifically.

Some of the near-panicky media coverage in this country was linked to clamour from the opposition parties, who invested much time and effort declaring what we were doing wrong. They were little help. Just as the negotiations were about to begin, the Conservatives and New Democrats issued a joint demand to the clerk of the Commons international trade committee insisting that an emergency meeting be held to reveal our priorities. This, I determined, would be a foolish act at such an early stage of the negotiations.

In an interview with CTV News, I said, "I'm not seeing where there's a huge advantage to laying out a list that says, 'We don't agree with this, we do agree with that,' because that puts us in a position where we've started at a place we might not want to start. What we want to do is put our best foot forward. We want to negotiate the best position for Canada."[35]

There are never benefits to carrying out international negotiations in public, and there was no reason at all to declare our priorities on the first day of discussions. To do so would severely limit our negotiating flexibility. Various groups seek to inject political positions into every event, especially those unfolding on the international stage, but this one didn't qualify. There are times

34 Known in the U.S. as the USMCA.

35 Joan Bryden, "No 'Huge Advantage' for Canada to Reveal NAFTA Plan: Morneau," BNN Bloomberg News, July 19, 2017.

when we need to speak with one voice, coming together as a nation knowing what our goals should be, and this was surely one of them.

Every Canadian recognized the importance of the negotiations, and most understood the need to revisit the agreement if only to ensure it reflected changing times and technologies. Much of the noise emanating from the Trump White House, however, sounded more intent on annihilation than negotiation. The original aim from the Canadian side had been to strike a balance between two nations whose economies were intertwined, but whose size and clout were out of balance. This had been Canada's goal for 35 years and it had worked, with much satisfaction on Canada's side and often grudging agreement in the U.S. We needed to maintain as much of the existing agreement as possible in the face of the Trump administration's demands.

The negotiating process was made more challenging by the involvement, direct or indirect, of President Trump. Whatever we may have thought of the ability of people appointed to conduct talks from the U.S. side, they were always responsive to the president's viewpoint and domineering personality. We encountered this directly at a White House luncheon early in our relationship with the Trump administration.

Things were set up in the fashion of similar meetings, the scene often captured in videos and photographs by the media. President Trump was seated in the middle of a very long table with his key cabinet members and staff flanking him. Prime Minister Trudeau sat facing the president from across the table, with me to his left and our team facing their counterparts.

President Trump dominated the room and all that occurred in it. He spoke of subjects that interested him rather than those related to NAFTA or any potential negotiations. Some of his pet topics astounded us, such as his unfavourable assessment of actor and former California governor Arnold Schwarzenegger's performance on *The Apprentice*. Donald Trump had hosted the show for several years and, the president claimed, he had been far more effective in the role than Schwarzenegger. He boasted of his success at avoiding environmental regulations that his golf course had been expected to adhere to, then surprised us by expressing his admiration for the Canadian immigration system. It was apparent that he didn't fully understand how our methods of determining immigrant qualifications worked, but this didn't prevent him from calling down the table to instruct his secretary of homeland security to "make sure our system is like theirs," pointing at us across the table. At a later White House session, the president noted the unusually cold weather in the Arctic at the time, citing it as proof that global warming was a hoax.

The impact of his behaviour was especially jarring to us when compared to the thoughtful commentary of his predecessor, President Obama. It also underlined the challenge we would be facing not only in our NAFTA negotiations but in our general relationship with the U.S. administration over Trump's term.

—

Once the negotiations began, it seemed every tremor created by demands from the U.S. side generated earthquakes of fear in Canada, especially among the opposition and the media. It was reminiscent to me of the men's gold medal hockey game between the U.S. and Canada at the Vancouver 2010 Winter Olympics. Each penalty against Canada and each shot on the Canadian net created fears that our country would lose yet again to the dreaded Americans, leaving us feeling beaten and bullied.

While most Canadians imagined the discussions taking place around a table in one room, the talks actually were conducted on multiple fronts over many months. Foreign Affairs Minister Chrystia Freeland had taken the lead at the negotiating table, exchanging positions and searching for common ground with Robert Lighthizer, the U.S. trade representative. At the same time, I was conferring with Steven Mnuchin, secretary of the treasury. As things progressed, Gerry Butts and Katie Telford made perhaps the most important connections with Bob Lighthizer, and with Jared Kushner in his role as senior advisor to the president. These sessions were rarely covered in the media as much as the high-profile discussions between Minister Freeland and Lighthizer, but as things progressed, they proved to be the key to successful completion of the talks.

The multi-layered involvement on our part was an all-hands-on-deck response to the U.S. president's bitter criticism of NAFTA, and it was more than justified. We and the U.S. side were discussing implications that could boost or hinder hundreds of billions of dollars in cross-border trade, each side prodded by representatives of industries ranging from hot-rolled steel to milk and butter. Our goal was to develop relationships that would enhance our negotiating opportunities, just as I had done for decades in my business career in the cultivation of clients.

It was easy for those in the media to present the negotiations as though they were a jousting match, a no-holds-barred contest involving long lances and snorting, charging horses, but the comparison just didn't work in my case. How can you picture knocking the other guy off his horse, even as an analogy, when he has just invited you as a guest to his wedding? My goal was to foster a relationship with the other side, be as clear as possible on our goals and push hard to achieve them. I have never believed that sustainable agreements can be built on anything less than healthy, respectful relationships.

The deal got done in the same manner that most complicated give-and-take discussions are resolved: through one-on-one sessions where each side was able to focus on its goals, searching for and finding openings that could be explored to the advantage of one side without involving backtracking by the other side.

In the complex state of affairs that characterized the NAFTA talks, these back-channel meetings provided an informal, practical means of exchanging views and positions out of the limelight of media scrutiny and within the shelter of personal respect and honesty.

Steven Mnuchin shared this assessment with me. He was even newer in his position than I was, but both of us grew dedicated to staying in touch throughout the negotiations, providing something of a stabilizing influence when and where it was needed. Although Mnuchin was a New York City native and working for Donald Trump, our backgrounds were not as different as they might have appeared at first glance. His political roots had been nurtured by Democratic Party values. After graduating from Yale, he joined Goldman Sachs, where his father had worked, becoming a partner less than 10 years later. Both of us had spent our careers in businesses where building relationships is paramount to success.

We both understood our roles in completing the NAFTA talks to everyone's satisfaction. In our sessions together, each of us could outline the thinking behind his stance on various issues free of emotional responses and misunderstandings, and both of us could express our frustration at assorted incidents ignited by others. We were open and direct with each other, free of concern that our comments might be misinterpreted and disseminated in the media. His points of view provided me with a new perspective on many U.S. positions and their rationale for taking them. This proved enormously valuable when assessing the motive behind their stance and devising a means of dealing with each issue. The exchange worked both ways, of course. Some aspects of Canada's economy — our regional challenges, our two official languages and cultures, our use of supply management to provide stability in dairy and other industries — were alien to the U.S. and needed explaining in detail when discussing each other's expectations from the revised deal.

For all of the challenges he presented Canada, Donald Trump's presidency made a point that we need to remember and respect in our future dealings not only with the U.S. but at a federal-provincial level within our own borders. The recent drift toward political partisanship and the growth of extreme populist views make it more and more difficult to get things done or even maintain a fruitful rapport. We need to focus our efforts on enhancing and expanding our relationships when dealing with other layers of government in Canada as well as with international friends and potential adversaries. That's what we strived to do during the NAFTA negotiations, and we generally succeeded, with one notable exception.

—

The relationship I shared with Steven Mnuchin was built on trust and a mutual interest in focusing on issues that would be consequential for both of our economies. That trust was tested during the NAFTA talks, not because of our relative positions on issues within the negotiations, but as the result of a speech delivered in June 2018 by then–foreign affairs minister Chrystia Freeland. Receiving the Diplomat of the Year award from *Foreign Policy* magazine, Minister Freeland commented during her acceptance speech upon President Trump's imposition of tariffs on steel and aluminum imports from Canada, citing U.S. security concerns as the motivation.

The president's claim about security was nonsense, as everyone involved knew, but it gave the U.S., via the Trump administration, an opportunity to pressure our negotiators. The price of imported steel had indeed fallen in the U.S., but, like so many events that occur in international markets, the changes in price and availability were linked to a range of causes. In this case China, which had developed a number of large, highly efficient steel producers, had suffered a deceleration in its economic growth. Not able to absorb the same volume of steel as it had before, Chinese producers placed the excess quantities on the international market at prices set well below the global level. This had a negative impact on U.S. steelmakers who had not taken advantage of the same new and efficient production technology. When the low-cost Chinese steel landed on American shores, some business and political leaders saw this as an assault on their industry, labelling it as an unfair trade practice that threatened their steel industry and steelworkers.

The 25 percent duty imposed by Trump on Canadian steel and 10 percent on Canadian aluminum dealt a blow to Canada's sale of the metals in the U.S. It also threatened price increases on steel products for U.S. consumers. Both measures prompted Minister Freeland to comment on them in her acceptance speech at the *Foreign Policy* banquet: "You may feel today that your size allows you to go mano-a-mano with your traditional adversaries and be guaranteed to win," she said. "If history tells us one thing, it is that no one nation's pre-eminence is eternal."[36]

Seated in the audience at the event, I grew immediately worried about the tone and substance of her speech. It's not that I or anyone else with Canadian ties disagreed with her perspective. But it's not easy to get what you want from your neighbour if you poke him in the eye while bargaining. Few observers, even in the U.S., bought the president's rationale about security concerns for applying the tariffs. Like many of his moves, they were made to display his support for domestic producers, something that played well among his political base. Minister Freeland's point of view may have been valid, but her timing couldn't have been worse.

Within a day or two I received a telephone call from an obviously irritated Steven Mnuchin. "How would you feel," he asked me, "if I was offered an award from people largely opposed to you, flew up to Ottawa to get it, gave a speech that roundly criticized you

36 Andy Blatchford, "More from Morneau: Canada Shouldn't Have Used Trump as 'Punching Bag'," Politico, June 2, 2022.

and your government, then got on a plane back to Washington without having talked to you about it? Do you think our relationship would remain the same?"

Canadians enjoy criticizing Americans whenever the opportunity arises. But the good feeling we get from doling out such criticism is like eating candy. You might enjoy the taste and maybe the sugar high you get in the moment, but if that's what constitutes much of your diet, your health is likely to suffer in the long run. It's true that sometimes we have to say no to the U.S., but we need to choose our rationale and our timing wisely. When Prime Minister Jean Chrétien was asked by President George W. Bush to support his country's invasion of Iraq, the prime minister took a moral stance supported by a majority of Canadians and refused to join in. Turning down the request was the right thing to do, as history confirms, but was contrarian and highly controversial at the time. Nonetheless, Chrétien made the decision while managing to avoid direct criticism of the U.S. and its leaders.

In time, the folly of the U.S. tariffs on our steel and aluminum became evident not through public lectures but as a result of frank discussion, reaching a solution based on information, trust and diligence. I come back to my point about imbalance between us and the U.S. in relation to the importance of trade to our respective economies. Like it or not, our relationship with the U.S. needs constant nurturing, accepting that it will always be far more important to us than to them.

There remain irritants in the relationship that can and should be addressed. Our pricing of softwood lumber and the supply management policy of our dairy industry are two prominent examples where we have had lots of talks but made little progress. Settling these to the satisfaction of both sides would be ideal, but it's clear to me that the solution lies in moving these negotiations off the high-profile government-to-government stage and resolving them at the industry level. The dispute resolution mechanism in the original U.S.-Canada free trade agreement (and lodged within CUSMA) is critically important to us, but things move much too slowly through this process. By the time issues are resolved, the individual firms impacted by the ruling have suffered severe losses that they may or may not recover from.

We cannot throw our hands in the air in a "What's the use?" gesture whenever our position goes unrecognized by the U.S., nor should we respond with undue criticism of our neighbour's policies and personalities. Neither is likely to succeed. The remedy lies in our effort to remain on the U.S. radar screen as a means, among other things, to avoid becoming collateral damage to actions taken by the U.S. that are not focused on our situation. This can lead to compromise, finding a give-and-take answer that satisfies both sides. Compromise isn't something, by the way, we should spurn. Not every encounter can or should be viewed as a zero-sum game. Let's remember that finding a comfortable middle path is something of a Canadian specialty. It's the basis of Confederation, and one way we have managed to keep this diverse and sometimes contrary but beautiful country together. It has taken effort to do that, and it will take effort to optimize our rapport with the U.S.

One of the easiest ways to strengthen our relationship with the U.S. would be to live up to the terms of our membership in NATO. Under a 2014 agreement, each member was to direct 2 percent of its GDP to defence capability within 10 years.[37] Eight years later the only NATO members to achieve the ojective were the U.S. and U.K. While not a NATO member (but under a collaborative arrangement), Australia reached the 2 percent goal, proving the target could be met without seriously undermining the nation's standard of living.

Buying guns, tanks, aircraft, ships and other weapons of war has

37 North Atlantic Treaty Organization, "The Wales Declaration on the Transatlantic Bond," press release, September 5, 2014, accessed online May 18, 2022.

never been appealing to Canadians in peacetime, but we need to adjust our thinking. Things have changed, as they always do, and building a closer relationship with the U.S., especially at the top level, has never been more essential. What's more, while we could assume de facto security all along our Arctic coast in the past, this is no longer the case. We claim sovereignty on paper, but that's only part of the story. We need a much more significant presence there, a policy of flying the flag to exert our rightful authority, and an important contribution to our partnership with the U.S. in the defence of North America.

One drawback we face is our continuing inability to effectively procure substantial volumes of military equipment to meet our NATO obligations and the demands of our geographic expanse. Our government was no better than previous governments in developing our capacity in procurement, and I was encouraged to see Anita Anand, our highly competent minister of defence, take on this issue. It's a skill we must acquire if we are to live up to our defence commitments and build a much more solid bond with the U.S.

—

It is vital to acknowledge that our relationship with the U.S. represents one of our most important priorities. This has not been the stance of many Canadian governments in recent years. Only in the face of an existential threat to our most important trading relationship did our government realize how essential the U.S. economic links are to us. Necessity drove us to assume an all-hands-on-deck approach to advancing our cause at a critical time. This was an absolute success story for the Trudeau government, and the prime minister deserves credit for remaining focused on this agenda through the NAFTA negotiations. It needs to be our regular, day-to-day practice in working with our closest neighbour and biggest trading partner.

Beneath all of this thinking is my view that the value of friendship is as important between nations as between people. Amid crisis and concern, when faced with situations that appear to offer no easy remedy, we tend to listen to our friends. By definition, friends are people we know and who know us, people with whom we share trust and respect.

Those are simple, but not necessarily easy, steps we can take to avoid blunt confrontations with the U.S. We are not likely to succeed by firing a directly negative response their way whenever a dispute arises, and the party in power on either side of the border must not drive our conclusions. We need to maintain an ongoing effort to cultivate positive relationships among all nations, with a special focus on those we count on to help ensure prosperity for us and for our grandchildren.

In my mind, it is the only feasible strategy.

Twelve

Promoting Human Rights and Trade

Paul Martin had alerted me to all the international travel I could expect to endure as finance minister. I assured him that I was prepared for it but, like many experiences associated with new responsibilities, I underestimated just how much time I would spend heading here and there around the world.

Literally within days of being sworn in to my new position I was off to attend the 2015 G20 summit in Antalya, Turkey. The following year, the G20 met in Hangzhou, China. Between these major international gatherings there were, of course, several other trips within and beyond Canada, but the most memorable was my meeting in Shanghai at the end of February 2016 with China's finance minister Lou Jiwei. Friendly and open, he clearly liked the idea of establishing closer connections with Canada. He also spoke a little English, enough that we began what I anticipated could evolve into a strong relationship.

Chinese president Xi Jinping's opening speech at the September 2016 G20 summit sounded like a direct invitation for countries like Canada to expand their trading volumes with China. His proposals included promoting global growth and upholding international financial stability, improving economic governance and strengthening institutional safeguards, promoting facilitation and liberalization of trade and investment and advancing sustainable development. There was more, but all of these nestled nicely within our own agenda if we could take him at his word.

Much of the world noted that Xi's comments did not speak to the issue of human rights. The question of China's treatment of its minorities, particularly its Uighur Muslim population, has gained a much higher profile since then. At the time, and over many of the years leading up to that moment, countries in the West assumed that China's membership in the World Trade Organization (WTO) and its growing number of trade relationships would lead to the country adopting some key Western policies on human rights and trading practices, but this belief was beginning to fray just as we embarked on our agenda of working to expand our trading opportunities with China.

Prime Minister Trudeau had commented about our relationship with China on several occasions before our electoral campaign, describing China in positive terms. I didn't share all of his rose-coloured views, especially the ones in which he admired China for its governance and ability to get things done. My perspective on China was positive in several ways but most noticeably on its economic advances; I did agree that the country's growth had been spectacular over the previous two decades and that the Chinese people had shared in the wealth the country had created.

In fact, China's economic growth since 1980 can quite deservedly be labelled miraculous. It is now the world's wealthiest nation,[38] having overtaken the U.S. on that measure in 2021. Until China broke with traditional communist principles to encourage private enterprise, the majority of its citizens lived in abject poverty. More than any other factor, China's international trading success generated sufficient wealth to lift them into comparative comfort. By 2015, when we assumed power in Ottawa, more than 400 million

---

38 "China Overtakes U.S. as World's Richest Nation," *the Financial Express*, November 16, 2021.

mainland Chinese were identified as middle class,[39] a number that likely exceeds 500 million today.

On a personal trip to China in 1988, I couldn't help being struck by the amount of poverty I encountered. It wasn't entirely a surprise. With more than a billion people, and an economy that was for the most part mired in the previous century, lifting its citizens to the middle-class level enjoyed by Europeans and North Americans looked like a long-term goal. But now they had done it. In 2000, half of China's population were living at or below the poverty level, defined as a daily income equivalent to US$1.90 or less.[40] Barely 16 years later only 4.5 percent of the population subsisted at that level, a remarkable achievement arrived at by building the economy and taking steps to join the global community through their membership in the WTO, and their ascension to positions of power and influence.

I was in agreement with the prime minister that we should forge closer links with China, although my previous direct contacts with Chinese authorities had generated less admiration for the way their society chose to work with Western companies. I had considered the possibility of investing in China years earlier from a business perspective and had little exposure to the human rights issue at that point. China's economic expansion, I mused, just might lead them to become more westernized to the point of depending upon businesses to serve as the source of social services, like pensions and employee benefits planning, and I thought we should at least consider how to get a foot in the door at an early stage. I quickly came to understand the likelihood that we would be forced to partner with a Chinese organization before being permitted to enter the market. I wasn't entirely opposed to partnerships, but

---

39 Trudy Rubin, "400 Million Strong and Growing: China's Massive Middle Class Is Its Secret Weapon," the *Seattle Times*, November 16, 2018.

40 The World Bank, "FAQs: Global Poverty Line Update," Worldbank.org, September 30, 2015, accessed online March 8, 2022.

under those circumstances there would be a clear danger of losing much of the value of the enterprise to the Chinese partner. On that basis, we continued to focus our business efforts on growing our U.S. business.

Once in government, I immediately found that the human rights issues were clearly stumbling blocks in the path of our hoped-for success. A large subset of Canadians would logically assume that a closer trading relationship with China would indicate at least tacit approval of its policies regarding minorities, dissidents, political prisoners and other persecuted groups. This presented us with a difficult balancing act if we were planning to expand our trade relationship.

Obviously, engagement with other nations is critical when seeking expanded trade volumes. But when your trading partner does something entirely antithetical to your values, whether it be the treatment of the Uighur Muslim minority or the kidnapping and imprisonment of your own citizens, it's time to think carefully about the merits and demerits of deepening your relationship. Does the economic advantage outweigh the repugnance of unacceptable human rights actions? Does the importance of dealing with climate change — a project that can be successful only if China, representing almost 30 percent of global emissions, is engaged — make the relationship essential regardless of other concerns? How important are questions of security when actions by one of our largest trading partners appear to infiltrate our domestic communications systems?

These were difficult questions to answer. I came down on the side of careful engagement because I put the climate change and security issues at the top of my list of concerns. Broadening a trade relationship can generate more than monetary returns. It can make each side aware of the differences between them, the first step toward understanding and tolerance, and a step away from tossing criticism and insults at each other. The Chinese focus on economic stability as a priority becomes easy to understand given a sense of their history. The need to bring the country up to the economic levels of the richest nations superseded their concerns about human rights and prevented us from sharing a set of mutual priorities. Did this represent an impregnable barrier to pursuing trade?

I decided it did not, and the prime minister was in full agreement.

—

A path toward a trade deal with China had been smoothed for us thanks to the China-Australia Free Trade Agreement, signed by both countries in June 2015. The full benefits for both countries were still unknown at the time, but expectations were high.[41] I also noted that negotiations on the deal had begun in 2005; that it had taken 10 years from first steps to completion was a harbinger of things to come.

Past experience cautioned me to be wary of engaging China in business matters. Agreements were complex to understand and difficult to navigate. By 2016, however, things had changed. For one thing, I was pursuing business opportunities not for my company but for the entire nation of Canada, a middle power with a reputation for honesty and fair dealing. Also, the U.S.-China relationship appeared to be growing frosty, so some opportunities for Canada and China to do business together, previously unavailable to us, might open up as a result.

For our part, Canadian businesses were generally in favour of

41 The deal worked out well, especially for Australia, whose exports to China leaped to more than $150 billion in 2019–20. China exported almost $80 billion in goods to Australia over the same period. But the reality of an increasingly assertive China now presents Australia with an extremely challenging problem, given their geography and economic ties.

building a relationship with China and many were already hard at work putting down roots there. I had close ties with several of them, including many of their CEOs. The Bank of Montreal had been one of my key bankers in the private sector for many years, and its then-CEO Bill Downe had preceded me as chair of St. Michael's Hospital. I had also worked closely with Sun Life, Manulife and Power Corporation, all of them hugely successful Canadian businesses with good reputations, strong balance sheets and ambitions to do more business with China.

There was a good deal of activity from previous government leaders as well. Former PM Jean Chrétien, former Quebec premier Jean Charest and former privy council clerk Kevin Lynch were hard at work developing our business ties with China. Their efforts and experience, I expected, would prove valuable in making contacts and setting up meetings with the people I needed to speak to in China.

For all the promise these facts seemed to offer, building an effective Canada-China relationship proved difficult. My Canadian contacts may have been able to identify the key personalities, but setting up meetings with them was still a challenge.

Part of the problem was the enormous cultural gulf between us, with a suggestion on China's part that they did not want to be slighted at any stage in discussions. For most preliminary sessions on subjects like this one, it would have been normal for François-Philippe Champagne, our international trade minister at the time, to take the lead. But this would not have given us access to the vice-premier level in China, an immediate problem. China expected us to send a senior minister, which was me. So I headed the economic and fiscal dialogue with China. And ran into a bit of a stone wall.

At the time, we were working on other trade deals, following up some of the work by the Harper administration, who had taken the first steps toward arrangements with Europe and Asia-Pacific nations. The European talks were being ably led by Chrystia Freeland, working very hard and effectively on the Comprehensive Economic and Trade Agreement (CETA).

China, however, was the big prize in our estimation. They were aware of this, which encouraged them to play hardball in discussing the idea. This wasn't entirely unexpected, but it became far more complicated with the election of Donald Trump as U.S. president.

Throughout much of his pre-election rhetoric, Trump had made clear his dissatisfaction with U.S.-China trade, his apparent general dislike for the country itself and his concern over the ascendancy of China at the potential expense of the U.S. Based on our location and close trading relationship with the U.S., Chinese leaders saw Canada as a U.S. ally who likely shared Trump's belligerent attitude toward their country.

In our first key meeting in Beijing to discuss a potential trade agreement, the U.S. president's words and threats were brought up by the other side with a clear suggestion that we supported his position. I realized they did not understand President Trump, his truculent style, his actions or where our government stood in relation to him. Instead of assuming that Canada was in lockstep with the U.S. administration's stance, China needed an honest broker who not only understood his comments but had been affected by many of them. We played that role, explaining how President Trump's comments on NAFTA were far off base and were meant to play to his right-wing supporters. This set the stage for pointing out some common concerns Canada and China faced.

On a subsequent visit I met with Liu He, the key economic advisor to China's president Xi and a man whose favour we badly needed. Like all of our China sessions, this one began formally, with a prepared script being read to us in Chinese and an interpreter simultaneously translating it to us. I couldn't complain because I had no command of the language whatsoever, but the formality was nonetheless alien.

Things were a bit frosty for a while, a situation difficult to correct due to the language and cultural differences. They remained that way until I mentioned that President Trump had unfairly made us subject to heavy import tariffs on our steel and aluminum. There was no basis for the move, I pointed out, and his claim that it had been instigated by security concerns was clearly untrue. The move had been made for purely domestic U.S. political reasons, and Canada was being punished unjustly as a result.

With that, Liu He's attitude changed. He began speaking to me in English, bypassing the interpreter and opening up noticeably. The slightly warmer attitude was reassuring, but it went only so far. Most Chinese officials still saw us — correctly — as being in the U.S. camp. Despite our disagreements with the Trump administration, we were always going to be much more closely aligned with the U.S. politically, culturally and economically than with China. No matter how much we stressed our objectivity where U.S. policy was concerned, every anti-China comment uttered by the U.S. president made the prospect of an agreement seem another step away.

It took an event in Vancouver to banish any doubt in the minds of the Chinese leadership about our affiliation with the U.S.

On December 1, 2018, I was attending the G20 meeting in Buenos Aires, Argentina, when a PMO staffer informed me of the arrest of Meng Wanzhou, chief financial officer for China-based telecom giant Huawei, on a U.S. extradition order. Along with her high executive position — Meng also serves as deputy chair of Huawei's board — she is the daughter of Huawei founder and CEO Ren Zhengfei. The dialogue with China about improving our trade relationship, along with other meaningful contact between us, was about to end. About a week later, China seized Canadians

Michael Kovrig and Michael Spavor in retaliation, deepening the crisis between us.

Who knows how far we might have gone without that incident and its repercussions? Perhaps not very far. I suspect we wouldn't have made much more progress on free trade talks anyway. China's hardball tactics and the tightening of mainland China's restrictions in Hong Kong were growing more concerning to us. Add its threatening tactics in Taiwan and the South China Sea, along with the U.S. strategic opposition to China as an emerging security threat and economic competitor, and the likelihood of real progress grew increasingly remote.

Whenever I think of the Meng-Huawei incident I recall a comment from former parliamentarian John Manley, who suggested that some savvy international observer should have warned Meng Wanzhou not to take that flight to Canada. A good idea. The benefits of having wise old hands near the PM had never been clearer.

At the time, we couldn't have anticipated that China's response to Meng's arrest would be to kidnap two innocent Canadians, charge them with serious crimes and hold them for almost three years. It has occurred to me that, had China detained the daughter of one of our most prominent citizens, tempers in our country would obviously have been hot. But even if we'd held the same power imbalance that China felt over us, our response would have respected international laws, norms and practices. Doing business with people who maintained such contrasting value systems was clearly not going to be easy.

As distasteful as China's seizing of the two Michaels was to Canadians, and as much as it turned many of our citizens off the idea of building a closer relationship with China, we were already beginning to realize that our hopes for success were far too optimistic even before the incident occurred. The window to China had already begun to close before we entered into serious trade discussions with them, and many people dismissed hopes that we and the Chinese could ever enter into a trade arrangement that would benefit both of us.

I'm not that gloomy now about the prospect. Meng and the two Michaels are home again, and, while the treatment of our citizens during their thousand-day undeserved imprisonment was abhorrent, Canada can legitimately claim it acted honourably and with respect to the rule of law. As time passes, both countries will share serious concerns related to climate change, energy transition and other matters. None will be solved or even seriously discussed without being able to speak to one another in a rational manner on important affairs. This takes engagement, and refusing to engage on subjects of concern to both countries is foolish and self-defeating.

I'm prepared to denounce China's egregious human rights actions. In return, I would point out that being able to face each day with prospects of nutritious meals, warm shelter, medical care and educational opportunity are also human rights, and they have been provided to about a half-billion people. Should we decry China's failings when it comes to their treatment of minorities and dissidents? Of course we should. But let's keep some facts in mind. One is the measure of how far the country has come in bettering the lives of its citizens within barely a quarter of a century.

While it is outrageous for the Chinese to use the example of Canada's failings regarding the treatment and status of Indigenous people as a justification for their actions, it is true that the progress we have made on that score is only fairly recent — one generation. When it comes to casting stones about human rights violations around the world, we Canadians first need to face the truth, and make amends for what has happened on our own soil. We need to push, and push hard, on reconciling to the extent it is possible. Without making that effort and achieving some hard goals in lifting Indigenous people to the status they deserved and were denied through the previous 150 years, our point of view about China's actions and values will have no impact at all if we seem to be simply shouting from the sidelines.

Canada needs to make its values clear and live up to them within our own borders. Wherever we see human rights abuses we need to call them out, both in private and publicly, with an avoidance of lecturing and condemnation except in the most severe cases. Poking people in the eye is not helpful in searching for agreement on any subject. The same goes for dealing with countries.

There are, of course, times when practising that philosophy appears difficult or near-impossible, such as Russia's invasion of Ukraine in the spring of 2022. The losses of human life and property go beyond anything the world has witnessed in recent years, and nothing can remotely justify Russia's actions. Canada's response to this atrocity reflected the outrage shared around the world. There is no question of our commitment to assisting Ukraine and its people, including opening our borders to the anticipated flood of refugees. But we should also, in my opinion, maintain links with senior government officials in Russia, remaining aware of and responsive to any movement that suggests the country is preparing to return to the values of a civilized nation.

—

Meanwhile, our economy remains subject to the whims and caprices of the U.S. How can we improve our trading relationship with the U.S. to make it more stable? One way would be to reduce our dependence on it as our largest export market. Anytime you count on 75 percent or more of your business from a single entity, that entity is neither a client nor a customer. It's an employer.

It doesn't take an introductory class in economics to make this obvious. However, given the reality of our geography, our culture and the tumultuous world trade situation that sprang out of the Trump administration, shifting our trading patterns to reduce our reliance on the U.S. won't be easy. Nor has it ever been. And of course it has to be done at the same time as we aggressively nurture our critical U.S. relationship — not an easy balancing act.

Developing new markets beyond the U.S. to strike a balance is not a new idea. Canada has taken a number of steps in recent years to achieve that goal, including our participation in the Trans-Pacific Partnership and CETA. Still, the U.S., for all of its challenges to us, remains right on our doorstep.

Much of my business career was spent growing my company. This could always be done with mergers and acquisitions, but I found the most efficient way to get it done was by expanding the strong business relationships we already had. Ideally, you have to do both, and the same holds true for adjusting Canada's trade volume, shifting things to reduce the imbalance we currently have.

So how do we shift so much of our trade reliance away from the U.S.? We are left with the uncomfortable reality that we need to continue working toward expanding our trade volume with China, now the world's richest nation. That's a simple answer, but not a simple task.

That old cliché about not ignoring the elephant in the room translates into refusing to ignore the giant in the marketplace. It's China, and any prospects for a country of Canada's size to maximize its trade and reduce its reliance on a single market has to involve China.

China has dominated almost every aspect of global trade relations over the past two decades. It is by far the world's largest trading partner as measured by the sum of imports and exports, and it has occupied that position since 2013. China does more trade with 124 countries in the world than any other nation, including their immediate neighbours. By GDP on a purchasing power parity (PPP) basis and almost every other metric available, China's economy remains impressive and dominant. [42] Since the U.S. is on a course to a constantly more challenging relationship with China, we can at least be helpful in maintaining the dialogue on the world's two most important challenges — climate change and security — by continuing to foster the relationship, as difficult as that will surely be.

—

My point of view was tested not only in China. We also encountered a different problem in a vastly different country whose approach to human rights, and to women's rights in particular, was so diametrically opposed to ours that we could only consider it deeply offensive. Just to complicate things, one of the world's leading defence manufacturers became involved.

Thanks to enormous petroleum reserves, Saudi Arabia's economy is by far the largest in the Middle East, and the 18th largest in the world. The money it earns is spent for the most part on behalf of its people and as a result it rates highly on the United Nations Human Development Index, a measure of a country's health, education and per capita income. Its human rights record, however, belies that favourable ranking. One of the few countries that has not signed the UN's Universal Declaration of Human Rights, it imposes capital punishment for offences ranging from drug use to adultery, and its restrictions against women are medieval in concept. Polygamy is permitted for men, who have a unilateral right to divorce their wives without legal justification. In Saudi

---

42 PPP measures prices of globally available products — from Big Macs to iPads — as a means of comparing the absolute purchasing power of the countries' currencies. In the opinion of many economists, PPP provides a more accurate measure of a nation's wealth than nominal GDP alone.

courts, the testimony of one man equals that of two women, and on and on.

So in 2014 when the Harper government announced it had signed contracts with the Saudis worth $14.8 billion for light armoured military vehicles built by the U.S. firm General Dynamics at its facility in London, Ontario, it generated a storm of controversy. The size of the arms order was unprecedented in Canadian history, with delivery of the equipment extending over a 15-year period.

Response to the announcement of the deal varied depending on your point of view. Supporting well-paying jobs for thousands of General Dynamics's Canadian employees over such an extended period was obviously good economic news. But equipping the Saudi Arabian military with vehicles that theoretically could be used to transport its soldiers into battle zones, and possibly quell demonstrations by its own people, didn't sit well with many Canadians.

At the time the contract was signed, the Saudis were leading a coalition of Arab states intervening in a civil war in Yemen that arose from long-simmering hostilities. Located on the southern edge of the Arabian Peninsula, Yemen could be mistaken on a map as a state or province of Saudi Arabia, but it is an independent republic whose economy, for the most part, is tied to its agricultural production. The country's minority Houthi population objects to the policies of the Yemeni government, particularly its close relationship with Saudi Arabia and the U.S.[43]

By the time we came into office, many Canadians had grown concerned that the Saudis would be using the Canadian-made vehicles to support the military conflict with Yemen. But it wasn't that simple. There were also reports of a large number of civilian

43 The roots of the conflict are multi-layered, linked to Shia-Sunni disputes and participation by Iran and other neighbouring nations. In addition, al-Qaeda and ISIS have also entered the fray, attracting interest and periodic support for Saudi Arabia from the U.S., the UK and France.

deaths attributed to Saudi Arabia's actions in the conflict,[44] and some people argued that the Saudis would use the vehicles to launch attacks against their own civilians.

Our government was unhappy with the deal for several reasons. From my perspective, the Harper government had handed us a political hot potato, a deal that our constituency was much less likely to approve of than Harper's Conservative supporters. We were also concerned about the conditions of the contract. Its details were cloaked in secrecy, the agreement so tightly bound that no public discussion was permitted about almost any aspect. Numerous critics, appalled at the Saudis' human rights record and suspicious of many of the Harper government's secret terms, began demanding that Canada cancel the deal almost as soon as it was publicly announced.

This became my problem. Dealing with crises like this was not a part of my official job description when I sat with the new PM and agreed to be his finance minister. However, the deal was important for our economy and involved a few thousand jobs, so it fell into my lap. Cancelling it might have felt good to the critics, but it was not at all practical. Under the terms of the contract, the Saudis would be free to sue Canada if we tried walking away from it. So rather than Canada earning $14 billion from the sale, we would be on the hook to pay the Saudis if we broke the contract. We could also expect a storm of protests to head our way from General Dynamics in the U.S., because cancelling the deal would have meant the loss of a significant contract for their Canadian subsidiary, not to mention the loss of thousands of jobs in London, Ontario.

There was also Canada's international reputation to be considered. If we wanted to expand our international trade, we needed to be known as a country that could be relied on to adhere to

---

44 BBC News, "Yemen War: UN 'to List Saudi Coalition for Killing Children'," October 4, 2017.

contractual agreements as part of an international rules–based trading regime. It's highly unlikely that our government would have signed the deal given its many objectionable conditions, but respecting the decisions of a previous government, however distasteful it may be to our constituents, was the reality of a grown-up nation. For a couple of years, I worked on finding a compromise between us and the Saudis. Through many twists and turns, the issue finally came to a head just as we began dealing with the severe impact of COVID-19 on Canada's economy. Did we really want to toss away all those well-paying jobs at a time when we were facing a tsunami of layoffs resulting from the pandemic? And there was that multi-billion-dollar IOU, payable to the Saudis, if we didn't live up to the terms of the contract.

Overriding everything was the question of Canada taking responsibility for the actions of a duly elected government once it was out of power. Like it or not, the contract committing this country to the international deal had been signed by the legitimate government of Prime Minister Harper. Whether he and his people had given serious thought to the moral concerns about supplying the Saudis with military weapons was not the core issue to me. The contract sealed Canada's commitment. If we, as the government replacing the Harper regime, rebuked the deal, would other countries rely on Canada to live up to its contractual obligations?

Things had already grown tense. Foreign Minister Freeland, in a Twitter message, had called for the release of women's rights advocates and other activists imprisoned in the Saudi kingdom. This prompted the Saudi foreign ministry to respond by labelling her comments "blatant interference in the kingdom's domestic affairs" and declaring our ambassador persona non grata, giving him 24 hours to leave the country. Threats were made to smother any future criticism from Canada, with the Saudis noting "any further step from the Canadian side in that direction will be considered as acknowledgement of our right to interfere in the Canadian domestic affairs."[45] A few weeks later, the brutal assassination of Saudi journalist Jamal Khashoggi in Istanbul added a chilling new chapter to things.[46]

I undertook the task of exploring how to make the Canada–Saudi Arabia relationship work. Was there a way to respect the terms of the deal and salvage its benefits to Canada without damaging our position on women's rights and on human rights in general? I had my doubts.

My first step was to deepen my relationship with the Saudi minister of finance. To my pleasant surprise we managed to build a practical rapport, sharing our countries' views and acknowledging our differences on subjects that included women's rights. Neither of us expected to change the other's mind, nor did we try. We did manage, however, to put things in context and, motivated by a mutual interest in finding a solution, settle on a plan that neither of us favoured but both of us could accept. And that my government would accept as well.

—

We in Ottawa were busy looking for a way to work with two very different countries with whom we had very different concerns. Saudi Arabia's treatment of women and minorities represented the biggest barrier to us forging closer bonds with them. China's emphasis on generating economic stability among their 1.4 billion

45 Ben Hubbard, "Saudi Arabia Assails Canada Over Rights Criticism, Sending Message to West," *the New York Times*, Aug. 6, 2018.

46 Mr. Khashoggi, a journalist, had visited the Saudi consulate in Istanbul to obtain documents related to his planned marriage. He was, according to all available sources, murdered inside the building, his body dismembered and disposed of. The Saudis at first denied the killing occurred, then claimed he died as a result of an assault inside the consulate. Later it was admitted the murder had been premeditated in retaliation for Khashoggi's criticism of Saudi Arabia's rulers. Eventually, eight Saudi citizens were convicted of the killing and sentenced to prison terms.

people shaped many of their actions and represented a primary motivation for their policies, as questionable as some may be.

Both countries were following their own paths, trying to manage their internal challenges. No way exists to persuade them to follow our path, in the short term at least, which means their approach to human rights will continue to outrage us. Arguing that China brought hundreds of millions of people out of abject poverty or that Saudi Arabia has made small steps in allowing more equality for women does not lighten our concern over their greater actions. So what is our best move?

The first thing we can do is to live up to our own standards in the field of human rights, celebrating our achievements and acknowledging our stumbles as each occurs, as well as those in the past. This is not meant in any way to make me an apologist for bad behaviour. It makes me a realist, and a practical one at that. We need to engage, cajole and nudge other countries toward those human values we consider essential.

Much of this belief grows out of my business experience. I always began a negotiation with the assumption that I could make progress by engaging the other side in discussions and understandings on the way to finding agreement. I would hold that belief until proven wrong. Did I get burned now and then? Yes, I did. But whenever this happened, I learned to come back at similar situations with the same intentions. This approach is even more important in dealings with countries than with corporations, since there is no choice but to find a way to get along.

That's where I believe we are with China. We need not stand back and wait for them to change. I think it's better to look for a new way to approach them and develop a relationship that benefits both of us, collaborating on climate change, sharing common concerns on economic stability and forging careful links on trade. We will need to be especially careful not to have agreements in sensitive technologies. We need to make our position clear without being confrontational about it. We can agree on the benefits of social equality, for example, and still express our severe concern over the removal of basic freedoms from those with a different point of view. And we should remember that being a model for others is always more satisfying and more productive than being a constant critic.

It's not an easy world out there, nor is it one where everyone is in total agreement with our values. The best way forward is to engage with others, regardless of the differences between us, and search for a way to resolve those differences to the benefit of both sides.

I see no other practical alternative. If you insist on living exclusively according to your highest principles, you'll find yourself living with a very small number of people.

Thirteen

The Trouble with Taxes

If you think your job is hard, imagine telling 20 million or so people how much tax they'll have to pay in the coming year. That's one of the unavoidable chores of a Canadian finance minister.

There are times when you can pass along good news, announcing that some taxes will be lowered or even, in certain categories, eliminated altogether. But even when that happens, you're reminding people about paying taxes, something they prefer not to be prompted about.

I understood this part of the job before I took it, but there's nothing like turning theory into practice to make it real. In his March 2004 budget Ralph Goodale, who served as finance minister in Paul Martin's government, introduced new tax rules designed to severely limit the appeal of income trusts as investment vehicles. The rulings from these changes were made just as I was about to launch the initial public offering (IPO) for Morneau Shepell, and I managed to get the IPO in just under the wire.

A year and a half later Jim Flaherty, finance minister under Stephen Harper's leadership, eliminated the tax benefits associated with income trusts. With what might be construed as devilish glee, he made the announcement on Halloween when I was out trick-or-treating with my three then-small children. This severely annoyed people who were running income trusts at the time, as I was. But I had mixed emotions. The new ruling had cost me a lot of money personally, but I also thought it was the correct move for him to make as finance minister.

Given my business background, I understand that taxes on their own are not the key driver in making business decisions. That being said, they're important for two reasons: they yield government revenues to get things done, and they signal how people should contribute to the public good.

—

I came into office with the understanding that whatever I and the federal government did on tax policy, we would never make everyone happy. People arrange their financial affairs according to tax guidelines. Change those guidelines — unless they involve substantial tax reductions — and you are likely to generate broadly based distress, much confusion and general irritation.

I had another perspective on taxes: Canada's personal and corporate tax rates needed to be competitive with those of the U.S. We compete with the U.S. for investment money, so if our tax schedule is severely out of line with theirs, it could limit the investment dollars available here and send billions across the border in response to lower-taxed opportunities there. What's more, notably higher taxes in Canada would make it difficult to attract capable individuals north for employment and cause a brain drain of Canadian talent heading south. I had run a business with substantial operations in both countries, with people who worked on both sides of the border, so I knew all of this first-hand.

I also knew from policy work done at the C.D. Howe Institute that consumption taxes, like the GST and HST, are among the most effective approaches to generating government revenue, even if they irritate consumers. I understood them to be progressive when shaped with exemptions to reduce their impact on those at the bottom end of the income scale. Coming into government made me realize that this is true only to a point. Eliminating sales taxes on food and other vital products and services can work that way. But purchases subject to consumption tax represent a much higher portion of after-tax income to those in the lower-income categories than those at the upper end. Income-tested refundable credits do a more effective job. My role would require me to balance all of these factors as I found the best approach to taxation.

One problem with these and the myriad other laws in our tax code is their number and complexity. I came into office thinking it would be great if we could strike a commission assigned to dramatically simplify the system and address the inequities that have grown out of decades of tinkering with the tax code, all while remaining competitive with the U.S.

An examination of our tax system conducted by the International Monetary Fund in light of the 2017 tax reform in the U.S. found some general coherence between the two systems and identified some aspects of Canada's tax policy that were coming under pressure. Here were some of the key observations:

- We have a sharply progressive rate on personal income tax (PIT) that runs steeply from a relatively low threshold at the beginning to a high top marginal tax rate. From my perspective, a progressive system made sense, but how progressive should the system be, and what should be the top marginal tax rate?
- We have an approach that has a close integration between corporate and personal taxes, representing an attempt to fully credit tax paid at the corporate level on payment of dividends to Canadians, a practice that is rare elsewhere in the world. While this seems to make sense, it creates a lot of complexity in our system.
- We have an unusually favourable tax treatment for small businesses. I saw this as encouragement for Canadians to start and manage their own businesses, but we had to

consider whether the continuing advantage of being small created a barrier to our aspirations about creating bigger enterprises.
- We have no taxation on a wide range of savings plans. Broadly intended to help Canadians prepare for retirement, it creates a complex set of arrangements that are entrenched and difficult to change.
- We have a relatively modest reliance on the GST for revenue generation, as compared to consumption taxes in most other advanced economies. This means we have not optimized a key source of revenue for government and need to tax Canadians in other ways (that is, through personal and corporate taxes) which are less effective.
- Finally, we have a high differential between the top PIT rate and the maximum corporate rate. This is the source of a lot of challenge; Canadians incorporate to reduce their tax rate, and we try to mitigate the problem with complex ways of recalculating the personal tax rate of people who get income through corporations. We also have a significant difference in tax rates for dividends and capital gains, which drives a substantial amount of tax planning.

Looking at this report, it was clear that a complete rethink of our system would make sense. That was what John Diefenbaker did in 1962 with the Carter Commission and tax practitioners across the land, including those in my department, considered it the best approach to dealing with some of our challenges. Now that I was in charge of the tax system, I realized it was not so easy. The barriers to considering another commission on tax policy were considerable.

—

Tax reform begins by eliminating targeted and poorly performing measures accumulated over the years, with the goal of lowering tax rates. As finance minister, I had to deal with the reality that the additional taxes earned as a result of other measures would not be enough to offset the revenue lost by reducing the rates (at least not by a meaningful amount), meaning we would be lowering the federal government's total tax take. And any commission would take time. The scope, complexity and importance of the tax system, and its impact on economic and social policies, make it virtually impossible to carry out a reform within a four-year electoral calendar. Picture a holistic tax reform effort being interrupted by a federal election. Whatever their rationale and progress, the reform plans would become a campaign football kicked up and down the field by every political party and position. There is, quite simply, no way to do this without making it a key feature of a focused government and with the fulsome support of the PM.

My agenda was already filled with other challenges. Through my first few months in office, I had advocated using the GST as a more important source of government income. I pointed out that a small increase in this consumption tax would help cover the costs of our agenda to assist lower- and middle-income Canadians, but it received zero support from the prime minister. Stephen Harper had reduced the GST by two points, and even though we and virtually every qualified economist saw this as a bad move, there was no desire to restore it to the previous level. The politics were too difficult.

Without political support to mine the GST for revenue, implementing a tax commission to review the system would occupy my entire agenda through our term in office. Reluctantly conceding that Trudeau's agenda was already far too ambitious and we would lack the focus needed for effective implementation, I shifted my attention elsewhere. I would deal with important tax issues as they arose, just as Jim Flaherty had done with income trusts during the Harper administration. In my case, I turned to the growing trend of personal corporations created by individuals solely to reduce their personal income tax obligation while limiting their personal liability.

Placing your earned income within a corporation is both legal and fair when your ability to earn that income involves participation by other individuals and the acquisition of support equipment and services. Medical professionals, for example, need staff and apparatus to schedule, examine, diagnose and treat patients. It's far more efficient to cover the related costs under the umbrella of a corporation than to assume the obligations on your own. Corporate tax rates are significantly lower than personal income tax, and the cost of many articles and services can be deducted from the corporation's taxable income. Both are justifiable in assisting companies to function efficiently but generally unwarranted for individuals.

Don't get me wrong. I firmly believe that operators of small businesses deserve respect and reasonable assistance from government. As we all know and appreciate, small businesses generate enormous employment opportunities, whether as corner grocery stores, automotive repair shops or medical and dental clinics. The contributions they make, not only to their community but to the nation as a whole, must not be devalued by government.

Unfortunately, too many high-earning small business operators, including medical, legal and accounting professionals, searched for advantages available to them within the tax guidelines in ways that were difficult to justify. One common method, referred to as *income sprinkling*, was to apportion the small business income among members of the owner's family, even if they were not involved in operating the business. Dividing the net income earned from the business among three or four family members can reduce the total tax payable by the corporation, sometimes by several thousand dollars. Multiply that figure by Canada's escalating number of questionable personal corporations, and it becomes clear that the country was losing hundreds of millions of dollars in justified taxes annually. What could we do about it?

Recognizing this unfair advantage and choosing to address it was neither a new idea nor an exclusively Liberal one. Prime Minister Jean Chrétien had dealt with it in 1999 when he had legislation passed to apply top-level tax rates on the distribution of dividends and other specified income to children under the age of 18. Later, Prime Minister Harper strengthened the rules on taxation of dividends even further.

Previous provisions to correct the situation hadn't gone far enough. We proposed a three-way approach that reinforced the rules against income sprinkling, removed the tax advantages of passively investing income from a private corporation and banned the use of artificial transactions to pull income from a private corporation at favourable capital gains rates. Calculations made by my staff indicated that the largest impact of proposed new rules would be felt by those making more than $150,000 annually.

I believed in making the effort to deal with the situation, but the first steps gave me some pause, knowing that tax rules are like sunburn: everyone knows they need treatment, but most people don't want you to touch them.

I didn't use that analogy with the prime minister in 2017 when I summarized my approach to revamping the small business tax rules. He understood my unease about the response to our proposed revisions that was likely to arise among the opposition, the media and, of course, owners and operators of small businesses. Not only that, but the solutions we would be proposing were necessarily complex given our attempts to create fairness.

I outlined my concerns to him during a flight to Seattle, saying, "This is going to cause significant pushback, and we should be prepared for it." I needed him to understand that opposition to the changes would be heated, directed at us from multiple sources. Along with small business owners we could expect farmers, high-net-worth individuals and others to express their disagreement with vigour, and while blame would fall on us as the government, I expected most of the sharpest attacks to be directed at me.

The PM nodded knowingly. This, he agreed, was the right thing to do, and we should move forward as planned. Then, in a gesture of understanding and support, he told me he had my back.

In theory, he did. We were in agreement that the policy was worth instituting and defending. But in practice his backing was irrelevant. I was not only assigned to shape and direct the program, but to lead the communications effort and deal with challenges to our plan. I was on my own.

—

The 2017 flight to Seattle with the prime minister was to attend a meeting hosted by Microsoft co-founder Bill Gates at his home outside the city. Along with other key business and political leaders, Prime Minister Trudeau also had been invited. We were working to find foreign investors for Canada, and the PM arranged for me to accompany him. Following a daytime session involving perhaps a hundred or so attendees, Gates invited the prime minister and me to join him, his then-wife Melinda, and Warren Buffett for dinner. It was a casual affair, set in Gates's impressive library, and led to one of the most memorable conversations I took part in during my time as finance minister.

Gates and Buffett were deeply interested in Canada, especially the country's political and economic environment. It was the first year of the Trump administration in Washington, and they were clearly concerned about the perils of increasing polarization in the U.S. They commented upon the absence of similar extremism in Canada, which they attributed in part to our social support systems, particularly our health care, government pensions and tax benefits such as the Canada Child Benefit. These, they felt, mitigated financial problems for lower-income Canadians, generally reducing the kinds of pressures and inequities occurring in the U.S.

The two men had contrasting personalities. Bill Gates was straightforward in his style. After asking questions he would listen carefully to the response, appraise it and offer an incisive, probing and deeply informed response. Warren Buffett, I sensed, was evaluating us in a different manner, measuring not only the facts but the personality of the individual supplying them. He framed his questions in his familiar folksy style — asking about Canada's business climate, and the successes we were achieving as a result of our resources, our people and our immigration policies. He was as interested in where we were going as where we were. Both men directed their questions about Canada's economy and business climate toward me because that was my area of expertise and responsibility. When they wanted to know more about Canada's objectives and activities on the international scene, they quizzed the prime minister.

In their opinion, the U.S. faced immense problems rooted in pervasive inequality, with many citizens so mired in poverty it was difficult for them to escape. I found it ironic that, despite their concerns about their country's ability to maintain its economic growth and domination, and the inequities that so many of its people faced, America had produced two of the world's wealthiest people, seated directly across from us. Yes, there were easily identifiable challenges, but the U.S. was also the most economically successful country on earth, generating enormous fortunes alongside societal inequities — fortunes, I should add, that both Buffett and Gates drew heavily upon to fund various social causes such as education, health care and assistance for poverty-stricken families. Clearly, we could learn just as much, or more, from these men as they could learn from us.

Interestingly, given my major preoccupation at the time, we didn't discuss taxes at all. They were more interested in people, our education systems and investments in key sectors of the Canadian economy. I left the meeting feeling more strongly than ever that corporate tax rates matter (obviously . . .) but they are not the primary driver in the economic equation. We needed to find our strength and ensure that taxes were not a deterrent to investing. What we didn't need to do was try to win with lower taxes. We just needed to be competitive.

And we are, at least in some areas. The marginal effective tax rate (METR) is an estimate of the taxation level on a new business investment. It takes into account federal, provincial and territorial statutory corporate income tax rates, along with other features of the corporate tax system, such as investment tax credits and key deductions, including capital cost allowances. Added to the mix are items including capital taxes and unrecoverable sales taxes paid on capital purchases.

All in all, it's a pretty comprehensive formula to judge our taxation policy against those in other corners of the world, and here's what it revealed:

- In 2019 our average corporate METR stood at 13.7 percent; in 2000 it had measured 44.1 percent. This made our average METR the lowest among all the countries in the G7, and below the OECD average. (Italy's may now be slightly lower.)
- We maintain an average METR advantage of 4.7 percentage points below the U.S. Recent U.S. tax changes reduced but did not eliminate our lead on the Americans.

- Our advantage over the U.S. stems from wider adoption of value-added taxes in Canada — our GST and HST. These do not add to business costs; taxes applied to capital inputs are creditable to the business. In the U.S., many states apply retail sales taxes on capital inputs.
- All of this gives our manufacturing sector a competitive edge over the U.S. The average METR in that sector stands at 16.4 percentage points below the average METR applied to U.S. manufacturing.

These METR levels give us an apparent advantage over other countries, creating the impression of Canada as an attractive place for business to invest, and offsetting drawbacks such as our small domestic market and the distances between major locations.

But we clearly have some issues that limit Canada's ability to attract corporate investment.

First, Canada's personal income tax rates are not competitive with the U.S. where highly skilled labour is concerned, particularly those earning $225,000 to $500,000 annually. Canadian firms in competition for employees at this income level may have difficulty attracting them to Canada without offering higher salary levels to compensate for higher personal tax rates. This was a difficult discussion to have in our government because we were rightly focused on ensuring that low- and middle-income Canadians realized gains from economic growth. Recognizing the importance of higher earners to our economy, I argued, was not inconsistent with our goals. Without doubt, a future government will need to thread this needle.

Of course, balancing our higher tax rate is our health care system, paid for through federal and provincial taxation. Some health coverage premiums in the U.S. are priced well north of a thousand dollars a month for individuals. Paying these high rates in the U.S. offsets to at least some degree our lower wage and salary levels and our higher income tax rates.

Finally, there are other issues to deal with. Some are not difficult, except for the political complications. For example, the provinces of Saskatchewan, Manitoba and BC maintain single stage retail sales taxes, which elevates the total tax paid by residents of those provinces notably higher than elsewhere in Canada.[47] So not all the work needs to be done at the federal level alone. Better coordination of our tax system with the provinces and territories represents one of our biggest opportunities for both simplicity and growth.

—

The memory of Warren Buffett's curiosity about and admiration for Canada stayed with me long after our session together. I was reminded of it when, shortly after returning home, I heard he had made a substantial investment in Canadian National Railway. I'm not suggesting that our depiction of Canada's economic promise influenced him to put down money as a bet on this country's economic future. He is not a man, I suspect, who makes a major decision according to another individual's comments. But I will always wonder . . .

—

Returning to Ottawa, we set the wheels in motion to make taxation changes affecting small businesses. Unfortunately, we bungled the task of communicating the principles and overall benefits of the package. One ground rule of politics dictates that setting policies

---

47 Single stage retail sales taxes, without an integrated system that ensures the tax is applied only once, produce higher retail prices and lower returns on investment. The integrated HST/GST approach eliminates duplication and improves business competitiveness.

to achieve your desired result is only half the job. Communicating the goals and the means to achieve them is equally important. As broadly beneficial as the tax changes were, the story became more complicated than it needed to be.

Response to the proposals was, as predicted, loud and negative from those affected, serving as fodder for the opposition in their criticism of us. Taxpayers impacted by the changes felt we were going after them — and we were, but only in pursuit of a level playing field. Many physicians believed that provincial governments had justified paying them less for their services in view of the tax benefits available to them through federal tax rules — benefits that were now about to vanish, unfairly reducing their income. They were correct in part, but we saw this as a matter between them and the provinces.

Some entrepreneurs and small business owners leaned on the fact that they are risk-takers and deserved some recompense in exchange for the risk they had taken. Launching and building a business that not only supports them and their families but provides employment for other Canadians is both beneficial to the country and risky to the proprietors. Some cushion, they suggested, should be provided in the tax laws to compensate for the gamble they had made.

I agreed with the facts. Choosing to start and run a business involves a gamble compared with seeking employment in a large, well-established corporation. Even after our proposed changes, there were still significant financial advantages to starting and running a small business, particularly the limitations on capital gains treatment that could be used to reduce taxation, especially on the sale of a business. But I also pointed out that hundreds of thousands of immigrants arrive in Canada each year with few assets and often no guarantee of employment. They abandon their homeland with the intention of starting a new, more prosperous and secure life here. That's also a risky decision, for which they neither ask nor receive any special compensation.

At the heart of the negative response was the realization that we were taking something out of the hands of small business owners they believed was rightfully theirs. They were correct — they had reaped tax benefits from doing something entirely lawful, and now they were being told it would no longer be possible. Farmers setting aside money they had earned each year in order to purchase a new tractor or combine harvester to dramatically increase their productivity would potentially be adversely affected. I knew some very high-net-worth people with private businesses who would be equally upset with me because they could no longer set money aside and defer tax on it for an extended length of time. Private corporations and small businesses of all kinds had been playing by the rules in the past and now we were saying the rules no longer applied. This didn't mean they had done anything wrong. It meant that the rules had been badly constructed.

I searched for ways to make the proposed changes palatable while retaining their original objectives. I simplified the income sprinkling provision, dropped revisions meant to curb access to a lifetime capital gains exemption and lowered the small business tax rate. The latter point, I hoped, would not only make the new rules more acceptable; it would enable small business owners to invest money toward improving productivity.

Good intentions in politics are never enough on their own. Almost everyone agreed with the goal of making our taxation policy fair regardless of the income level and source, but few wanted to stand up for the idea. Along with questioning the basis of the concept, some critics aimed their fury at my personal financial situation. They argued in a firestorm of outrage that I had no need of the advantages that small business owners, doctors and others were objecting to losing, so how could I possibly appreciate the impact the new rules would make on them?

The insults didn't stop there. Attention was paid once again to my decision to follow the guidance of the ethics commissioner about not needing to place my assets in a blind trust and my failure to identify the corporation managing our property in France. Little attention was paid to our original goal of making the system fair to everyone. That's the harshness of politics.

My adventure with small business taxation taught me an important lesson: if you adjust a tax rate upwards, you had better find a way to give something back, or your words and rationale will be swamped beneath furious objections.

We had already encountered other hurdles in revamping the tax system in search of fairness. The Canada Child Benefit program had been an important pillar in our 2015 election platform, delivering benefits to working parents everywhere in the country. It would support our intention of bringing more women into the workforce and assist young families to earn and save money by providing them with safe, affordable child care services. The objection at the time was, how did we plan to cover the expense?

We had addressed this in our election platform, which included proposals to raise taxes on the highest-income Canadians as one source of income to cover the CCB cost. I believed that top-level earners could afford it, and it would help us ease the tax burden on middle-income Canadians. I disagreed, however, with the mechanics of the plan, which depended on raising the income tax level on those in the highest tax bracket. I felt it would be better to establish a new top bracket, where the higher taxes owed would apply. The optics would be better: instead of drawing more tax from everyone in the bracket, we would impose the higher taxes only on those at the pinnacle of taxable earnings.

In the U.S., the top tax bracket kicks in at a much higher level than ours; the same was true in several other countries with which we did business. Aligning many of our tax levels in that manner made sense to me and should be a serious consideration for a future government.

The truth, however, is that boosting taxes on the wealthy is not all that effective in terms of absolute dollars gained. Raising taxes on those in the peak income bracket means, by definition, that the number of taxpayers affected will be quite small. If the upper bracket, for example, includes 2 percent of the taxable citizenry, how much will be harvested by setting a higher tax bracket in search of larger contributions from the top 0.5 percent? The math just doesn't work. There is also a psychological barrier of sorts when the taxation level meets or exceeds 50 percent of income in any country, even though levels in the past have been higher than that threshold.

We looked elsewhere for a fair means of funding the CCB, reviewing unfair advantages made available for subsets of taxpayers, such as the ability to pay no tax on capital gains from the sale of a primary residence, with no limits — a nice perk for those who own a home, but one not available to renters. Or our preferential treatment of capital gains rates, in which only 50 percent of capital gains is taxable, reducing the effective rate to half of the regular income tax rate. I didn't favour changing or eliminating either of those rules, which would have been extremely difficult to introduce, in any event.

My main takeaway? Changing tax rules is hard. So is growing the economy, but it produces advantages that everyone can embrace, like increasing the flow of tax dollars into government coffers.

So much for history. If launching a tax review commission with the forlorn hope that it could make and apply its recommendations within a single four-year electoral cycle is out of the question, what other steps might be available?

Here are the moves I would advocate. They would not involve a total revamp of the system to the extent that I believe it needs, but taken together they would make the system more fair and make the country more competitive when it comes to attracting investments:

1. Retain the current top marginal tax rate, but raise the income level that attracts the highest tax rate to make it more consistent with the U.S.
2. Raise the GST/HST to the level it was prior to the reduction made by the Harper government.
3. Simultaneously lower the overall corporate tax rate to more closely align it with the small business tax rate, creating an incentive for more investment.
4. Maintain the exemption on capital gains due on the sale of a principal residence. Removing the exemption for gains above a high threshold makes sense, but it would be very difficult to implement, administratively and politically.
5. Keep a separate capital gains tax rate to accommodate inflation and other concerns. About a 50 percent inclusion makes sense.
6. Assume a policy of incremental changes to the tax system while striving where possible for simplicity and staying prepared to deal with loopholes introduced by creative tax planners.
7. Most important of all, in my opinion, would be to keep tax rates down for low- and middle-income earners. We need to keep recognizing that our capitalist market-based democracy only works if everyone sees benefits from

> growth. Overcoming stagnant or low growth in incomes for hard-working Canadians has to be an important government priority.

Canada faces a number of problems in shaping and administering a tax system that is equitable while generating a sufficient income for the federal government to carry out all of its obligations. We can, I suppose, take comfort in the fact that virtually every other industrialized nation encounters similar challenges for a similar reason: many people take greater pleasure in avoiding taxes than they take satisfaction in paying them.

It's all reminiscent of an amusing quote attributed to American humorist Mark Twain. "Everybody talks about the weather," Twain reportedly said, "but nobody does anything about it."

Replace "weather" with "taxes" for a taste of reality.

Fourteen

Navigating Crises and the PMO

History will likely record the SNC-Lavalin affair as the most explosive incident in Prime Minister Justin Trudeau's first term in office. It may even rank as one of the most notable events in Canadian federal politics, thanks to the openness of the dispute and Jody Wilson-Raybould's high profile as the country's first Indigenous justice minister.

SNC-Lavalin, a large engineering-construction firm headquartered in Montreal, was charged in 2015 with fraud and corruption by the RCMP and Public Prosecution Service of Canada. The raw facts are well known, distilled down to what was seen as Jody's refusal to consider whether a remediation agreement could be a good solution to the charges that SNC faced. This would have been an entirely appropriate remedy for her to agree to or at least consider under the relevant statute. A remediation agreement (similar to a U.S.-style deferred prosecution agreement) is essentially a plea agreement between Crown prosecutors and alleged perpetrators of criminal acts. Such an agreement forces the company to pay a hefty financial penalty and demonstrate it has corrected any previous bad corporate practices that enabled wrongdoing. In exchange, it would be allowed to continue pursuing contracts; and it would avoid the stigma of a formal criminal conviction, which would make it difficult to compete with other companies for international contracts. It would also save the viability of one of Canada's few truly global corporate champions, an outcome that I thought made a lot of sense. Canada had adopted the remediation agreement regime in part because most of our allies had similar remedies, and we had a gap in our criminal law when it came to corporate wrongdoing. Prime Minister Trudeau favoured this approach, as did I, on the basis that it would punish the firm while avoiding the loss of thousands of jobs.[48]

But long before the SNC-Lavalin scandal erupted in February 2019, the challenge on this file came down to relationships. As much as I admired the prime minister for selecting Jody to fill the position of justice minister and attorney general, it soon became obvious that things were not working. Had the PM been proactive in engaging to build a relationship from the start, it could have prevented the entire scandal from happening.

Jody was clearly a champion for certain issues that she cared passionately about, and she had worked on them for much of her life. And she was obviously qualified for the job, or at least as qualified as any of us first-time cabinet ministers could be. But a challenge arose when it became clear that Jody's views were often not aligned with those of the broader team. This created a breakdown, on both sides, in the ability to understand where people were coming from and what they were worried about.

Some of the prime minister's weaknesses as a leader, including his inability to develop significant relationships with his colleagues, aggravated the situation because he did not provide Jody an outlet to raise her concerns directly with him. Having kept her in that job as long as he did, despite many signs of problems in their relationship, the PM was left in an impossible position. If he kept her on, he accepted that a key portfolio was being managed in a

48 Just for the record, I shared that opinion with then–Conservative leader Andrew Scheer (Alex Boutilier, "Andrew Scheer Met with SNC-Lavalin Chief over Criminal Charges," *Toronto Star*, February 10, 2019).

way that was inconsistent with his direction. But any attempt to move her from that role would invariably be seen as a demotion (at least by her) that she would not tolerate. The ingredients for the SNC affair were set, and in my estimation the resulting fireworks had little to do with the file itself.

Most Ottawa watchers were aware of the frayed relationship between the justice minister and the prime minister by the time the SNC-Lavalin matter arose, one not likely to be mended given Jody's fierce independence. When the prime minister demoted her to minister of veterans affairs in the January 2019 cabinet shuffle, it was like dropping a lighted match into a tinderbox, and she and Jane Philpott resigned. They were followed by Gerry Butts who, without identifying himself as a primary role-player in the drama, basically fell on his sword. With him went the key role he had played as intervener, managing to guide projects among political machinery and personalities.

With Gerry's limitless energy gone, we were left with the persona of Justin Trudeau and the political savvy of Katie Telford. The failure to recruit someone with Gerry's vision and abilities to fill his role critically weakened the team. If you're going to centralize all decision-making in the Prime Minister's Office, you should at least focus on having a complete team of advisors. More importantly, from my perspective, it left me without a key interlocutor in the PMO. Given the PM's inability or unwillingness to cultivate direct relationships, it became harder to get things done. Clearly this was not a reassuring indicator of what would come in a second Trudeau term.

Following the October 2019 election, I expected 2020 to be a year focused on our commitments to deal with climate change. The election had been, in my opinion, largely devoid of substance with the campaign focused on introducing small items intended to reinforce our successful first mandate initiatives. We talked about raising the carbon price, increasing the Canada Child Benefit and making commitments on housing, immigration and Indigenous reconciliation. All worthy, but there was a dearth of new ideas. We were fighting a Conservative team led by Andrew Scheer, an uninspiring leader who had no coherent message on the core issue of climate change. The lacklustre campaign became more interesting (not in a good way) when Canadians discovered, at the same time I did, that our prime minister had dressed up in blackface on several occasions.

When I returned to work as finance minister, I hoped to focus on energy transition as my central issue. I was prepared to help manage the reduction of our carbon footprint while balancing the economic imperative of jump-starting a slow-growth economy. It wouldn't be easy, but I was looking forward to the challenge, confident that I had passed the steepest part of my learning curve in the role and ready to find a pragmatic middle path on this challenging file. Making climate commitments would be the easy part of the job. Delivering on plans and promises was always going to be the hard part.

The scale of our resources sector, and the reality of thousands upon thousands of Canadian families who relied on it for their livelihood, meant we were going to have to push on multiple fronts at the same time. We needed to address carbon pricing, renewable development, decarbonizing our industry and resource sector, and finding a way to increase the anemic level of corporate investment in our country. It was a major challenge, but it also served as an inspiration to me. I was anxious to get started.

But crisis intervened, and we were soon launching the biggest economic assistance package in our history, reaching every stratum of society in every region of the country, to provide the help needed to survive COVID-19. The size of the aid, in absolute dollars, dwarfed anything else the government had done since Canada's involvement in the Second World War.

Looking back at our economic response to the COVID crisis, I believe we got the big things right despite some serious errors. We served Canadians well in an extraordinary moment in our history, and I'm proud of that.

—

There were two phases to the early COVID economic response. The first phase was difficult but important and largely successful. The second was equally difficult but much less successful, and ultimately signalled the end of my time in government, shattering my ability to work with the prime minister and the PMO. By that point in the pandemic, after the initial policy responses were put in place, the PM permitted himself to be led by people who treated key decisions on real policy as though they were mere talking points in political debate, free of any monetary costs. With time, too many decisions on serious policy problems were no longer based on or even associated with the hard work of analysis and economic insights. It became all about sound bites, not sound policy.

Gerry Butts's departure in February 2019 had left a gap in our ability to conceive, plan and execute new ideas in response to the needs and interests of Canadians. When no serious effort was made to replace him with someone possessing similar skills and insights, many of the PMO's activities became managed by Trudeau's communications team, with policy taking a secondary and clearly neglected role. This might have been barely acceptable in a period when our goal was to formulate and implement policy, but it was clearly inadequate when we were faced with a crisis as all-encompassing as a global pandemic.

Once the scope and impact of the pandemic registered, we

quickly agreed to focus on helping Canadians survive the massive financial impact that lockdowns, isolation and other necessary steps were certain to have. We needed to put substantial sums of cash into the hands of individuals and businesses, and keep providing them for an unknown but likely significant length of time. Only the federal government had the financial resources and systems to marshal both the money and the means of distributing it. Our first action was to create the Canada Emergency Response Benefit (CERB) to satisfy the income needs of Canadians during at least the outset of the pandemic. Funds would be delivered through the Canada Revenue Agency (CRA), a decision that proved critical to the success of our entire COVID economic response. There was simply no other way for us to get money to people quickly, because our systems were not set up to deal with a sudden shutdown of our economy. The benefit would tide people over, shoring up markets and incomes to avoid a downward economic spiral.

Providing enormous amounts of money on the basis of perceived need alone was a disturbing idea to some. Many saw it as something akin to what economist Milton Friedman called "helicopter money" — cash distributed widely to people with little or no conditions as though it was thrown out of a helicopter in the sky. Whatever the label, it meant tens of billions of dollars would be dispensed by the federal government. We accepted the very real possibilities of fraud (although using the CRA system had the benefit of somewhat mitigating this problem), and the risk that thousands of people could get access to funds with little oversight to determine the criteria for needing it.

Other groups voiced other concerns. While the urgency was obvious, voices and eyebrows began being raised, questioning the wisdom of plunging the country deeply into debt — not a pleasant prospect for fiscal conservatives, or for anyone who worried about our capacity to sustain a high standard of living and still provide broad social support. The opposition was particularly unhelpful, spending more time criticizing measures when we urgently needed to come together and agree on solutions.

As we saw earlier, there are three ways to evaluate debt: its size, in dollars; the benefits of using it; and the ability to service the debt over an extended period. Obviously, we were in a position where the benefits of using debt to support Canadians who suddenly had no capacity to pay for groceries and rent vastly outweighed the downside of increasing our debt load. With that settled, we still needed to maintain the ability to service the debt and grow our economy. Canada was in a strong fiscal position to provide assistance. Our balance sheet assured us that we could handle the debt resulting from the emergency payments, and my department and I began assessing the amount to be paid to individuals and corporations.

It's worth noting here that over the years since my arrival in Ottawa I had heard warnings from various quarters that our debt was too large. In case of a dire emergency, I was told, Canada would lack the capacity to take whatever measures were necessary to deal with the crisis. Yet here we were, facing a calamity of unprecedented scope and able to manage it well thanks to the financial footing provided by our strong debt-to-GDP ratio. The lessons gained from Jean Chretien's and Paul Martin's aggressive deficit fights enabled us to take difficult decisions in addressing the crisis.

We had a good start — a big idea that dealt with the need. The breakdown began when the details needed addressing. How much money should be dispensed? My team and I started on the calculations, determining how much aid should be given and to whom. We based our work on the need to support the huge cohort of people who were off work due to the COVID restrictions, and literally unable to earn any income. The figure needed to be substantial enough to satisfy the bulk of their income needs without serving as a disincentive for those who were able to work but might be tempted to claim CERB funds instead.

After looking at all the options and variables, we submitted a range of weekly incomes justified by our carefully considered calculations, only to be overruled by the prime minister and PMO, who rejected our recommendations in favour of distributing $2,000 per month or $500 a week because the numbers "sounded good."

Supporting people off work was critical, but we recognized that the amount decided on by the PMO was over the top. For many part-time workers or those in low-income jobs, this amount would exceed their regular take-home pay. I wanted to be generous, but the PMO's figures, chosen with no regard for our detailed calculations and justifications, meant we would be distributing billions of dollars more than was actually needed under the circumstances. We were under pressure, it's true, and mistakes can be made in that kind of situation, but a billion-dollar mistake was something I didn't want to make.

Nevertheless, the PMO had its way, and when we began developing a similar program for business the pattern was repeated. We had already started to design the Canada Emergency Business Account (CEBA) and I had been working with the banking sector to ensure that funds would be available at terms guaranteed by the government. Before long, demands arrived from the PM and PMO to deliver an immediate answer on direct support to businesses in response to cries for support from business leaders. We added the Canada Emergency Wage Subsidy (CEWS) to supply 75 percent wage support for businesses to help keep their staff employed and connected to the organization if revenues were suspended due to the pandemic, and for the biggest corporations we introduced the Large Employer Emergency Financing Facility.

The problem was delivering the funds according to the prime minister's and the PMO's expectations. The introduction of CEWS, we realized, would be made before we figured out how to put the money in the hands of the businesses. The CRA system became our fallback option for the business support programs as well, but we had yet to determine for each how much money would be provided and to whom and for how long. Once again, my team worked through the night to make our calculations and shape our recommendations on how much money businesses would actually get. I managed to deliver our report to the prime minister at 10 p.m. one evening early in the pandemic. At a press gathering the next morning, about 12 hours after he had agreed with all aspects of the program I had presented, I watched and listened as he introduced the program to Canada. With great pride, he announced the amount of money made available to individual businesses via CEWS . . . a figure significantly higher than we had agreed was the highest we should go the previous evening!

It was one of the worst moments of my political life.

—

This became our daily routine: address a problem, consider how to support Canadians in a time of unprecedented need, come up with a range of appropriate solutions, debate the best alternative with our team and the PMO, reach the conclusion that made the most sense under the conditions, submit it to the prime minister and the PMO . . . and then discover that the decision announced by them to the public was framed according to the impact the PMO believed it would make on the daily news cycle.

The prime minister launched a series of morning news briefings, which was good political strategy in the context of the pandemic — if the content of his announcements had been measured and meaningful. The team around him began demanding a constant flow of information from us that the PM could show as evidence of the action he was taking on behalf of the nation. In some cases, they wanted solutions to problems that didn't exist.

As an example, I was petitioned to develop an income support package for seniors. No one could deny that our seniors were hit hard by COVID, harder in fact than any other sector of our population. The health risk was much higher for them, confirmed by a soaring death rate, and the need for them to stay home was doubly important. The sacrifice was real, and it was impacting seniors everywhere. But we were talking about seniors' *incomes*, not the essential health care they needed and would be receiving. Almost by definition, seniors were not likely to be in the workforce; their income was more likely to come from private pensions, CPP, withdrawals from Tax-Free Savings Accounts, Registered Retirement Income Funds and other investments, and payments from Old Age Security (OAS) and the Guaranteed Income Supplement (GIS). None of these payments would be financially impacted to a meaningful degree by the pandemic. The money would continue to flow into seniors' accounts undisturbed, whereas millions of working Canadians faced a total loss of income over the coming months.

To the prime minister and the PMO, seniors were an important and highly visible constituency who, to be blunt, also represented a large block of engaged and informed voters. Announcing a benefit to them would have a major psychological impact on Canadians and could serve as one more positive announcement in the PM's morning briefings. I made the point about seniors not being at the same risk of economic deprivation as working Canadians in this situation. I wasn't playing Scrooge. I was emphasizing the wisdom of putting funds where they are needed most and that, unlike working Canadians, seniors had a steady source of income and no expectation of it being lost. My point was ignored. Once again, policy rationales were tossed aside in favour of scoring political points.

We lost the agenda. During the period when the largest government expenditures as a portion of GDP were made in the shortest time since the advent of World War II, calculations and recommendations from the ministry of finance were basically disregarded in favour of winning a popularity contest. We were relegated to a secondary status as merely an analysis team, trying to devise support measures to match the demand and to taper the established programs as the disease ebbed and flowed, but the communications agenda remained more important throughout the pandemic.

Experience is what you get when you were expecting something else. The team at finance was expecting to function as part of a group dedicated to dealing with the crisis in a responsible manner. Instead, our experience was as spectators to a drama where "enough" lost out to "more," based not on need but on political expediency.

—

I shared alarm for the health of seniors as much as anyone in cabinet, but I was also concerned about the pandemic's impact on students. The anticipated widespread unemployment was certain to hit them as hard as any group, and I began raising questions about the dilemma they would be facing. How could we assist others and assume that university and college students would somehow get by on their own? Students depended a good deal for their part-time and summer earnings on industries that were likely facing closure — restaurants, bars, entertainment facilities, recreation and leisure activity and so on. It would be a cruel blow to students if COVID meant that they could not afford to continue their studies.

Should we simply hand over cash to students, as we were about to do for others with the Canada Emergency Response Benefit? I wasn't comfortable with a student version of that program, preferring a plan that would involve employment or service of some kind. Why, I wondered, couldn't we develop a program where students would contribute to the country through volunteer work or help us somehow in our COVID response? Participating students could apply many of their own skills and interests to something worthwhile and personally satisfying, while earning an income from the government benefit and acquiring valuable experience and contacts.

Nothing existed within the federal structure to manage and direct these activities, and we were already committed to solving too many other demands stemming from the pandemic to build such a program from scratch. Was there an entity somewhere that could link with student groups, assess and employ volunteer projects and handle the disbursement of funds to those who qualified?

That's when the public service team working on this issue proposed selecting WE Charity to administer a Canada Student Service Grant (CSSG) program for qualified participants. The prime minister agreed, and a contract was finalized in June 2020. The quick decision, driven by the constant communications cycle, revealed a serious lack of political due diligence. Crisis or not, we were dumping a substantial amount of money into the hands of an outside organization without the usual oversight from within the halls of government. WE was awarded the contract to oversee the distribution of $900 million under the CSSG, a decision made without a full probe of any baggage that may have accompanied — or *appeared* to have accompanied — two people associated with the decision, and one of them was me.

In the middle of constant 16-hour days and unending crises some things were overlooked, including the fact that I had previously personally donated funds to WE and gone on a trip in which some of the expenses were, unbeknownst to me, covered by the charity (which I paid back immediately once I was made aware of them) — facts that the ethics commissioner acknowledged while waving away any hint of a quid pro quo. Unequivocally, I should have recused myself from a decision to move forward with the plan on that basis.

The prime minister's problem seemed larger than mine. He, his wife, mother and brother had all publicly participated in WE events, using the stage to promote themselves, either personally or politically, and in the case of his mother and brother, receiving significant-sized honorariums for their appearances, creating a question of bias and favouritism.

Much of the criticism from the opposition and observers landed on my head. Like it or not, their perception was that I had either made or approved the decision to select WE, influenced by my previous involvement with them. No serious person truly believed that I was financially influenced by these connections — it was all about politics. Still, accusations and revelations echoed through much of the summer, leading to the inevitable cancellation of the contract and the entire program and, in early September, the announcement that WE Charity was winding down its operations in Canada. I felt a sense of sadness that an organization that had done so much to engage young people in community involvement found itself in the crosshairs of partisan politics during a pandemic.

Perception, we are often told, is reality in politics. Reality arrived in a detailed report issued by Ethics Commissioner Mario Dion in May 2021, a report that confirmed I had no opportunity to further my own interests, but that a *potential* conflict of interest meant I should have recused myself from the decision on WE. You may have missed the story.[49] Most people did.

—

Other events came along to trip us up. A dramatic drop in oil prices brought the danger home in that sector, making its biggest impact on the western provinces. Suddenly, in the midst of everything else we were dealing with during the pandemic, we faced a

49 Ryan Tumilty, "Ethics Commissioner Clears Justin Trudeau in WE Charity Scandal," *National Post*, May 13, 2021.

new conundrum: How could we offer special support — or any support — for oil companies while opposing continued payment of fossil fuel subsidies? Our solution was to make all industries eligible for the wage support programs, and to support the Alberta and Saskatchewan petroleum industry with funds to be spent on cleaning up abandoned wells.

We faced frustrations galore. Some developed from the simple challenge of helping small- and medium-sized businesses make their rent payments. Our CEWS and CEBA programs helped the companies retain their staff and purchase goods and supplies, but one of the largest expenses they faced was paying their monthly rent, which ran us headlong into questions of jurisdiction. Rent is a provincial concern, so the federal government was prevented from taking action against landlords who treated business tenants unfairly during the crisis. Rent is also a link in the financial food chain. Tenants pay rent to landlords, who in turn use a portion of it to cover mortgage payments with banks and other lenders.

We decided the best way to deal with this part of the crisis was shared responsibility by all involved. We established a program to cover 50 percent of a business's rent if the landlord forgave 25 percent of the total. This would put 75 percent of the rent into the landlord's pocket, the majority of it provided by Ottawa. It was intended as a program to lessen the pain among all three participants — tenants, landlords and the government. Things grew complex when too many landlords reacted negatively to the idea that they should make a sacrifice for the common good. In the end we modified the program, dispensing with the idea of landlord support.

Large corporations presented other challenges. We expected small businesses to use the funds provided to pay their employees, which would keep money circulating because the employees would spend it on food, rent and other essentials. The situation could change with funds provided to large corporations. They could easily move it around internally rather than injecting it into the economy. Instead of covering employee salaries and operating expenses, the money could theoretically be directed to pay executive bonuses and shareholder dividends. Neither of these matched our goal to keep the economy spinning, yet some large businesses were under pressure with a legitimate claim for assistance. How could we offer assistance to one firm and refuse aid for another? In the end, we realized that the only response was to have economy-wide programs; an expensive decision, but the only way to protect employees and companies in the face of an unprecedented crisis.

The conflict and disappointment that arose from the prime minister's and PMO's actions aside, when I look back at the first six months of the crisis I am surprised by how many positive steps were taken. That record is even more impressive when taking into account the fact that most decisions were made on the fly. None of us had experience in tackling anything like the pandemic and the multiple threats it represented to our economic and physical health, and decisions had to be made quickly. While the process confirmed our capacity to respond to crisis conditions, it also revealed serious flaws resulting from the conflict between doing what was best for the country and what was best for our Party's political future.

My job of providing counsel and direction where fiscal matters were concerned had deteriorated into serving as something between a figurehead and a rubber stamp. That's not why I wanted the position of finance minister, and it's not why it was created in the first place. There was neither productive tension nor appropriate consultation between the finance department and the prime minister and PMO at this critical time. There was only revision of my recommendations, ever upward, toward funding levels that the PMO believed would play well the next time Canada went to the polls.

Every country in the world was forced to grapple with these same issues, but of course the most important focus was on the main impact of the pandemic, dominated by the tragic deaths of millions. The shocks of these losses and their emotional impact are certain to resonate in various ways over many years. While the final assessment remains to be measured, I believe the majority of Canadians dealt with the challenges, the setbacks and the limitations on their social lives with acceptance and determination.

Earlier I mentioned my concern about the massive size of the benefits we provided to assist Canadians through their financial difficulties, and the speed with which we responded. Our hasty reaction was necessary to avoid the risk of an unprecedented economic collapse, and it did its job. As for those Canadians who received funds they didn't need, within weeks of launching the CERB program, 190,000 Canadians chose to make voluntary repayments of money they were not entitled to receive. I find that reassuring.

The most disturbing note arising from the COVID experience was evidence of weakness in our federation. We were dealing with an economic downturn triggered by an international health crisis. The federal government had the capacity and the responsibility to assist Canadians facing pressures they could not have handled on their own. Those pressures extended beyond the sphere of financial means. They included justifiable concerns over health care and the importance of both preventing and treating the spread of the virus.

Health care is a provincial responsibility, and during the crisis a dichotomy arose between the federal government assuming leadership and the provinces responding negatively to Ottawa's perceived encroachment on their turf, leading to unnecessary delays and frequent frustration. It wasn't easy persuading the provinces to do more testing for COVID, launch contact-tracing programs, provide funds for long-term care homes and establish links with municipalities to identify areas where assistance was needed. Much time was lost and many resources were wasted as a result.

I understand the reluctance of provincial premiers to discharge any of their constitutional rights, even if the move was a temporary means of dealing with a critical problem. These disagreements can be, and usually were, solved through dialogue and negotiation. I was not as sympathetic, however, to cries of poverty made by some provincial leaders. Of the hundreds of billions of dollars distributed by the federal government to assist individuals and businesses during the early months of the crisis, much of it flowed into provincial coffers and helped the provinces manage their primary areas of responsibility, including health care and education.

The lessons learned from COVID-19 will likely launch a small library of books. For me, the most important takeaway is the need for senior levels of government to set aside trivial concerns and turf wars in times of major threats. No one had a clear and unequivocal response to the potential disaster we faced in 2020. There was no off-the-shelf solution. In the face of that reality, we needed to adopt an inclination to accept, understand and respond to the situation. It could be solved with federal and provincial entities providing assistance in a spirit of cooperation, minimizing concern over matters of jurisdiction that can be dealt with post-crisis, when calmer heads prevail.

Is that naive to propose? Not if a healthy working relationship has been cultivated and maintained on both sides. But that work has to be done in advance.

We don't need to talk past or at each other to achieve this kind of cooperation.

We just need to start listening. Carefully.

Fifteen

Heading for the Exit

Our efforts to deal with the pandemic had played out in an atmosphere that was something less than inspiring and reassuring. In fact, had I followed some of my instincts in the months leading up to the 2019 election, I might not have been in the government to assist in dealing with the COVID crisis.

Gerry Butts's resignation in February of that year left me doubting our ability not only to win re-election but to govern with an acceptable level of competence. This is not to suggest that Gerry was irreplaceable. No one should assume they are, in government or anywhere else. I knew, however, that without him, or someone with his skill set, we would be missing two vital elements critical to our success.

One was likely unavoidable. We had been swept into office at least partially due to contagious enthusiasm over an appealing young leader who brought new ideas that reflected the needs and concerns of Canadians. Justin Trudeau's upbeat personality, contrasted with the staid Stephen Harper, was one measure of the appeal. However, it alone would not have been successful without a platform of programs that spoke to the country about climate change, Indigenous rights, immigration, social assistance and other concerns. It was a package of sunshine versus shadow, fresh ideas versus stale beliefs, and the promise of responsive government.

Prime Minister Trudeau provided the sunshine and spirit, and his team was supposed to add substance and structure. By 2019 much of the sunshine had faded, and his team was depleted.

We had succeeded at getting the big things right — the introduction of the Canada Child Benefit, the enhancement of the Canada Pension Plan, the introduction of a carbon price nationally, the continued increase in our immigration levels, the renegotiation of the NAFTA deal and the initial economic response to the COVID crisis. Yet I grew more frustrated about failing to prudently manage our bottom line. I suspected that my concerns were increasingly being felt by a broader cross-section of Canadians.

It's a Canadian political axiom that governments scoring a majority in one election should be prepared for reduced success in the next one. I'll leave it to political scientists and pundits to explain the phenomenon, but history tends to confirm this is the case. Lacking the same level of momentum in 2019 from the two elements that had brought us to Ottawa in the first place, we could hardly expect to avoid a similar experience, and evidence of this appeared early in our second term.

—

One of our most satisfying achievements in the first term had been the successful creation and implementation of our Canada Child Benefit plan, which I referred to earlier. The CCB had stood as a cornerstone of our 2015 election campaign. It enabled us to raise an enormous number of children out of poverty and was among the first of our campaign promises to be fulfilled.

Our plan had been to offset the cost of the program with an increase in marginal tax rates applied on the top 1 percent of taxpayers, measured by taxable income. We would supplement this with the elimination of universal child benefits and tax credits for sport and fitness programs introduced by the Harper government.

When we arrived in office to find that the math on this balanced promise didn't work, I was assigned to find an alternative solution.

This process was reassuring, but things soon changed and the disciplined practice of having a defined policy goal and a specific fiscal envelope wasn't maintained through our term where the budget process was concerned. Our success on achieving key policy objectives was blemished by a lack of proper design and management of the process. The unwillingness of the prime minister and the PMO to agree on the setting of financial targets at the beginning of the budget process meant we were not forced to make difficult choices between competing policy priorities. It's easy — or at least easier — to deliver on policy commitments if there are no fiscal guardrails. Budgeting is a foundational element of government, but it only really works with targets and constraints, just like any budget.

As time passed, I realized we were unlikely to achieve the fiscal targets I might have liked because many decisions were being made outside of my control. I remained committed to our policy objectives, but I could not persuade the PM and the PMO that fiscal discipline meant we had only limited capacity to move forward on our goals. I knew that were being forced to reduce our expectations in some areas or even abandon important objectives. Facing up to and dealing with the choices imposed by our financial situation was essential; failing to do so would produce worse outcomes down the road. I wanted to invest in the next generation, not leave them with a challenging hole to dig their way out of.

The failure to set and abide by targets for the 2017, 2018 and 2019 budgets proved challenging for me to accept. I had managed to retain control over the process, but without budgeting targets it was difficult to achieve a proper outcome. Responding to proposals from various ministries in preparation for each budget, I would agree to those that were appropriate from a fiscal standpoint and propose alternatives to those that weren't, all while attempting to manage the overall picture with the PMO. This often resulted in a three-way tug of war, with a ministry making its case with me for budget-based funding, me dealing with the PMO on the ministry's rationale and the ministries selling their positions to the PMO through whatever back door they could find. As long as I was in the centre of this triad, I was able to maintain some control.

Things had limped along in this manner through the first term, becoming progressively more challenging with each budget, but with an election looming on the horizon the game changed.

Obviously, we couldn't campaign for re-election in 2019 on the 2015 platform. We would build part of our case on the things we had achieved over the previous four years, but that was only part of our story. We had to adapt. With the driving force behind our 2015 campaign missing, the prime minister and the PMO were left to craft our appeal to voters. Lacking the guidance of Gerry Butts's political instincts, they appointed political advisors to prepare the 2019 election platform.

With four years of budgeting experience under my belt as the sitting finance minister, I assumed I would have at least some control over shaping the platform from a fiscal standpoint. It soon became clear that this would not be the case. Two PMO staffers arrived in my office and informed me, politely but firmly, of the items to be placed in the election platform.

I got the message. Canada would essentially be guided through the next four years by the apparent wisdom and reflection of policy staffers who would shape the elected government's direction and goals without much in the way of consultation. The experience and wisdom gathered by cabinet ministers, most of whom would be seeking re-election based on the platform, were to be dismissed.

Scanning the list of items that I was advised were to be included in the platform, I recognized several that had been proposed over the previous four years, and which I had persuaded the PM and PMO to remove from the agenda. I argued against them once again. They were still inappropriate from a fiscal viewpoint, in my opinion, scattered as they were among some new and equally impractical ideas.

One of them endorsed raising the amount of basic personal income tax deductions, an idea proposed often in the past. Each time it had been submitted I responded that it represented both an expensive measure and an inappropriate use of funds, available to everyone across the income spectrum in a way that would almost surely be missed, or misunderstood, by most. Some people would benefit from the move while others would feel no effect, and since virtually no one understood the tax form well enough to notice the change, there wouldn't even be a political advantage. And clearly, the measure would not be the best approach to identify and target those in most need of additional support. For three years in a row this proposal had been submitted, assessed and removed from the agenda with broadly based agreement, including from the PM. Now it was back, and it was clear that despite the evidence of its unsuitability and the consensus that had been reached over the previous three years to set it aside, it was going to be incorporated based on the singular perspective of one of the staffers on the campaign platform team. Hardly a way to run a country.

Based on policies like this, I was anticipating a second term of even less control of the fiscal agenda. From my perspective the ideas being proposed were hugely expensive and not likely to gain much political advantage. It was certain to challenge our ability to get to a reasonable bottom line, since I knew there would be many more demands for funding on the horizon.

I was also informed that imposition of a luxury tax should be inserted in the platform budget, slapped on expensive cars, boats and aircraft. We could agree there had been an increase in wealth among the top 1 percent of Canadians, but this new tax would serve only as a populist wedge, an issue that might play well in some media quarters but was unlikely to generate any measurable benefit among Canadians, whatever tax bracket they were in. I agreed with the issue of addressing the country's changing wealth dynamic, but I never liked the idea of creating an us-against-them situation, which this proposal would do.

There were other proposals as well, all previously considered and rejected by cabinet members after deliberation. Now here they were again, submitted to me with the assumption that I, a candidate seeking re-election, would quietly approve them.

I made my case opposing the ideas — again — and left the meeting severely disillusioned. Not only had I lost control of the process, but the prime minister was effectively saying that the duty of shaping our campaign platform had been taken out of the hands of elected representatives and given to advisors assigned to compel agreement from cabinet members whatever their point of view, for or against.

Keep in mind that this was prior to the 2019 election. In the midst of preparing our platform, I began asking myself if I really wanted to stand for re-election. I was already dealing with the lack of privacy and personal freedom in my role, something that other elected representatives were grappling with as well.

One evening I told Nancy about my reluctance to run again. I was not searching for total autonomy in my job, I explained. I would never promote that idea for any elected representative. I believe very strongly in building and maintaining relationships with others who bring experience and involvement to a defined role they were assigned to fulfill. This did not appear to be the case prior to the election, and I feared things were unlikely to change in the post-election period.

But I liked the job otherwise. I liked the notion of expressing and implementing my vision of Canada, what it was and what it could become, in partnership with others whose values were similar to mine. I believed that I could continue to make an impact within government. I saw my service in Parliament as perhaps the most important thing I would ever do in my life. And I was aware that if I, as the finance minister, chose not to seek re-election it would be a major blow to the Liberal Party and to many of its values that I continued to share.

Nancy and I even talked about the possibility of my running for the leadership role at the OECD, which would enable me to continue focusing on key public policy issues. But on balance, I decided to run for re-election. My campaign proved successful, but the Party lost 20 seats; despite failing to win more votes nationally than the second-place Conservatives, we managed to achieve minority government status. This was when the prime minister and the PMO went silent for weeks about cabinet appointments, leaving those of us returning to Ottawa who had been ministers wondering if, having secured our seats, we would once again be serving in cabinet in the same or a different capacity.

I had considered myself a key member of the team for four years and now I, and many others, were left in limbo. Whatever the cause of this extended period of non-discussion, I considered it a huge dereliction of the managerial process. Had the prime minister yet to determine the assignment of ministers for the new term? I could accept that premise, but it would still require some form of communication through that period.

As disappointed as I might have been over this lack of communication, I was not entirely surprised. It had not been the prime minister's practice to meet regularly with cabinet ministers in the past or have any ongoing engagement with us. Fine — that was his prerogative. But with several dozen experienced individuals anxious to get down to work but unsure if they still held their areas of responsibility, we faced the reality that the PM's governing team was not the cabinet, as it should be, but the PMO. We saw none of the transparency expected from a manager dealing with the closest members of a team. In private business his actions would be like a CEO having guided his top executives through a critical restructuring or economic crisis and choosing not to discuss its impact and effect on the company and the team running it. That would be disturbing in a business setting. In an elected government, it was intolerable.

Whatever the cause and however it can be assessed, the effect of this non-communication was to lose the engagement with, and dissolve the enthusiasm of, key team members. Eventually, the decision in my case was finalized, delivered in a meeting between the prime minister, Katie Telford and me. I would remain as finance minister.

—

The frustrations motivated me to assert more autonomy and to assume more authority over my department as a means of filling the void in managerial competence. I began by choosing Elder Marques as my chief of staff. An experienced lawyer, Elder was highly competent and had served in the same capacity for Minister of Innovation, Science and Economic Development Navdeep Bains before moving into the PMO. Elder's familiarity with the PMO would enable me to manage my portfolio, using his insight and ability to see around corners when needed, to judge and anticipate the PMO's actions in situations that might arise. I saw it as one means to ensure that I would play an active role in insisting that our actual policy conclusions, notwithstanding our campaign platform, would be drafted with attention paid to fiscal concerns.

Elder and I were aligned in our outlook, and we agreed that a pragmatic, centrist approach to managing Canada's financial controls was in keeping with a long and storied Liberal history. I still had to deal, however, with the reality of a PMO that had created a campaign platform far to the left of my instincts and largely bereft of prudent fiscal targets. With that in mind I concluded that I also needed to draft some of the key platform architects into my team so we could debate the merits of the policies. This would also enable me to add a fiscal dimension to the discussion, not unlike our successful efforts on the Canada Child Benefit with Jean-Yves Duclos. To ensure that the final policy conclusions reflected financial consideration, it would be wise to have the PMO policy advisors working in my office as opposed to being in the PMO arguing against my points.

By now it was early 2020, and the COVID-19 pandemic crisis was upon us. We needed a policy with substance to address a uniquely threatening situation very unlike the re-election challenge we had faced a few months earlier. The first instincts of the PMO were to focus not on hard assessment and sound decision-making as much as on image and communications, which I considered evidence of the dearth of management skill sets among the group at the top. As I've already pointed out, in almost every case my recommendations for the levels of benefits to be assigned to specific groups were disregarded in favour of whatever would look best in the media releases.

I began asking myself if my presence in the cabinet was making a difference.

—

When stories describing the prime minister's dissatisfaction with my performance began leaking from the PMO, I seriously assessed my position, counting all the problems I faced and the few means at my disposal to solve them.

One was my disappointment at the lack of management skills demonstrated by the prime minister. It's no surprise that the lack of attention paid to fiscal matters loomed as the most acute concern from my point of view, but there was more to it than that.

Good leaders in politics, business and sports are never aloof or uncommunicative. They grasp the significance of relationships, the value of transparency in their methods and the worth of keeping their word. These are elements of trust, and there is no more treasured quality in a leader than the measure of trust he or she builds among their staff and supporters. If the entire operation was being run by the PM and the PMO with decisions based almost entirely on their political considerations and communication concerns, what was the point?

I saw no path forward as finance minister.

Sixteen

In Pursuit of Productivity

My five years in national politics led me to conclude that Canada works not despite our federal-provincial relationship but *because* of it.

Given the apparent unbroken list of federal-provincial disputes that appear to dominate so much of our national media coverage, this may appear like a wishful dream, but it's true. Our future success depends on getting this relationship right, or at least making it the best it can be. And our leadership, at all levels, needs to make this an absolute priority, especially when it comes to the crucial necessity of elevating our productivity from its current bottom-of-the-barrel position.

You read it right: Canada occupies the very bottom of the list when it comes to measuring our productivity growth against all the other nations in the OECD — which, of course, represent the competition when we're trying to sell products to the world.

And as much as or more than the other nations, we rely on trade for our economic health. So what should we do about the situation?

—

Canadians take pride in belonging to a nation governed by a highly decentralized government structure in which each of 13 regions holds substantial power. Our decentralization is also financial:

Canada has by far the highest sub-national (that is, provincial and territorial) tax revenue as a proportion of total government revenue among all OECD countries. The provinces and territories generate slightly more than half of all government tax revenue and account for two-thirds of total government spending. About 20 percent of sub-national income is accounted for by federal government transfers.

In most countries on the globe, this blend of decentralized political and financial power would be considered a drawback. In Canada, I see it as a strength. Placing a good deal of power and responsibility in the hands of the provinces yields dividends because the provinces are best positioned to provide services that meet the specific needs of their population. They can also choose to function like laboratories for new ideas that can, in turn, be adopted nationally. Saskatchewan's pioneering health care plan and Quebec's child care programs are two prime examples of provinces exploring and implementing concepts that led or are leading the way toward national implementation.

Our structure also encourages compromise, the country's greatest asset. Canadians work at finding compromise because, frankly, we can't get things done without it. Our understanding of that fact, and our ability to use it wisely in most governing situations, contributes to our Canadian exceptionalism.

—

Compromising to achieve goals may be a Canadian tradition, but it demands a framework in order to reach decisions and get things done. My experience in government revealed that not enough focus is placed on establishing an accepted framework to deal with situations that are complex, involve multiple jurisdictions and are vital to the country's economic performance. The primary reason? A lack of leadership attention to managing our most important set of relationships — with each other.

During my time in office many flashpoints of challenge arose between the federal and provincial governments. The most significant was the conflict between British Columbia and Alberta on the expansion of the Trans Mountain Pipeline, and the federal government's decision to purchase the asset in order to resolve the conflict and maintain our ability to move our resources to international markets.

Just about every hot button you can name was part of this file. We had Indigenous groups both supporting and opposing the project, environmental advocates demanding it not go forward, energy sector leaders explaining the necessity of transporting our resources to market, premiers from two provinces exerting their authority over what each saw as their responsibility to their constituents and the federal government maintaining its constitutional right to be in charge of interprovincial trade. With all of that, we lacked a process for bringing the many constituents together to resolve their different perspectives. No federal-provincial discussions took place until the crisis grew hot. Would a more systematic approach to federal-provincial meetings have led to a different outcome? Maybe not, but the absence of upfront discussions created a potential for conflict that likely could have been foreseen. Instead, we left it all to a private sector company to resolve the disputes between implacable foes.

Eventually, we were left with no choice. Canada purchased the pipeline from its U.S.-based owner-operator for Cdn$4.5 billion in 2018. It was a decision I didn't want to take — owning a pipeline was not part of our plan — but that was necessary to complete the project and show international investors that Canada is a place where things get done.

That haphazard and episodic approach to our federal-provincial relationship is a fundamental problem. It fails to start with the recognition that we have essentially a partnership, one sometimes fraught with different perspectives and objectives. Journalists often speak about prime ministers choosing to avoid provincial meetings because the premiers inevitably demand either more funds or restricted federal jurisdiction, and occasionally both. Staying away from the meetings has never solved the problem, and never will. Its only effect is to delay the inevitable while building momentum for bad feelings that make agreement that much more challenging.

A better way exists. My experience with the expansion of the Canada Pension Plan can serve as an example of how the federal-provincial relationship can work effectively. The CPP process worked because rules and an enforced mechanism existed to guide the decision-making procedure. Seven out of ten provinces, representing two-thirds of the population, are needed to approve any change in the Canada Pension Plan. That's not necessarily the ideal mechanism for every decision (for starters, the territories have no say), but it forces both the federal government and the provinces to work together in a structured manner. I take some personal pride in the 2016 enhancement to the Canada Pension Plan because it was the product of good-faith negotiation that found and applied creative solutions to provincial and federal concerns. And because we had an effective framework to guide our decisions.

We lacked a similar framework to guide the way forward for projects like Trans Mountain or to deal with other conflicts. This has proven burdensome when managing long-term issues like health care spending or interprovincial trade. In place of a framework, we depend on informal procedures. First ministers' meetings can be called by the prime minister when necessary, and federal-provincial-territorial (FPT) meetings occur once or twice a year. They have proven valuable at laying the grounds for agreement on projects like enhancing the CPP and dealing with recurring five-year agricultural policy questions. FPT first ministers' meetings and bilateral consultations between the prime minister and premiers are supported by Intergovernmental Affairs, out of the Privy Council Office.

First ministers' meetings tend to focus on health funding, along with issues of immediate political interest or recurring fiscal matters. They typically don't involve consideration of longer-term challenges, nor does the format lend itself to making deliberate progress on structural issues, such as the need for tax coordination or bringing the private sector into infrastructure funding.

That's the structure, as such. But where's the management? Where is the guiding hand that builds, confirms and employs good working relationships, revealing each side's needs and expectations, to ease the way toward a compromise? And where is the framework to define both the means and the goal?

Consider interprovincial free trade. Canada's inability to function as a fully open economy, with products crossing provincial boundaries free of charges or regulatory concerns, may appear a nuisance to an individual purchasing beer or wine. But it is more than that. On a wider scale, these barriers represent obstacles to the growth of companies that operate nationally. A company based in one province, prepared to scale up its operations by hiring more employees and pursuing export markets, may find its plans foiled by another province's legislation. That's not the way to raise national productivity. Labour and capital ideally should be able to move freely according to need and opportunity, contributing to the efficient operation of the economy overall.

We lack a common market within our own country, one that permits the free and undistorted movements of goods, services, labour and capital across provincial borders under a harmonized system of regulatory policies. If we could achieve this goal, while ensuring that all Canadian citizens would have access to social services regardless of their provincial residence, the improvement in economic efficiency would be substantial. According to the

International Monetary Fund, we could see up to a 4 percent improvement in our economic results.

And this may come as a surprise to you: the constitution already favours this harmonized approach. Section 121 provides that "All Articles of the Growth, Produce or Manufacture of any one of the Provinces shall, from and after the Union, be admitted free into each of the other Provinces." Sounds cut and dried, doesn't it? It is and it isn't. The clause has been left to interpretation in a way that allows provinces to restrict the free flow of goods for legitimate policy objectives, and it doesn't even address trade in services.

Steps to solve the problem have been taken in the past, but they amount to little more than voluntary agreements between governments, assembled once again on an ad hoc basis. Formal efforts to deal with the situation include the 1982–1985 MacDonald Commission, which led to the Agreement on Internal Trade signed by federal and provincial governments in 1994. This proved ineffective thanks to general noncompliance among the participants. When it became obvious that the agreement wasn't delivering the intended results, pressure built up for a new approach, leading to a 2016 Senate report proposing features that included a harmonization of regulations among all provinces and territories, a dispute settlement mechanism and mutual recognition that products conforming with the standards of one province be deemed to be conforming with the others.

The Canadian Free Trade Agreement, which became effective in January 2017, largely reflects these recommendations. But without regulatory harmonization, the giant steps needed to foster a genuine internal common market are unlikely to occur.

The list of interprovincial barriers continues. Licensing of professionals across Canada remains another problem in search of a solution. A fully accredited physician in Nova Scotia, for example, needs a provincial licence to practise in Alberta or PEI or Quebec or anywhere else in Canada other than her own province. Surely this is a solvable situation. But it won't happen without a sustained effort. We also need a national securities regulator to preside over cooperating jurisdictions, manage systemic risk, identify potential criminal activity and generally serve as a cooperative capital markets regulatory system.

The urgent need for better management of federal-provincial cooperation goes beyond these economic considerations to our long-term national advantages. Canadian openness to immigration is one of our great strengths, making our country one of the most diverse and vibrant nations on earth, and it takes on added importance in the face of an aging population. Immigration is a shared jurisdiction under the acknowledgement that, should conflict arise, federal law will trump provincial law. The federal government retains exclusive power to deal with issues of naturalization, while the provinces retain legislative rights over housing, health and social services on behalf of immigrants. Settlement services for immigrants, such as employment assistance, English and French language training, mentorship and other supports, are provided by the federal government via non-profit organizations, educational institutions and private business. In the 2021–22 period, Canada budgeted about $1.7 billion for these services. Quebec funds its immigrant settlement costs with a separate federal grant.

Canada's track record on immigration policy, and the integration of new residents, is often held out as a success. To a large degree that's correct, but immigration levels are certain to grow, sharpening the need to attract the optimum mix of immigrants and increasing the costs for settlement services. The assortment of federal and provincial streams is certain to make the process more complicated, requiring greater coordination between the two levels of government.

Even in areas where cooperation is well established between the federal government and the provinces, we have more work to do. Substantial cooperation exists in the funding and legislation of major stabilization programs for agri-food production. They function under a succession of five-year frameworks that balance federal and provincial concerns in the interest of reaching agreed-upon economic, social and environmental goals.

These efforts have to work within the confines of our restrictive production and marketing policies. In dairy products, for example, market-entry and production are controlled through a quota system, preventing dairy farmers from expanding their operation beyond a fixed threshold. Producer prices are regulated by the Dairy Commission, which effectively limits imports via tariffs. The result is a system ensuring predictable and stable conditions for producers without the need for direct government intervention. Sounds good, but in the process market conditions are distorted, interprovincial trade is limited, Canada's international trade negotiations are constrained and Canadian consumers pay a higher price for dairy products than necessary.

—

Meaningful systemic discussions will help us deal with other challenges that we will be facing as a nation but are not fully prepared to tackle in a unified manner. Surely the most pressing issue is Canada's and the world's response to climate change and the entire sphere of environmental concerns.

As critical as it may already be today, the magnitude of the problem and the complexity and cost of dealing with climate change are certain to grow in the future. It's imperative to avoid duplication between levels of government, or provinces and territories may opt out of programs to deal with the issue. Complicating things is the fact that environmental issues are not specifically dealt with in the constitution, leaving the power to regulate them loosely allotted between federal and provincial jurisdictions. In some cases, both levels of government may claim authority.

One of the most important moments in my time in office was the day we received clarity on our approach to pricing carbon. The implementation of carbon pricing represented a historic achievement, as did the Pan-Canadian Framework on Clean Growth and Climate Change. A decision by the Supreme Court of Canada established the authority of the federal government to regulate greenhouse gases under the "peace, order and good government" provisions of the constitution, related to issues of national concern. As a result, all provinces and territories need to adhere to carbon pricing guidelines, with a federal backstop to use where necessary.

This sounds better in theory than it works in reality. Differing federal and provincial perspectives result in a sub-optimal system. Multiple systems directed to achieve the same objective rarely if ever reduce costs or the burden of administration.

A more efficient approach to carbon pricing would see a single national pricing system (or at least a single system outside Quebec) that would return proceeds to the provinces under an agreement to ensure basic principles are followed. Consider the advantages: more investor certainty that the system would continue over an extended time period and on a given trajectory; a reduced burden of compliance for large emitters operating multijurisdictional locations; and a better facilitating market for earned credits. And most importantly, it would allow the provinces to receive the proceeds from carbon pricing and rebate the money back to their citizens. We price what we don't want — carbon emissions — and give rebates back to people who are free to choose how to spend their own money. It's simple, motivates all of us to consume less and leads to a better environment. When I described it to my colleague at the G7 table Bruno Le Maire, the finance minister of France, he immediately concluded that our approach might have worked to reduce the French resistance to carbon taxes that led to the gilets jaune movement in his country. But there is no way any of this will be achieved in Canada without leadership from the top, along with an open and collaborative approach to federal-provincial relationships.

—

One of my early successes as finance minister was working with Jane Philpott to get to an agreement on federal health care funding with the provinces. It was an arduous job that fell to me and my team because, although Jane and her team were the leaders on the policy issues, negotiations inevitably come down to dollars. We saw getting to an agreement with each province as critical; the only way we could have a reasonable chance of coming close to our deficit targets would be to ensure that the federal health care transfer was manageable. An agreement with the provinces would be a win, we thought, especially if we could force agreement on our priorities, which included a more focused approach to mental health and home care.

We were willing to agree to a long-term commitment for federal funding of health care. It would apply a formula less generous than the 2004 Health Accord, which had a 6 percent escalator, conditional on a commitment from the provinces to achieve measurable progress on health care reform with the focus on mental health and home care. In 2017 we continued the pattern of negotiations where the federal government gives money while accepting a fiction: that the provinces will apply the funds to the system for which they are responsible, which is something that often fails to happen. Clearly, progress on real reform, dealing with long-term cost issues and ensuring the universal access that is so important to Canadians, does not occur in these money-focused negotiations.

Not dealing with the fundamental challenges and priorities of health care is increasingly irresponsible. Public health care costs represent about half the expenditures of provincial governments, and they're constantly under pressure from an aging population needing increased attention, as well as the need for capital investments in advanced technology and demands for higher compensation from medical professionals.

For their part, the provinces contend that federal funding for health care programs needs to rise from its current level of about 20 percent of total provincial outlays to 35 percent. Increasing the Canada Health Transfer to that extent would put heavy pressure on the federal government's fiscal situation. Suggestions have been made to fund the system at least partially through an approach in which the provinces formally request the federal government to increase GST levels to pay for the increase in transferred funds. This has some attraction because the GST is the least distortive of the taxes we pay. It raises a logical question, however: Why wouldn't the provinces raise their own sales tax rates and retain full control over the revenues generated?

—

That's an intimidating and still incomplete list of concerns for us to deal with as a country, and none will be easy to solve. But that's only, I submit, because the search for solutions has too often been mishandled. Different political philosophies, deep-seated historical grievances, staggered electoral timelines, varying fiscal capacity, questions of provincial sovereignty and myriad other issues all intrude into FPT relations.

We need an approach that acknowledges the cost pressures facing provinces are profoundly different from those facing the federal government. Let's begin with the fact that provincial governments, either directly or indirectly, are responsible for providing most of the services their citizens receive. As I said, public health care costs represent about half the expenditures of provincial governments, and they're constantly escalating. It doesn't stop there. K–12 education costs, social services and infrastructure renewal all place extra pressure on provincial budgets.

Conversely, spending in areas of federal jurisdiction tends to be relatively static over the long term or even in some cases subject to decline, as with defence spending (although as I mentioned previously this should be reassessed in a world growing ever more security conscious). In fact, the share of federal spending as a proportion of total public spending in Canada has declined steadily over time. From a fiscal perspective, this leaves the provinces more vulnerable than the federal government.

Stability and predictability in funding arrangements are key considerations for provinces. Constraint measures installed by the federal government in the mid-1990s, as necessary as they might have been, resulted in unilateral reductions in transfer payments. Their impact remains on the minds of provincial fiscal planners. What's more, while federal cost-shared programs offer additional support to provinces, they tend to be driven by federal priorities which are, of course, subject to change. Like it or not, this creates a sense that ongoing provincial programs are being held hostage by Ottawa.

None of these thorny issues can be effectively addressed with short-term solutions to constrain spending at any level of government. We badly need meaningful dialogue focused on identifying and planning for longer-term challenges to our fiscal and economic policies. Admittedly, some attention is already paid to these issues at both government levels. What's missing is a coordinated approach recognizing and taking into account the key roles that each level of government plays and tailoring actions accordingly.

To move forward in a spirit of true cooperation, I suggest a strategy with three key principles.

First, the federal government should not introduce new programs requiring joint funding without agreeing with the provinces and territories on policy rationale and program development. Advance discussions are not preliminaries; they are essential planning steps and should be treated that way.

Second, there is no path forward for constructive discussions without addressing health care costs for longer than one political cycle. This requires a long-term commitment on the part of the federal government for health care funding, applying a formula less generous than the 2004 Health Accord of a 6 percent escalator but more generous than the previous amount of 3 percent. Transfers would be conditional on a commitment from the provinces to achieve measurable progress on health care reform, with a joint forum overseeing the progress.

Finally, a commitment is needed from both levels of government to begin ongoing discussions that will identify and implement new ways of improving Canada's productive capacity and economic growth. We urgently need to refocus the management of FPT relations to permit a truly collaborative discussion on the long-term economic challenges facing Canada.

—

Our decentralized structure was built on a 19th-century constitutional model reflecting the roles played by governments back then. But from time to time the guidelines have successfully been redrawn to make room for changes requiring wide support, including a national employment insurance system, national principles underlying our health care system and the establishment of the CPP, OAS and GIS. The challenge we face today is no less serious: we will not be able to support our cherished social security systems, much less compete with a developed world that is exceeding us in growth rates, unless we take a fresh approach to working together.

This will require disciplined and focused leadership, a recognition that the provinces and the federal government are partners and a time commitment that vastly exceeds the current one. I note that the European finance ministers normally meet each other more than a dozen times a year, and the Canadian finance ministers meet once or twice a year, often grudgingly. Meeting much more often not only allows for progress on big and consequential issues, it creates windows in which small wins may be possible, like my CPP experience.

Improving Canada's weak productivity level will require coordinated and calculated action by both levels of government, and it must be both sharply focused and well structured. The standard solution would be to begin by identifying the challenges and building consensus around those most critical to solve in order to achieve success, much like the work done by my Advisory Council on Economic Growth. I suggest we go further, with an organization similar to Australia's Productivity Commission mandated to develop not short-term patchwork ideas but strategic steps taken with fixed targets and objectives in mind, plus a schedule to measure progress toward success. To more accurately focus it upon its objective, I would propose labelling it a *Growth Commission*.

We need a Growth Commission that can report simultaneously to federal and provincial governments, creating a non-partisan and provincial-federal approach to getting at things that matter. And we need it urgently. Our job in government is to improve the economy for Canadians, and we must do better, together.

Seventeen

Choosing Between Transition and Tragedy

You have encountered the horrifying predictions elsewhere — oceans with high acidic levels and lower oxygen content causing severe depletions in fish and marine animals; more recurring (and more deadly) storms, floods, wildfires and droughts; and shocking declines in the population levels of birds, mammals, reptiles and other life forms. The impact appears overwhelming in its tragedy and dangers. And we have to stop just talking about it. Taking little or no action today will inevitably lead to future disasters of biblical proportions.

Canada has an unwelcome status as one of the world's largest emitters of carbon dioxide, the leading contributor to global warming. We generate enormous amounts of CO_2 per capita. Among advanced industrialized nations only Australia (15.30 tonnes) and the U.S. (14.24) exceed our annual CO_2 output of 14.20 tonnes per capita. In an industry-by-industry comparison, our largest source of carbon emissions is oil and gas production, followed by transportation, buildings, industries, agriculture and electricity generation.

We can rationalize our CO_2 production from fossil fuel usage in various ways. Our cold winter climate demands energy to heat homes and businesses, primarily with the products of our carbon-intensive oil and gas sector; our country's vast size dictates extensive use of vehicles to reach far-flung communities, driving up emissions from transportation; and our heavy industries employ fossil fuels to mine, smelter and process raw materials for assembly and shipping. But explaining it doesn't solve the problem.

This is the most urgent file facing our government today.

While serving as minister of finance, my many speeches on the topic included reference to the increasing number of climate-related natural disasters our country faced. I repeatedly explained that I had the dubious distinction of writing more cheques, at a higher dollar value, for relief after climate disasters than any finance minister before me. The worst part is that I'm pretty sure a future finance minister will beat this record. The world is getting hotter, and the consequences are very real. We cannot sit by and do nothing. Even if we considered that a morally acceptable response, it is not a politically viable response. No topic brought a more visceral reaction among young people when I spoke to them on university and college campuses than our need to deal with climate change.

Our government set out in 2015 to ensure that addressing climate change would be a key priority. We demonstrated our intent with our participation in the 2015 Paris Agreement, in which 197 countries agreed to set targets for reduced CO_2 production by 2030. Canada's original target was a reduction of 30 percent from our 2005 levels, increased to 40 to 45 percent in July 2021. Ultimately, we have committed to net-zero emissions by 2050. The Trudeau government continues to make the reduction of our carbon emissions a central goal. However, I am not convinced that we will see the results we need to see without a more effectively managed process. The commitment is there, but the job is enormously complex and difficult. It won't happen without collaboration between the federal government and the provincial and territorial governments, nor without global coordination and cooperation.

So how do I believe we should start the discussion? First, we need to be realistic: we will not achieve our goals by switching from fossil fuels virtually overnight. That's not a viable option when an overwhelming number of homes in Canada are heated by fossil fuels and a similar proportion of vehicles are powered that way. We also have to face political reality: in a country with an enormous resource sector and a lack of consensus on the urgency of the climate change problem, the federal government can't simply dictate that we eliminate our use of fossil fuels immediately. It just won't happen.

We will find the path to reducing our carbon output through an energy transition, an idea many people find more comforting than stopping cold turkey. A well-managed energy transition involves a gradual shift away from fossil fuels and toward renewable sources of energy. It would be made over a determined period of time without seriously disrupting the economic prosperity that is deeply dependent on energy access and consumption. There is no practical alternative. We must work together on this, as challenging as that may seem based on the disputes over the imposition of carbon pricing and attempts at developing pipelines to get our resources to market. But "challenging" is not the same as impossible. If we need more incentive, consider this: leading the world in energy transition will enable us to maximize our economic potential and reverse our declining productivity performance.

Most of us grew up relying on gasoline and diesel fuel to power our vehicles, and natural gas and petroleum products to heat our homes. It's difficult for many of us to imagine these energy sources no longer being universally employed to provide transportation and comfort. Do electric vehicles, solar panels and wind generators really represent the future? Yes, they do. Our challenge is to get there by reducing the carbon footprint from our current sources of energy and aggressively decarbonizing as much of our lifestyle as is practical.

Think of life back when Shakespeare was acting in his own plays. Most of the energy available came from wind, water and muscle power, both human and animal. All of it was renewable. The Industrial Age changed things with its emphasis on coal, gas and oil as sources of energy. This was good news for working people and horses, but bad news for the quality of air, water and the environment generally. It's time for another energy transition, this one a downshift from the production and use of fossil fuels.

Much of the world has already started down that road, and the size of the investments made by participating countries is impressive. More than $500 billion — half a trillion dollars — was spent globally in 2020 by companies, governments and households to cut carbon emissions. The money was used to develop and install equipment for renewable energy (solar panels, wind farms and hydro power), electric vehicles and related infrastructure, energy storage, energy-efficient heating systems, carbon capture and storage, and hydrogen production. But this is only a start. The true scale of the investment needed to deal with the climate crisis vastly exceeds current expenditures. If Canada doesn't ramp up spending now, we will not have any chance of meeting our 2030 and 2050 goals. More critically, we won't be able to invest enough to meet our goals if we don't increase our spending today. Trying to catch up all at once in later years will be too much for the economy to handle.

The idea of *transition* implies an initial period of mediocre progress, not an overnight event. The world will take a few decades to move from the finite sources of petroleum, gas and coal to wider use of renewable power sources — solar, wind, geothermal, hydro and others. To some it will seem that we are pushing and pulling at the same time, which is a recipe for sowing confusion, frustration and anger. Doing more than one thing at a time seems counterproductive, but sometimes you have no other choice. We are dealing with a complicated management challenge.

The first and most important part of the transition is the imposition of carbon pricing. In my opinion, the most consequential policy achievement of the Trudeau government during my term was the nationwide adoption of carbon pricing, with the proceeds being returned to Canadians. Our August 2017 introduction of the Pan-Canadian Framework on Clean Growth and Climate Change leaned heavily on carbon pricing as a tool to accomplish our goal of reducing emissions. I worked closely with then-minister of environment and climate change Catherine McKenna, who brought a massive commitment to the project, and Gerry Butts, who considered it the most important policy initiative of his life. We also relied on some very capable and committed people from the PMO, led by Sarah Goodman, a smart and effective policy advisor.

This was an extremely difficult file, and it went all the way to the Supreme Court when the provinces challenged the federal government's jurisdiction to impose carbon pricing. All in all, a quintessentially Canadian formula for getting things done: get broad general agreement, bring some key provinces on side, use the federal government for a backstop and — the pièce de résistance — put money in the pockets of ordinary citizens.

Of course, just because it worked doesn't make it ideal. We need to do better than that. We need a means of achieving agreement and commitment from all the stakeholders instead of our familiar patchwork style. This will take federal government leadership, federal-provincial coordination and private sector investment, enabled in many cases by government policy, to get to the place we need to be.

—

Of various alternative strategies to support energy transition, carbon pricing is fundamental. As a market-based approach to the problem, it produces an economic incentive to reduce carbon emissions, which we don't want, and motivation to develop carbon reduction practices and technology as a profitable investment, which we need. In the face of future environmental disasters likely to occur in the absence of reduced carbon emissions, it appeared an ideal solution.

Few things in life, however, generate a more negative emotional response from people than a directive from authority to change the way they live. And when the change is made in search of a goal they neither support nor fully understand, while threatening their immediate economic interests, the emotional response deepens and darkens. Waves of vitriol were aimed my way when the program was introduced, and while I obviously resented the threats and labels, I understood their source. On top of people's concerns about the blows to their income they expected to feel, they were asked to make these adjustments with the admission that the ultimate payoffs might not be realized in their own lifetime.

Attitudes toward our efforts to address climate change differed according to geographical location and local impact. Giving a speech in Calgary in 2018 to announce the closing of the deal to purchase the Trans Mountain Pipeline on behalf of the federal government, I was inundated with applause approving the measure. At the airport on my way back to Ottawa, strangers approached me to share a high-five of congratulations. Good thing I wasn't flying out of Vancouver. Many insulting comments were directed at me from British Columbia. Curiously enough, both provinces were administered by NDP governments at the time.

Politics in Canada can be a confusing experience.

—

Weaning ourselves from petroleum needn't mean closing down our own production facilities. We and the rest of the world will continue to need natural gas and petroleum for the next two decades, constantly lowering our consumption until carbon emission goals are reached. Between now and then we can and should support our domestic resource industry on condition that it becomes an active participant in our decarbonization efforts. There is no cold-turkey option. We cannot hand down an edict to Alberta and Saskatchewan ordering them to forgo the production of petroleum and overnight wave goodbye to the jobs and facilities associated with oil and gas. That's a formula for blowing the country apart.

Nor can we assume that setbacks and snags will vanish as a result of fostering cooperation between the federal and provincial levels. Life isn't that simple, in or out of government. But engagement at any level and on any topic is important, if only to alert each side to concerns that are likely to arise on future events and prepare them for important, sometimes difficult, discussions.

Besides, in many quarters the transition away from fossil fuels is already well underway. What follows is one example.

Among the most visible sources of CO_2 emissions, especially if you live in the Greater Toronto Area, are the steel companies in Hamilton. Steelmaking is a messy business involving massive amounts of iron ore, coal, limestone and other ingredients loaded into furnaces where the mixture is heated to about 1,400 degrees Celsius (2,550 Fahrenheit). The amount of energy needed to reach this temperature is, of course, enormous.

In early 2022 ArcelorMittal Dofasco, one of the country's largest steel producers, announced a plan to eliminate coal as a heat source, replacing it with electric arc furnaces. The company estimated that the move would cut its annual CO_2 emissions by 3.5 million tonnes. Reportedly, that substantial reduction will be equal to taking one million cars off Canada's roads. It is an interim step toward the firm moving to hydrogen as a heat source on the way to a zero-emissions target. The move will cost an estimated $1.8 billion, with the province of Ontario committing $500 million toward the capital cost and the federal government contributing $400 million. An estimated 2,500 construction and engineering workers will be employed to complete the changeover, which the company forecasts will enable it to move away from the traditional steelmaking methods it now uses exclusively and expand into more technically advanced, and cleaner, manufacturing operations.

While a good deal of lip service has been paid to reducing CO_2 production among Canada's heavy industrial facilities, the capital costs involved, as illustrated above, are substantial. Gathering the funds required a partnership between the private company and both levels of government. If the new facility proves as successful as expected, it is likely to motivate similar changes in the sector and among other industries. But what about all that public money being spent to assist a private corporation? It's hardly a new action, but is it necessary?

Battling climate change is too important and frankly too expensive for private capital to make such massive adjustments on its own. We can expect, and should encourage, similar public-private joint investments that promise advances beyond the goal of zero emissions. To do this will involve an ongoing search for the biggest opportunities to reduce carbon production, determining how to create the incentive for private investors to make the required financing. As a starting point, the government will need to ensure that every business in the country, large and small, understands its carbon footprint. We can't manage what we don't measure. This will enable us to come up with appropriate incentives to persuade businesses to move down the path toward decarbonization.

Carbon pricing creates the financial imperative, but we will need to do more. Some situations may require the government to assure investors that they can have confidence in the rising price of carbon. Businesses will invest in the process only when they can fully trust that the price on carbon will increase. This will require a guarantee from the government, one that contractually ensures that if some future government lowers the price on carbon, or reduces the pace of price increases, businesses will recover the investment they made on the expectation that the carbon price would be higher.

In addition, the federal government will need to implement carbon border adjustment taxes that prevent our businesses from losing market share to competitors operating in countries that lack carbon pricing. These would arrive in the form of selective tariffs applied to the products of nations rejecting the carbon pricing formula. Eventually, as other countries catch up to our carbon pricing strategy with their own, this approach will become unnecessary. In the meantime, our businesses will grow adept at decarbonization, giving them a long-term advantage on a global basis.

Most of this country's efforts to slash our CO_2 emissions are linked to carbon pricing, considered by many economists to be the most efficient way of reducing emissions. People will decide to choose less carbon-intensive sources of energy only if it works for them financially. Our decision to return the funds received from carbon pricing to Canadians means it is *not* a regular tax — instead, it is a way of ensuring that we can reduce our impact on global warming by changing both our investment decisions and our day-to-day behaviour. Frankly, that is the only sustainable means we have to reach our goal.

Electric-powered vehicles, solar panels and wind farms are a beginning, and, like with most beginnings, there may be stumbles. Many people unfortunately focus on the missteps without seeing the long-term benefits of energy transition, which extend beyond the critical motive of suppressing global warming. The benefits include positive socio-economic impacts on employment, industrial development, health and access to energy. In rural areas, solar mini-grids can significantly improve the availability of electric power, while the elimination of coal- and natural gas–powered electric generating plants reduces premature deaths from air pollution and lowers health costs.

All of these attractive long-term goals will need a period of time to make their impact felt, thus the term *transition*. But the world cannot wait for developments like electric-heated steel plants and highways busy with electric-powered vehicles before taking necessary steps. The time to cut fossil fuel consumption is now, and carbon pricing represents the best first step toward it.

Energy transition is important for another reason, this one closely associated with Canada. Much of our economic performance is derived from our resources sectors. At least three of our provinces are highly dependent on locating and refining their natural resources. As critical as carbon reduction is to Canada and indeed the balance of the world, we cannot ignore the impact that restrictions are likely to make on this key portion of our economy. Our best move is not a sudden tire-screeching stop, but a steady slowing down on a fixed schedule.

Our commitments to meet carbon reduction levels by 2030 are critically important not only to us but to the rest of the world as well. We will not make the necessary energy transition, either within Canada or on a global basis, without working together. We can begin with efforts to help our oil and gas sector decarbonize, a move they have taken with good and sometimes spectacular results.

Decarbonization by petroleum producers is already a worldwide movement, with several Canadian companies leading the way. They're doing it through a series of steps, all designed to cut carbon emissions during their processing stages. One source claims that the global petroleum production industry is poised to cut carbon emissions by at least 3.4 gigatons annually by 2050, which would represent a 90 percent reduction in current emissions. They'll do this in a number of ways, including an extended system of maintenance procedures; use of renewable energy sources to power production equipment; elimination of flaring gas and methane leaks; carbon capture, utilization and storage; and other steps. Little of the technology is revolutionary, and all of it is currently available. History teaches that once a new technological approach gains ground and grows wider in application, more efficient means of achieving the same goal will be developed.

We need to take these steps not only in the interests of the world generally, but to our own advantage. The movement toward cutting carbon emissions may not yet be universal, but it encompasses virtually all of the industrialized world. Countries will gradually transition away from petroleum products through much of the balance of this century. During that period they will make a choice among suppliers, and nations whose petroleum producers are not making serious efforts to cut carbon generation in their operations will be bypassed.

Our goal must be to set an example for the world. We don't have to pose as a paragon of virtue. We need to be seen rolling up our sleeves and getting the job done by introducing carbon pricing that returns the money to citizens; decarbonizing what we manufacture, produce and consume; and lobbying international bodies like the IMF to advance policies among national governments that will both address climate change and reduce our risk from its impacts, which is a very real macroeconomic issue.

If Canada is not in step with other oil-producing nations in minimizing carbon production (or ahead of them, given our energy-intensive oil sands operations), we will not only be out of the line to deal with climate change, we will watch other countries become favoured suppliers, which I would define as a lose-lose proposition.

Finally, and perhaps most challenging of all, we will need broad political advocacy to promote energy transition in pursuit of our goal. Getting to net-zero carbon emissions is attainable. It is essential, it is accessible, and it is far too critical to us, our grandchildren and their descendants to be used as a jousting stick brandished by one political party against another. But achieving this objective will involve tough discussions between the federal and provincial governments. There is no point in having a carbon price if provincial premiers reduce gas taxes to offset the added cost to consumers whenever the carbon price goes up. We will need to be clear on the repercussions of not working together. The federal government has negotiating tools, including federal transfers, that are important to the provinces. If we truly believe in climate change as an existential issue — and my experience says that is how Canadians feel — we have no choice but to have the tough discussions. This means making a major transition, and an expensive one, and it can only be done with mutual support and involvement. Let's start the discussions, however heated they may become, and reach a conclusion. Because if we don't do it — as individuals, as a nation and as a global society — the conclusion will be determined via horrifying circumstances beyond our control.

Eighteen

Facing the Future

One reason I took to the idea of running for office in 2015 was Canada's slumping economic performance. I was attracted to the possibility of applying my business skills and experience to help make a difference in critical problem areas such as our response to climate change, reconciliation with our Indigenous population, and the need for a national child care program. All of these, to one extent or another, could only be fully addressed if we had the funds to invest in them. So dealing with our economic objectives, in my mind, had to be a key priority.

Canada's economic growth had been stalled for two decades or more, and it needed to be resuscitated. According to the OECD, Canada had been outpaced in the recent past by 138 countries including Australia, Mexico, New Zealand and the USA. While growth had been sluggish through the Stephen Harper years, this was not a partisan issue. In my mind, it was a fundamental problem needing immediate attention.

It wouldn't be easy to solve. The policies needed to pull us out of our economic doldrums would be hard to implement and involve significant expense. They would also require a clear focus, strong discipline and a willingness to collaborate in new ways. That's a formidable shopping list.

On the upside, we accomplished some important things from 2015 to 2020, highlighted by the CCB, expansion of the CPP and the launch of a national approach to pricing carbon. And, of course, barely into our second term we encountered COVID-19. Despite all we achieved, we didn't do nearly enough to stimulate economic growth, however. This is not surprising, perhaps, because restoring Canada's economic performance wasn't a major plank in our election platform. A talking point, yes. But it needed to be more than that. We needed a clear-eyed view of the challenges ahead and a determined approach to changing our growth trajectory.

Let's be brutally honest about it: with all the national attributes our country has been gifted, we shouldn't be lagging behind so many other nations with similar levels of industrialization and development — we should be at the head of the class. That realization prompted me to create the Advisory Council on Economic Growth. The council did some significant work, drawing attention to the importance of immigration and its impact on our demographics; identifying key economic sectors where Canada held a competitive advantage; focusing on how we could stimulate lagging private sector investment with ideas like the Canada Infrastructure Bank; advocating for the expansion of international trade in Asia, where growth was likely to continue; and pushing for a focus on skills development and training.

As happens so often in political life, the ideas were good but their application proved a challenge. Building and renewing infrastructure demanded a large amount of capital and extended time frames to complete projects, plus provincial and municipal buy-in. On the international front, our strategy to expand trade opportunities with China ran up against hard-nosed geopolitical realities, and implementing other promising initiatives encountered obstacles that couldn't be easily sidestepped.

The focus on economic renewal deserved to be sharpened and directed by the prime minister, but it was not. I was prepared to play any meaningful role to reach the goal, but responsibility for economic growth cannot be delegated to the finance minister alone. It requires attention at the very top. In my view neither the PM nor the PMO saw the need to address our anemic growth record as a first priority, despite a raft of statistics confirming it and the need to treat it as a priority.

There are many ways to define true economic success, but any way you slice it, it is based on productivity. That formula works for countries the same way it works for people. If your and your family's economic situation is good, it's probably the result of your personal productivity. Many things contributed to it — your education, your location, your choice of career, your natural skills and, of course, your persistence and energy.

It took more than applying those attributes to succeed. Over time, you needed to improve them. You completed or extended your education and training, chose a career that was both rewarding and satisfying, sought and accepted promotions and other rewards associated with your work and stayed focused on goals that mattered to you.

It's all about building from one success to the next and learning how to deal with setbacks and challenges. In a word, it's about *growth*, for individuals or for countries, and in recent years Canada's productivity growth has not been what it should be. Unless we take action to reverse the trend, many of our defining national qualities will weaken or vanish. If this occurs, we will be unable to generate meaningful increases in wealth, either as individuals or as a nation. We will lack the means to fund key social programs to a globally competitive level. The comparative quality of our public education, our universal health care system and our valued social programs will all be threatened, along with a litany of other valued benefits.

This makes it absolutely necessary to reverse our deceleration in productivity growth. It won't be easy. It will involve changing old methods that many people value and introducing a few new ones that may make them uncomfortable.

Change is never easy for people. Changing fundamental practices for an entire country is even more difficult. But it needs to happen.

From the end of World War II to the mid-1970s, few countries exceeded Canada's rate of economic growth. As one measure, the weekly earnings of Canadians grew at an average of 2.54 percent annually over that period after accounting for inflation, more than doubling our earned income. Pretty impressive, but from 1982 to 2019, our country's real GDP rose an average of just 1.3 percent annually, which is not impressive at all.

The slump is directly related to a downward trend in productivity growth over those years. Out of 36 OECD countries measured from 2000 to 2019, Canada rated in 25th place when it came to productivity growth. Assessing real output per hour worked, we were less than mediocre in comparison with similar OECD nations: 10 percent lower than the UK, 22 percent lower than France and Germany and a giant 27 percent lower than the U.S., our best partner and our biggest competitor.

One reputable study noted that Canada's productivity from 2000 to 2019 grew at an average of 0.9 percent annually, half the annual rate it had grown over the years from 1961 to 2000. Had we maintained the same productivity growth from 2000 on, the average annual income for Canadian workers in 2019 would have been about $13,550 higher. That's pocketbook proof that greater productivity benefits everyone.[50]

Unfortunately, it's not just the past we need to be worried about.

---

50 David M. Williams, "Pay and Productivity in Canada: Growing Together, Only Slower than Ever," *International Productivity Monitor*, No. 40 (Spring 2021): 3–26.

In 2021 the OECD projected the real change in GDP to occur in most of the world's nations over the next 40 years. Long-term forecasts like this deserve to be viewed with caution, but they provide a reasonable interpretation of the future based on what we know for certain today.

The contrast in potential is startling. Over the next few decades we're likely to see explosive growth in emerging economies like Indonesia, Turkey and several African nations. But in Canada, our relatively weak level of capital investment per worker and lower labour efficiency, measured according to GDP per person, are clearly holding us back.

There's more, all of it sobering from a Canadian perspective. India's GDP growth was projected at 150 percent over the 40-year period, while China's would double over the same time. Developed nations showed lesser but still impressive potential: Australia and the U.S. were expected to rise by 45 percent, Denmark and Japan by 50 percent, Hungary by 60 percent and so on. The country with the lowest projected GDP increase over the same period? Canada. And it wasn't even close: about 30 percent.[51]

Projections aren't reality, and even small annual improvements can make a significant difference over the extended period covered by the study. Still, it's a chilling assessment worth heeding and confirms that maintaining or, more importantly, elevating Canada's living standards will depend on increasing our capital investment, an essential part of improving the country's productivity level.

A closer look at Australia reveals even more sobering comparisons. (Aside from our contrasting climates and that country's distant location from the U.S., we share several qualities including reliance on resources as a major component of our economies.) Using 1985 as a starting point, Australia's improvement in productivity per

51 Yvan Guillemette and David Turner, "The Long Game: Fiscal Outlooks to 2060 Underline Need for Structural Reform," *OECD Economic Policy Paper* No. 29 (Paris: OECD Publishing, 2019).

hour soared 85 percent by 2019. In Canada, our productivity rose barely 50 percent over the same period. These numbers imply that, without successful efforts to correct our performance vis-à-vis the rest of the world, our standard of living is likely to decline relative to other countries in the OECD.

What's behind the drop-off in productivity growth? Have Canadians become lazy? Do we no longer understand the importance of being productive as individuals and corporations? Are we content to let the rest of the world race past us?

I don't buy any of those theories. Instead, I count several factors that explain our weak performance. One has been our declining level of capital investment over the years. Let's remember the point I made earlier about change and understand that other countries will change according to their needs and abilities without waiting for us to catch up.

The amount of money invested to keep our productivity competitive with other countries has at best been stagnant over recent years. Canada spent about $5,000 per available worker on that goal in 1991. We were outpaced by the U.S., which invested around $7,500 per worker, and by other OECD countries whose investment levels were almost double our own. Thirty years later our investment level per worker was under $10,000, while in other OECD countries it had climbed to almost $15,000, and the U.S. easily surpassed $20,000.

Associated with this less than stellar record has been our poor performance when it comes to innovation; we depend too often on others to lead the way. That's a bronze medal approach that may make us feel good but achieves little of substance. Canada's subpar performance is linked with a lack of investment on vital issues. Our funding of research and development is not only unimpressive, it has been declining over the years. In 2018, OECD countries spent just under 2.5 percent of GDP on research and development, flowing from private businesses, higher educational institutions and government. Canada spent barely 1.5 percent, a number that is still falling.

As difficult as this reckoning may be, historically and for the future, we can expect it will become harder to grow our economy given the challenges we'll face. Much of our success over the post-war period can be attributed to our position as a trading country during a time when globalization expanded trading opportunities. Now, facing populism and geopolitical issues, we can expect deglobalization — a new headwind that will impinge on our ability to grow (see the Biden administration's "Buy American" policy as an example very close to home).

These obstacles are challenging enough on their own. Facing them in the context of a world moving out of the COVID crisis doesn't make it any easier. Like every other industrialized country, our primary focus will be on restoring business activity and economic performance back to their pre-COVID levels. But this doesn't make focusing on future growth any less necessary either. We have to get the job done with confidence, not complacency.

Improving productivity is not about maximizing our labour force participation, as important as that may be. Increasing the labour force helps promote growth, but it doesn't necessarily improve productivity. Nor should our goal be about working harder or working with fewer people to do the same amount of work. It's about working smarter, which is not the same thing at all. The best way to elevate labour productivity in the 21st century is through the application of technological advances and ensuring the ability of the labour force to adapt to them.

It is impossible, on a long-term basis, for any society to earn or spend more than the value of whatever they produce, whether goods or services. That's a basic rule that one doesn't need an economics degree to understand. All you need to grasp the idea is your experience at balancing your household budget. The key to long-term prosperity is productivity, and the reality of our aging demographics will make it ever more important over the coming years.

Rather than maintaining the age of retirement, we should encourage older Canadians to remain in the labour force as long as they choose. Why should we discard their talents, experience and contribution? Those are enormously valuable assets. We need to ensure people have an incentive to continue working while their health and interests favour it, and we should encourage them to apply their skills to the job of expanding Canada's wealth-generating growth.

Productivity growth will help us improve our current standard of living in the face of growing competition from other nations. But we also need to ensure that the benefits of economic growth are enjoyed broadly by Canadians. Improvements in living standards, while measured on an average basis, must be enjoyed by all income levels.

The goal of improving our productivity and, by association, our economic success is related to far more than financial benefits. Our once solid commitment to tolerance and democratic principles has been challenged here in Canada and elsewhere. There are various causes for the widespread discontent, but many are clearly linked to insecurity. Many people fear that their economic future is not promising. They believe that political parties in power are unresponsive to their concerns, dismissing them in a "just trust us" manner.

At heart, it all comes down to financial security. Other aspects of modern life create uncertainty, but few make an individual feel good about the future more than confidence in their opportunity to earn a healthy income into the foreseeable future.

I'm not suggesting, by the way, that all of our problems can be solved through economic growth. I'm certain, however, that those same problems are less likely to arise if Canadians are confident about the financial future — their own and the country's.

—

One reason improving our economic growth has not been elevated to top-drawer status is because of all the complications associated with it. You've seen it written before on these pages: much of politics is hard, and tackling some policy initiatives can be especially hard. But that's not a reason to avoid them by setting them aside for some other administration — or some other generation — to deal with.

Stimulating our economic growth upwards so it is at least equal to that of other countries at a comparable stage of development is not an overnight task, nor one that can be realized a year or two from now. It is a long-term goal requiring a long-term approach. It cannot be launched with expectations of success by year's end or even before the next election cycle, and that can be a debilitating factor to those in favour of a flag-waving, vote-getting celebration every week or so.

And it's complicated. Economic performance results from the efforts of many actors, both public and private. To the extent it's influenced by the federal government, it's not just about policies. It's about the approach to management and actions taken collaboratively with the provinces, which puts us back at the federal-provincial negotiating table again. This shouldn't be intimidating. On the reasonable assumption that steps to improve Canada's productivity will adhere to expanded standards of environmental protection and carbon reduction, few groups in or out of politics will seriously question the goal. Higher productivity yields higher personal incomes, more economic security and larger government coffers to fund key social programs such as health care, retirement incomes, infrastructure maintenance — the things we want. That alone doesn't ensure hassle-free discussions, but within an established relationship it serves to launch negotiations on a positive note.

Improving our economic growth is not, and should never evolve into, a partisan issue. There is plenty of scope for partisan debate about the size and role of government and redistribution, but everyone should agree on the goal of raising our living standards through growth. Making that goal a reality is, I believe, one of our most significant challenges in an increasingly partisan world.

It was never difficult to convince business and industry groups of this perspective. Whatever their political tendencies might have been, they all grasped the importance and urgency of getting on with the job of improving Canada's productivity. Yes, you could argue that self-interest was the motivation. But isn't that the point of a capitalist market-based democracy? Wasn't that how we got to the place where we could have one of the best lifestyles in the history of the world? I was always impressed by all the suggestions originating from those in the private sector who immediately saw the benefits awaiting us if we managed to hit some growth targets. My challenge was building a consensus within the government on the urgency of the problem, and providing enough incentive to seriously tackle it. There is always an important short-term problem to be solved, a social problem that should be dealt with. Often I agreed, but the reality is that without the focus on growth, all of those other goals will be more difficult to achieve — we will be constantly fighting for our pet priority with more limited means. Breaking the cycle, to focus on growth first and programs after, is the leadership challenge.

Notwithstanding the hard work and practical recommendations from the Advisory Council on Economic Growth, keeping a focus on growth proved a constant challenge. Most of my time was spent evaluating spending proposals. So, each time the annual reports on economic performance were released by the IMF or the OECD, I felt a little more like the proverbial frog sitting in the pot, doing nothing while the water temperature gradually crept toward the boiling point. Our complacency compromises our ability to compete and even to govern effectively; progress is meager, and the results underwhelming.

We cannot do nothing and just assume we'll muddle out of the situation. The world doesn't work that way, nor has it ever.

So, what should we do?

Our first move must be to acknowledge that the problem exists and take steps to deal with it in response to the OECD projections on our future prosperity. Economic projections are not weather forecasts. The difference is that we can change the future, by taking the right decisions today and tomorrow. And creating our economic success is a duty no one else but us can assume.

Let's also accept that there is no quick fix to the problem. We did not lose the economic success we enjoyed overnight. The slide was slow and incremental, and we were accompanied on the ride by other developed countries who saw their own productivity growth lose speed and momentum. Misery may love company, but that's not the kind of company we need or want because on the ride down we dropped faster and further than the others.

Other industrialized countries have identified the need for economic growth and have taken action to produce it. Australia's Productivity Commission is described as "an independent research and advisory body on a range of economic, social and environmental issues affecting the welfare of Australians."[52] Its mandate includes improvement of the country's productivity and economic performance, reductions in unnecessary regulations, the development of

52 Australian government, Productivity Commission, pc.gov.au

efficient and competitive industries and other means of elevating their success at competing in global markets. As a reflection of its importance, the commission reports directly to Parliament.

Australia is not alone. Chile, Denmark, France, Mexico and other nations have set up similar government bodies whose function is to develop methods of making their countries more competitive, more productive and more successful at building their economy. The success of these initiatives prompted the OECD to recommend that all its member countries consider launching their own productivity commissions. They can contribute significantly, the OECD noted, to policy discussions on ways to improve production efficiency and lay the groundwork for their adoption.

Extensive studies indicate that while a broad range of factors could help improve the rate of productivity growth, there is no simple recipe for bending the curve. Some consensus suggests that deliberate actions taken across multiple fronts over a sustained period of time may prove the best strategy. The OECD also identified a series of factors to boost the success of the productivity commissions they recommend, based on experiences shared by countries that had launched similar organizations. Among the guidelines are some that can be instructive for Canada:

- Establish the commissions under legislation that includes an appropriately crafted mandate. In our situation, this means considering the need for federal-provincial engagement.
- Provide the ability, readiness and capacity to supply informed analysis and advice, even when it does not always align with the policy priorities of the government in power. For us, this means recognizing that we need to somehow create momentum for policies that will be considered by any party in power, meaning we need to generate studies, ideas and policy options that are presented to Parliament

rather than just the government of the day.

- Ensure leadership from a chair or board of commissioners who bring real-world experience to their function, are appropriately qualified, avoid partisanship and have demonstrated high competence and independence. In our case, we've seen the benefits from groups like my Advisory Council on Economic Growth, bringing together experts from different places, including scholars, Indigenous leaders, experienced industry leaders and world-class investors.
- Stipulate that advice submitted by the commission be responsible and implementable, ideally incorporating alternate means of moving forward on a defined problem. This means that we have no choice but to consider political realities, creating a need for former partisans to contribute practical advice on implementation — and to be bold when the moment arises.
- Confirm an appropriate connection point with government, ideally the minister of finance or equivalent. Also verify that individual's ability to focus the work of the commission on areas of particular interest to the government while providing the commission with the capacity to initiate work on its own. I would argue that in the Canadian reality, the finance minister should be central, but the prime minister must endorse the importance of the work or it doesn't keep the required status.
- Affirm that the commission possesses sufficient data from the public sector to perform quality analysis as well as the ability to build and operate its own models. In Canada, we have a strong public service. My experience with putting experienced public servants in the room with industry leaders gives me confidence that the differing perspectives lead to better insights, on both policy and implementation.
- Verify statutory requirements for the commission to

> release draft reports for public consumption as a means of assuring that benefits accrue from a range of perspectives, lending further credibility to the findings. In Canada, this transparency will help other leading think tanks to criticize, affirm or build on the commission's work, bringing momentum and public buy-in.

The mandate for such a commission would need to include consideration of equity and environmental sustainability. The principal focus, however, must be fixed on growing Canada's economy.

Whatever form the mandate takes, it is important to ensure that the role of the organization be intended not to supplant consultations on policy issues or duplicate research by existing think tanks but to stimulate and complement them. The OECD's note about the commission's primary government contact being the minister of finance or equivalent seeks to place government administration in the hands of a senior representative with responsibility to table the organization's reports in Parliament within a defined period of time. This adds formality and accountability to the process, ensuring the material is made available in a timely manner for an informed debate. In Australia, the treasurer consults with colleagues on the terms of reference for questions referred to the Productivity Commission, helping to achieve buy-in across all government bodies.

Governance in structures like this is always a concern, and an appropriately qualified and independent commissioner would be essential to success. A fixed term in office should be long enough for the commissioner to establish proper management principles and provide continuity to the programs — seven years would seem ideal. Another qualification for the first commissioner would be a demonstration of his or her competence and experience to build the organization from scratch.

Other aspects should be established and adhered to in

designing and establishing the commission. In Canada, federal-provincial-territorial considerations need to be formally acknowledged and built into the mandate. This could be as simple as appointing federal, provincial and territorial ministers of finance to the board of directors, an effective means of involving them not only in the governance of the organization but in the reports and recommendations submitted to Parliament. Regular meetings of FPT ministers of finance could serve to support this function. The federal minister could seek input — but not exercise a veto — on questions directed to the commission for study. While there is always a risk of the federal government or the provinces attempting to steer the work of the organization away from sensitive issues within their jurisdiction, the risk can be overridden by the benefits of mutual engagement.

Engagement by the public would represent another vital element to ensure success. Turning once again to the Australian model, public comments would be sought on draft reports. Building mandatory public consultation into the process would bolster the prospect of generating a broad range of perspectives, lending credibility to its conclusions.

The resources available to the organization should be sufficient to provide quality analysis and guidance. The Australian Productivity Commission receives annual appropriations of $35 million, with a staff of approximately 170. For those who might question the expense, it's been calculated that a similar organization in Canada raising annual productivity by 0.1 percentage points over 10 years, starting from 2020, would boost the country's output by $23 billion by 2030,[53] making it a highly worthwhile investment.

Guidance for the commission at the outset would emerge from a work plan covering a broad range of issues. The organization could begin by examining factors contributing to lower levels of

---

53 David Crane, "Post-Pandemic Euphoria Will Not Last," *the Hill Times*, July 5, 2021.

productivity in specific sectors versus those in the U.S., and lower levels between firms in different sectors. This would lead to the assessment of issues such as

- areas of government regulation along with the overall effectiveness of the regulatory system;
- taxation (while a broad-based commission on taxation would be politically challenging, detailed study by a commission on growth provides a strong basis for considering appropriate amendments to our tax system);
- competition policy, including the impacts on productivity performance resulting from the protection of various sectors;
- intellectual property protections;
- performance of insolvency and bankruptcy protection systems; and
- reasons why Canadian firms appear to struggle to achieve scale, an important predictor of productivity performance.

I have spent considerable time on this topic because my years of experience in office convinced me that productivity improvement is the most important issue on our agenda, and *we are not focused on it.*

The implications of ignoring this aspect of Canada are more than significant — they are critical.

Without focusing on our economic growth to produce an improvement, we will not be able to engineer the energy transition process. Nor will we be able to seriously address the problem of polarization without expanding opportunities for everyone. Our next prime minister, reflecting on the key elements in the party's platform, must consider economic growth as the most important goal of the federal government.

Absent that objective, every other policy initiative must be, by necessity, constrained.

Reflections

Someone commented that I looked totally relaxed after I announced my resignation in my meeting with the prime minister in Rideau Cottage that August afternoon. And I was. It's difficult to relax when you're struggling to make sure you are getting to the right answer on issues that are consequential for the future of your country while not being distracted by various crises, turf wars and partisan politics. All of that was behind me.

There would be no more crises or conflicts for me to deal with on Parliament Hill. As much as the odds were against winning, I was looking forward to seeking the appointment as secretary-general of the OECD. Wayne Gretzky famously quipped that you miss 100 percent of the shots you don't take. I was taking a shot.

If that didn't prove successful, there were other things to accomplish. I was interested in starting new business ventures that could make a private sector impact on some public sector challenges. I also looked forward to getting more involved with my university-aged children and reconnecting with friends back in Toronto. I also considered perhaps doing some teaching. And I wanted to find time for volunteer work on behalf of kids, refugees, university students and others.

I had spent five years trying to make a difference on behalf of 38 million Canadians. If I didn't win the OECD position, I could make a difference to the same people one at a time.

—

You don't shrug off a major government position the way you unzip a jacket and toss it aside. It had been an enormous privilege to work on behalf of Canadians as their finance minister, and I will never regret the time and effort I invested in the job. Those years of burying myself in responsibilities important to the welfare and future of the entire country provided a legacy of memories, images and ideas, and they stayed in my mind through the weeks and months following my resignation. Freed from the clouds of frustrations I had encountered for the past five-and-a-half years, their impact remains clear and intense.

Among them is the memory of the months immediately following our election victory in 2015. We were, in a word, euphoric. That's no doubt the reaction of every team after defeating a powerful and entrenched competitor, but it was enhanced in our case by the force of Justin Trudeau's personality, his wide celebrity-like appeal and his vision of restoring Liberal values to mainstream politics in Canada. He believed deeply in the goals we had set and sincerely cared about the members who accompanied him to Ottawa.

He proved unable to convert his promises into reality not by any lack of resolve or weakness of spirit but by an inability to apply good management skills to the political process. He was hardly the first politician to encounter this challenge, and he won't be the last. For that practical reason we must think about new approaches to governing and managing in the 21st century. Finding ways to support democratically elected leaders in areas requiring a long-term focus is critical to addressing our need for growth.

—

Out of my experience as finance minister came five concerns that drew my attention over those years in office and, with the perspective of time, they coalesced into themes that have been woven throughout this book, and they deserve reviewing now.

First is the management of our relationship with the United States, something that has been an issue for us since Confederation. I believe we did well on this matter during our first term, not as a direct result of any strategy but through our renegotiations over NAFTA or, as it's now called, CUSMA (or USMCA in the States). It's ironic, but one of the biggest difficulties we have in dealing with the U.S. is that they take us and our relationship for granted. Why shouldn't they? We're good friends and neighbours. We're neither a security threat nor a problem to them, so sometimes we have to stomp our feet and speak a little louder to get their attention.

I'm not suggesting that will always be a good strategy in the future, but we'll need to raise our profile in Washington as time passes. To some degree I'm echoing Brian Mulroney when I propose drawing closer to the U.S., but it's a practical reality given the scale of our relationship. Many developments are putting a strain on that relationship, including deglobalization and the disturbing drift toward political polarization and populism. These will make a significant impact on the economic, political and cultural life in both of our countries, and the stronger our links and the clearer our voice, the better we will be able to grapple with them.

Next, we need to change our approach to federal-provincial relationships and cooperation, a demand that will grow in urgency for a multitude of reasons over the coming years. Changing demographics, for example — a larger proportion of retired seniors and a reduced number of younger employed citizens — will affect the provinces in different ways and with an impact greater for some than for others. The result will be varying fiscal concerns that will inevitably cause some provinces to seek federal assistance.

Federal-provincial conflicts over funding and responsibility have become something of a rite in recent years on an increasing number of files, but they needn't be. Our success with revisions to the CPP program is proof that we can work together on consequential issues, but only if we take a determined approach to reworking our forms of interaction. True collaboration requires intense and sustained communications, agreement on objectives and a willingness to work together through difficult issues. The need for coordination and cooperation is evident everywhere, from interprovincial trade to management of our tax system and encouraging more significant investment in our collective future.

The biggest risk to long-term fiscal health for the provinces remains our valued health care system, which will continue to need our attention for some time. Educational costs also continue to rise while our universities are growing in stature and global reputation each year, many of them achieving great advances in research and development. Our openness to immigration provides a unique opportunity to attract talent to our country in a world where many nations are closing their borders. Our resources and our initiative provide the opportunity to lead the world in energy transition if we wisely employ our investments in decarbonization, renewables and technology. Unified federal and provincial support can only enhance our success on these issues, with benefits to be shared everywhere.

The climate crisis is my third theme. I have direct experience with the impact of climate change: I wrote more cheques to fund disaster relief from the effects of climate than any finance minister in Canadian history, and the unfortunate reality is that droughts, floods and fires continue to happen frequently. Their impact ensures that climate policy will dominate global dialogue for the next generation or two. In Canada, our success in addressing our carbon footprint will either enhance or inhibit our ability to manage the increasingly polarized debate. Our success will also depend upon the degree of federal-provincial cooperation we achieve. Overcoming deep provincial differences of opinion, we were able to set and launch a carbon pricing program that represents a critical first step in Canada's role. The outcome of that action will be enhanced if we are able to move to a more coordinated national approach on pricing carbon, one that provides coherence and certainty to encourage potential investments in carbon reduction. Government guarantees of the carbon price trajectory will play an important role for investors. So will continued rebates to Canadians of the proceeds generated from carbon pricing, preferably at the provincial level. We will need similar cooperation as we move more deeply into the next stages of energy transition.

Creating the investment environment to produce business opportunities for the next generation of scientists, geologists and engineers is, in my estimation, the only way forward. We cannot expect people to agree with a policy that negatively impacts their economic situation unless they can see a brighter future resulting from the change.

My fourth theme has been threaded through every chapter of this book: the upsurge of polarization and populism that has swept through Canada and other democracies in the past decade, exacerbated, most observers concur, by social media. In Canada, we felt somewhat immune as we witnessed waves of often violence-prone demonstrations taking place elsewhere, but they were brought home with noisy impact during the truckers' protests in the winter of early 2022. These protests were inspired not for the most part by mandates and restrictions arising out of the COVID pandemic, but by feelings of helplessness and alienation sustained by fables of conspiracies fuelled by social media.

People who feel their concerns are being addressed by government, and whose future appears bright and promising, do not grow polarized in their beliefs and stampede toward extreme corners. They prefer the comfortable centre. Populism is not a political movement on its own. It is a reaction to feelings of alienation, a sense that power resides within some definition of social elites, unavailable to "ordinary people." It is, in short, a loss of trust in government's ability or inclination to meet the needs of its citizens, and a loss of control over much of their lives.

Suspicion and concern about power at the upper levels of government are not new. Many will argue they are part and parcel of free expression within a vibrant democracy, when expressed by peaceful protest. No disagreement there on my part. These first decades of the 21st century, however, have seen a historic shift in Canada and elsewhere in the targets, the hostility and the impact of the protests to the point where the claimed goal of the protesters — freedom itself — is in peril.

For much of our history, the impetus for political protests was policy, ranging from trade with the U.S. to Canada's position on nuclear weapons. Today, the focus of the threats and shouts — often delivered in gutter language with racist and misogynist overtones — are elected officials and public servants. No one in public life or working to serve Canadians in any capacity should expect either fealty or fawning deference from citizens. But neither should they have to tolerate hateful personal attacks.

Too often, comments from anonymous sources in social media create headlines that help destroy public trust in our democratic institutions. In social media almost anything goes, and many forums encourage controversial statements regardless of their disassociation with reality. Advocates of social media claim they provide expressions of free speech, and I buy that. I hesitate to suggest that opinions be censored, especially where politics are concerned. It simply comes with the job. "If you can't stand the heat, stay out of the kitchen" is one way of putting it.

But.

A 2019 University of Toronto study of incivility toward politicians discovered that about 10 percent of messages sent to federal politicians were uncivil in content — not just negative or disagreeing but insulting, abusive, offensive and frequently obscene.[54] About 2.2 million Twitter messages to Canadian politicians and U.S. senators were evaluated for insults and disparaging content. About 11.7 percent of tweets directed at male office holders at the federal level were abusive and insulting, while approximately 8.6 percent of those sent to female office holders had similar content, although women in more highly visible positions were more heavily targeted. I witnessed the effect at close quarters. Watching the deeply offensive social media attacks on some of my female colleagues in Parliament was one of the most disturbing aspects of what passes for our current political dialogue.

Many people in political life can shrug off insults with the old children's adage about sticks and stones, but social media exerts serious damage with its plethora of views growing out of rumours, speculation and outright lies. It fosters extremism when large portions of the population are pushed off centre positions and into dark corners by inexcusable claims. Extreme actions and spurious allegations are detached from accepted levels of tolerance, open-mindedness and cooperation. They threaten what I believe are our country's most valuable characteristics: our tolerance, our openness to differences and our ability to reach compromise.

The world is far too complex to provide the degree of individual control that populists demand. Our political parties need to restore trust in the minds of Canadians with deeds, not words.

---

54 Ludovic Rheault, Erica Rayment and Andreea Musulan, "Politicians in the Line of Fire: Incivility and the Treatment of Women in Social Media," *Research and Politics*, January–March 2019: 1–7.

They need to extend their sense of care and concern via policies responsive to the very things that so many populists feel have been missing. Engaging and listening are essential to easing the tension. The steps we took to acknowledge such needs and fulfill expectations — like the Canada Child Benefit plan and CPP revisions — speak to their concerns about security and risk. But we need more. We need an attitude of engagement, even among those with whom we don't agree.

It will be difficult for the federal government to engage with provincial governments of different political persuasions, just as it's difficult to listen to people who don't share our point of view on the efficacy of vaccines. But a lack of engagement is certain to keep each camp in its own comfortable corner, and that's not an effective way forward.

Finally, I have invested much space and many words on identifying new ways to create greater growth and higher productivity in Canada. These are needed not for their own sake but as a means of funding the features of Canadian life that we value.

Growth, achieved within the boundaries of environmental protection, human rights and social values, permits many things to happen, all of them good. I usually explain my concept of growth by returning to my earlier metaphor of a pie to be sliced and shared among friends. (Any analogy between federal and provincial revenue sharing in Canada is purely intentional.)

If all of us gather around a table, each one anticipating a larger slice of a pie than the others, we'll likely get more tension and frustration than pie. What we need is a bigger pie, which is best achieved by growing our economy through greater productivity.

I rarely encounter serious objections to the concept of growing our country's productivity and wealth while respecting energy and environmental concerns. Too often, however, I discover that while many people nod in approval when hearing about the idea, they shake their heads at the suggestion that they take steps to make it happen. While I was frustrated when apparently financially literate opposition Conservatives argued against clearly advantageous economic policies, my concern is not only about a partisan political response.

Provincial Liberals in Ontario and my Federal colleagues recognized the potential benefits in rebuilding our infrastructure promised by the Canada Infrastructure Bank. When I proposed two archetypal structures in their province that would be ideal to launch the concept — rethinking the ownership of Pearson International Airport and funding improvements to the often-reviled Gardiner Expressway — the response was inflexibly negative.

It's not easy to get things done in politics. I suspect it never has been. But that doesn't mean we should abandon our efforts to find a way toward success. We are among the lowest of all OECD countries in future growth prospects and productivity improvements, and we need to begin reversing that trend now. It's a major challenge that will need new institutions and serious engagement across the political spectrum and throughout the country, an urgent national project that will require both new thinking and strong leadership. The latter quality is, in my estimation, a key attribute that has been sorely lacking.

—

Canada faces big challenges, but I don't know of any other country more capable of overcoming them. We are the best-educated and one of the most stable nations in the world.[55] Fully 60 percent of Canadians have successfully completed post-secondary education, substantially higher than Japan (53 percent), South Korea (51 percent) and the U.S. (50 percent). That's a resource that enables us to set and achieve goals beyond the reach of other countries.

---

55 World Population Review, "Most Educated Countries 2022," accessed online March 2, 2022.

My international experience reinforced my view that Canada is almost universally respected, and I know that we have the capacity to listen and learn from advances and ideas spawned by other cultures and nations. What we lack is principled, experienced and disciplined leadership to tackle major items on our agenda, and that can be a challenge. It is not easy to get the right people in the right roles. We need an active agenda to help make it happen.

Among the most critical goals is something we have achieved with success over much of our history. Canada has built a reputation for creating relationships with and among other nations, even when their values and actions conflict with our own. Nothing good happens between people or nations without engagement. This is a policy we have practised with success over many years, and it has helped build our identity as honest brokers.

At heart, everything we need is available for us to ensure a bright future for Canada if we can capitalize on our assets. The key ingredient is leadership. The most important elements to look for in choosing our leaders are an ability to build relationships on the way to achieving a constructive compromise and sufficient experience to gain a new outlook on what needs to be done and the means to do it.

The experience quotient cannot be overemphasized. Experience tells good managers, for example, not to set 30 different goals and promise to achieve all of them. Because you won't, whether you make the goals in business, in politics or your personal life. (And, of course, in politics the goals you don't achieve are likely to carry more weight and generate more media coverage than the ones you do.)

What we have lacked at the federal level in recent years has been a narrowing of focus on a few key things that are important not as a means of creating impressive sound bites and video moments on the news channels, but for the good of the next generation. That's a challenge to those whose minds are fixed exclusively on approval ratings, opinion polls and election schedules. Politics isn't, or shouldn't be, a sporting event that pits competitive teams against each other in a stadium crammed with devoted fans, all with the intent of crowning and revering the winner. It's not about winning; it's about *doing*. And the doing — applying the time, effort and determination to fulfill the promises that enabled you to achieve victory in the first place — is never easy. Nor should it be.

There is an immense void, a wide and deep chasm, between the work involved in getting elected and the work needed to justify the triumph you achieved. The effort invested in the first stage is essentially selfish — you are working for your victory. In the second stage you are working for others — the people who entrusted you with the responsibility of guiding them toward the vision you shared together.

At that first stage we should expect practical policies. The second stage demands strong principles.

Exceptional policies are of little value when promoted by people with unexceptional principles.

—

I have one more enduring memory of my venture into federal politics, one that I described earlier but remains important to me.

It's the young girl who approached me with the scrap of yellow paper at my headquarters during my first election campaign. She and the other five members of her family were living in a one-bedroom apartment. They had been waiting months for admission to a community housing facility, one with sufficient space for them to live comfortably. Through my five years in Parliament, I kept that small piece of paper as a reminder that Canada had enough resources, and a big enough heart, to provide her and her family with adequate housing and all the opportunities they had come to Canada to enjoy.

We have the capacity to provide them for her, and for everyone who treasures this country. She, and thousands like her, are our future. If we remember that, and invest in her, our future will be bright.

Index

Note: BM stands for Bill Morneau and MFM for Morneau as finance minister. JT is used for Justin Trudeau.

Acknowledgements

No one ever succeeded at politics without the support of a talented hard-working team, and the same holds true for writing a book.

My political team proved as invaluable to me in preparing this book as they were during my years in government. Many thanks to Elder Marques, Sharan Kaur, Marion Pilon-Cousineau, Robert Asselin, Ian Foucher, Justin To, Pierre-Olivier Herbert and Matt Barnes. They deserve enormous credit for all that we accomplished, and I bear responsibility for the goals we were unable to achieve. Their recollections of our time together were invaluable in the development of the book. Yet, just like during our time in office, they don't necessarily share my opinions and conclusions.

I owe a great deal of gratitude to those who provided guidance and counsel in reviewing the stories within these pages, most notably Michael Denham and my aunt Eleanor Cronk. Their contributions of time and wisdom spent reading multiple drafts helped shape the story I wanted to tell. I am also indebted to insights offered by former colleagues at the Department of Finance who, following their policy of impartiality, must remain nameless.

My wife Nancy and daughter Clare were enormously supportive and candidly critical of material I asked them to review — their honesty and perspective is invaluable to me.

Assembling the text took place over months of discussion with my co author John Lawrence Reynolds. John worked with me to craft this account of my time in office and my views on effective policy out of untold hours of probing and discussion, maintaining his unflappable manner even when I edited something for the 17th time.

All of it was entrusted to the editorial team at ECW Press, who made sure the book was completed on time. Along the way they provided valuable insights into the publishing process as well as counsel on how to shape the book to reach the right audience from an appropriate content perspective. Many thanks to Jennifer Smith, Karen Milner and Rachel Ironstone.

This book is also available as a Global Certified Accessible™ (GCA) ebook. ECW Press's ebooks are screen reader friendly and are built to meet the needs of those who are unable to read standard print due to blindness, low vision, dyslexia or a physical disability.

At ECW Press, we want you to enjoy our books in whatever format you like. If you've bought a print copy just send an email to ebook@ecwpress.com and include:

- the book title
- the name of the store where you purchased it
- a screenshot or picture of your order/receipt number and your name
- your preference of file type: PDF (for desktop reading), ePub (for a phone/tablet, Kobo, or Nook), mobi (for Kindle)

A real person will respond to your email with your ebook attached. Please note this offer is only for copies bought for personal use and does not apply to school or library copies.

Thank you for supporting an independently owned Canadian publisher with your purchase!